The Battle for Fallujah

The Battle for Fallujah

Occupation, Resistance and
Stalemate in the War in Iraq

VINCENT L. FOULK

McFarland & Company, Inc., Publishers
Jefferson, North Carolina, and London

All of the photographs were taken by the author

LIBRARY OF CONGRESS CATALOGUING-IN-PUBLICATION DATA

Foulk, Vincent L., 1950–
    The battle for Fallujah : occupation, resistance and stalemate
in the war in Iraq / Vincent L. Foulk.
        p.   cm.
    Includes bibliographical references and index.

    ISBN-13: 978-0-7864-2677-5
    ISBN-10: 0-7864-2677-2
    (softcover : 50# alkaline paper) ∞

    1. Fallujah, Battle of, Fallujah, Iraq, 2004. 2. Iraq War,
2003—Personal narratives, American. I. Title.
    DS79.766.F3F68   2007
    956.7044'342—dc22   2006033537

British Library cataloguing data are available

On the cover: U.S. Marines of the 1st Division take position
overlooking the western part of Fallujah on November 13, 2004
(AP Photo/Anja Niedringhaus)

Manufactured in the United States of America

McFarland & Company, Inc., Publishers
  Box 611, Jefferson, North Carolina 28640
  www.mcfarlandpub.com

To my loving wife Claudia,
who has supported me through many deployments,
and to my son Matthew,
who is serving as a Signal Officer
in the United States Army.

Also, to all the honorable men
and women serving our country.

Table of Contents

Preface

On February 14, 2003, I was called to service from the United States Army Reserves as a colonel in the Army Civil Affairs. I was given a small team of remarkable young men and women, and together we set about to defend our nation and perhaps naively committed ourselves to expanding the blessings of democracy and freedom. We came prepared to fight one kind of war and soon found ourselves confronting challenges for which we were not trained or equipped. After a short and brilliantly fought advance, the American military found itself faced with a skeptical population who could mouth the terms of democracy but often had no concept of what they meant and had little confidence that anything other than raw military power could govern. In those early days in Baghdad it quickly became apparent that after the fall of Saddam Hussein's military, things were going wrong.

After a period of frantic attempts to rebuild a nation that had literally been plundered by its own people, I was reassigned to support the newly created Coalition Provisional Authority, which was created as the occupational authority of Iraq. From that position, I watched as the coalition struggled to apply its under-resourced military, an unresponsive civilian bureaucracy and slowly arriving reconstruction funds. I also watched a civilian population rapidly fall into disillusion following wildly optimistic promises and predictions.

After I'd spent as much time in the field as possible, it was also clear to me that a different picture was forming between the one on the ground outside of Baghdad and the one seen in the office of Ambassador Paul Bremer and the command post of Lt. General Sanchez. The military trained for one fight was now asked to confront a new enemy and new problems in which every act seemed to only make things worse.

This book looks at the difficulties of the American military as it struggled to confront an enemy for which it was unprepared. It shows the evolution of an enemy that took hold and grew from the ground up, often enhanced by America's early mistakes and lack of planning. It also

The author on a mission in Iraq.

shows the daily struggles of the common soldiers and their lives in confronting a new and dangerous enemy who nearly instantly adapted to America's every move. In that atmosphere local insurgents combined with foreign jihadists to wrestle away control of the city of Fallujah. From there a newly independent city-state confronted the might of the world's superpower, America.

The city of Fallujah became a model for the insurgency throughout Iraq and a threat to America's strategy to hand over power to an Iraqi government that actually had control of its territories. This work details the evolution of the American military as it too adapted to confront and crush the de facto insurgent city-states that sprung up after the uprising in Fallujah. Upon seeing no alternative, the U.S. military developed new tactics and turned on the insurgency with a vengeance. In the end, the autonomous cities each fell to the American offensives, paving the way for elections. But these new tactics failed to win over the Arab Sunni population or eliminate the foreign fighters organized under the banner of Abu-Musab al-Zarqawi. Thus, with the fall of Fallujah a new Iraq stood ready for elections but still infected with enemies from within.

CHAPTER 1

"...They are occupiers and infidels"

Fallujah, Iraq, was a dingy city sprawling across the desert to the Euphrates River. Mostly of cinder block buildings, it was a colorless sea of gray stretching from Highway 10, the road coming up past Baghdad some forty-five minutes away. From the houses, low-hanging power lines bowed haphazardly across the streets in an amateurish tap for electricity. On a good day they gave power for only twelve hours.

In the heat along the roadsides, vendors set up stands made of woven reeds and scrap wood. Upon them a carcass of a sheep dangled, butchered and dressed, ready to have a piece cut off for a buyer. Around each stand grazed several other live candidates should sales be good that day. This was a common person's town, not easily taken to new ideas.

An industrial town of profitless factories making products no one wanted to buy, its people were long dependent on fellow Sunni leader, Saddam Hussein. Propped up by the Iraqi government, the industries were heavily subsidized. In the days before the Americans came, the people of Fallujah looked to their tribal sheiks to solve their problems, get them their jobs, or protect them from others who thought they had an "in" with the government. They would in turn go to the local Baa'th* appointed Muktar.† In accordance to principles of loyalty and reward, they got their share.

In Iraq, wealth did not flow from talent but in accordance to the group. Loyalty was everything. You could see it in who had fine houses and cars and who received respect from others. It was also evident in the shoddy construction of public buildings. All of the Saddam-era buildings had wiring exposed on the outside of the walls and unfinished sides. The contract on each required a 30 percent skim-off of the price to the sheik,

*The Baa'th Party was Hussein's political movement based upon Arab nationalism.
†A Muktar is an official similar to a Chicago-style alderman.

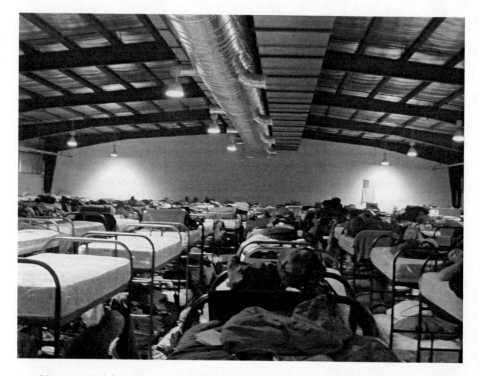

Upon arrival for the invasion of Iraq, most soldiers were housed in warehouses. Privacy was impossible. Men and women were housed together.

muktar, and Baa'th official, making finishing the work impossible. It showed in the products they produced from the state-owned industries. The local glass factory, which produced nearly all of the plate glass in Iraq, turned out a film-like sheet with so many distortions and blemishes that looking out a window made of the stuff sometimes gave a fun-house image. Not that the people spent much time making the glass. At around sixty dollars a month salary, most spent only a fraction of their time at work, having other ventures on the side to provide for their families.

It was not that the people lacked pride, far from it. Pride was the central aspect of Fallujan life. They were Sunni Muslim and proud of it. Fallujans referred to their city as the City of Mosques. They were warriors who fought bravely against the Iranians and repeatedly put down the Shi'a and Kurdish rebellions, smashing their cities into submission. Most did not love the dictator of Iraq, Saddam Hussein, but they admired his strength. When he spoke defiantly or acted decisively, they were proud of him. Many joined the Republican Guard, and the ideal of a Pan-Arabic superpower had currency.

During the advance to Baghdad, the Americans had no need to take

Destroyed Iraqi equipment was a common sight for the first year of the war. In fact, most were simply abandoned as the Iraqi army melted away.

Fallujah. The only early vision of the Americans was what others told them as they fled the disintegrating army. It was not that they were afraid of the American army when they deserted. The military formations that fell apart, often at the mention of the approaching Americans, did so because Saddam had fallen from the sight of God. It was Saddam's weakness, not America's strength, that brought the invaders to their city.

There were the radio broadcasts of the Americans and British. To the ears of Fallujans, the announcements of a coming democracy and freedom sounded like local control. Rumors of getting the electricity up, clean water plants, and jobs for everyone rebuilding the infrastructure came repeated as official promises. To their minds, the timetable was months, not years.

Just prior to the war, the Baa'th party formed a militia called the Saddam Fedayeen. By sheer numbers the militia had managed to occupy the 101st Air Assault Division protecting the supply lines on the advance on Baghdad, which in turn was able to suppress the amateur force with remarkably few casualties. The Fedayeen were lightly armed and had minimal training. What tactics they knew were centered on hometown defense, not coordinated offense. The American Third Infantry Division came in a lightning advance towards Fallujah but turned east towards Baghdad.

The local Fedayeen commanders ordered attacks on the Americans who hunkered down at the Saddam International Airport, about a half-hour's drive away. Few answered the call. Without loss to themselves, the Third Infantry Division's rear guard slaughtered the ones who climbed into automobiles to make disjointed attacks. As was obvious to even the bravest of Fallujah, a private automobile was no match for the American tank-like Bradley Fighting Vehicle.

The people of Fallujah listened to their few battery-operated radios and the refugees from Baghdad to hear that the capital had fallen. Then their sister cities of the Sunni Triangle fell with hardly a fight. Many took in relatives from Baghdad and the southern Shi'a areas, fleeing looters or vengeful relatives of those whom the Baa'thists murdered. Some were fearful, resentful, or took a wait-and-see attitude towards the Americans. Almost nowhere was there gratitude or optimism in the traditional Sunni city.

In Baghdad, the first officials of the newly created Office of Rehabilitation and Humanitarian Assistance (ORHA, later to be called the Coalition Provisional Authority, CPA) under former General Jay Garner* moved in. They were overwhelmed. The entire Iraqi bureaucracy collapsed and ceased to exist. Newly appointed senior officials floundered about, searching for a government that no longer was, not knowing who to trust, and with no money to spend. There was much discussion prior to the war, and there were plans all over the place. But there was not *the* plan. The Department of Defense had taken over the planning that was worked over by the State Department and it was only now that the personnel requirements were seriously being studied.

The military was declaring victory and EndEx.† Everywhere, combat commanders turned to civil affairs and other non-combat leaders saying, it's yours now; we have to go home. Soldiers were calling home making plans; staff officers were preparing schedules to move their equipment back to Kuwait. The principal concern in many headquarters was to get in the paperwork for their Bronze Star medals before the deadlines. Almost nowhere was there a mention of what would happen should the expectations of the people of Fallujah not be met.

The 82nd Airborne Division arrived April 23, and occupied a local school. These American soldiers were an oddity in Fallujah. Although

---

*The appointment was short-lived and not well received by the Arab world. Garner's ties to Israel were so open that the English-language Jewish Forward headlined, "Pro-Israeli general will oversee reconstruction of postwar Iraq." Given little to offer but promises, the local Iraqis would not cooperate. He was replaced by L. Paul Bremer.

†EndEx is a common military slang for End of Exercise. Military exercises were regularly conducted with a set ending point with no thought of what would happen next. The soldiers would just clean up and go back to cantonment.

nearly every household had an AK47, there was not an armed uprising at their appearance. To the soldiers it was a routine of patrolling and taking possession of critical public buildings. For the most part, their interactions with the people were limited to contending with curious boys begging for money and nearly every male trying to sell them Iraqi dinars as souvenirs.

In other places Baa'thist officials fled, but in Fallujah there was no stigma in association with Saddam's political party. Some government officials fled from Baghdad and now lived in Fallujah. Most of the city's male population had joined the Fedayeen, and unlike other places the sometimes-amateurish force had not fought in any serious way. Thus, the Americans had not defeated them. It was only a matter of time before the Americans' tolerance would be tested.

Five days after the Americans moved in, a demonstration called to protest the military presence in the town turned violent. On April 28, a small group of Iraqis protested. It was not clear what was the complaint. Some called for an end to the occupation of the school. Some said they were celebrating the birthday of Saddam Hussein. In the crowd were people with AKs* who fired in the air in what was termed as "celebratory gunfire."

The troops had heard the shooting many times before but always at a distance. On Thursdays, the shooting was particularly heavy because it was the favorite day for an Iraqi wedding. Even then, it was a question as to whether the shooters were actually celebrating or trying to intimidate, saying by the un-aimed bursts, "We are here, armed, and not going away." This was the first time the shooting was openly in the soldiers' presence.

The soldiers in an enclosed schoolroom were frightened and with justification believed they were endangered. The soldiers in the school opened fire into the crowd. It was unclear if any in the crowd shot back. The soldiers killed seventeen and wounded another seventy. There were no reports of soldiers injured.†

After the initial panic, instead of being intimidated, the people in the area remained. As the troops left, the schoolboys shook their shoes at the soldiers, an insult in Iraq, threw rocks, and yelled in English, "No, No, USA," and other slogans.

"We won't remain quiet over this," said one father in a hospital room with his 18-year-old son who was shot in the stomach. Doctors told him that his son would likely die. "Either they leave Fallujah or we will make them leave."[1]

An AK is the Russian-created assault rifle popularly known as the AK47.
†*Arab-language news network al-Jazeera and other media reported U.S. soldiers fired unprovoked into a crowd.*

The next day, a military convoy driving through the town ran into another demonstration. It fired on the protesters, killing three and wounding at least sixteen more. The soldiers believed they were under fire. The Fallujans insisted that the Iraqis fired no shots. They admitted throwing rocks at the army vehicles, breaking the window of a truck, and injuring a soldier. The stage was now set for a bad relationship.

On May 1, several grenades were thrown into a military base, wounding seven U.S. soldiers. Starting in mid–May, there was a steady stream of attacks by small groups on U.S. forces. On May 27, an ambush at an army checkpoint in Fallujah left two U.S. soldiers dead[*] and nine injured.

Meanwhile, in Camp Victory just outside of Baghdad, the commander of CJTF-7, the highest military command, insisted that the war was over. Lt. General William Wallace repeated this even while a growing number of incidents came through the chain of command. With the declaration on May 1 that hostilities had ceased, as far as Baghdad and Washington were concerned, the fighting was over.[†] Orders for new armored vests for the troops were canceled; no thought was given to the reality that nearly all of the support troops were traveling the roads in unarmored vehicles.

Part of the problem lay in the under-reporting of attacks. Attacks regularly occurred that were not reported to the commanding generals. The reporting channels came through the units that "owned the ground." Most of the attacks were aimed at the supply convoys that were always passing through terrain under the responsibility of combat units. These transportation units were regularly attacked and unless they called for help from a surrounding combat unit, the ambush was not recorded. With some combat units, shooting and shelling became so common that they simply stopped reporting unless casualties were involved. Throughout Iraq, the daily report of sixty or so incidents to higher headquarters was masking many times that number experienced by the troops on the ground.[‡]

For the common person in Fallujah these were hard times. Food was available but at high prices despite the Oil for Food Program. Every adult with a memory back to 1978 could remember a proud Iraq with electric-

---

*KIA: Staff Sgt. Michael B. Quinn, Sgt. Thomas F. Broomhead
†This was common throughout the theater. In the Sunni Triangle, as his soldiers were regularly being ambushed, Major General Ray Odierno, commander U.S. 4th Infantry Division, said: "I will never downplay Americans being killed in combat.... But from a military perspective, it is insignificant. The [attacks are] having no impact on the way we conduct business on a day-to-day basis in Iraq." June 18, 2003.
‡In the scores of occasions the author was under fire in Iraq, only once did the attack make the incident report for CJTF-7. Complaints about the reporting problem were regularly dismissed by the general staff.

ity 24 hours a day, a dinar that could buy nearly a dollar's worth of goods,* good medical care, and a future. Now, they sweltered in the over-100-degree heat, in the dark, lucky to have a job, and if so lucky to be paid.

The Americans were not a big part of their lives, seen only occasionally riding around in convoys of Humvees or manning the checkpoints impeding their travel. The Americans hardly spoke to them because of the language difference and often stared wearily at them through metallic reflective sunglasses.†

There was one change that was a revelation to the average Fallujan. Anyone who could scrape together the money bought a generator and a satellite dish. For the first time in thousands of homes in Fallujah, real news beamed into households. They stared into TV sets receiving Egyptian soap operas, game shows, and other light entertainment. They watched old movies and one of at least four pornography channels. They also watched the news, and by far the most popular stations were al–Jazeera and al-Arabiya. On both these channels was a drumbeat of anti–Zionist news and anti–American stories. The Americans or British had nothing remotely capable of competing.

With the print media, there was a more even playing field as newspapers sprung up all over Iraq. Many were openly anti–American, but there were others that presented a balanced view and a few others favorable to the Coalition's aims. But in general, the people did not get their views from the news media. The clan, the street, the family, and the mosque were the gospel here. Iraqis had been lied to all of their lives. Here, relationships counted most, and information from a trusted person was what was most likely true. One thing was for sure, anything an American said was not credible if only for one reason: no one knew an American.

Throughout Iraq, army civil affairs teams fanned out, making assessments and trying to reach out to the population. Exceptionally vulnerable with unarmored Humvees and lightly armed, they immediately became the target of the remnant Baa'thist cells, who on first sight understood that these teams were among their greatest threat. U.S. military commanders, faced with having to divert forces to escort these teams, often tied the C.A. teams to the schedule of the combat forces. This constricted their operations and reduced the outreach to the people. To make matters worse, there was a desperate shortage of civil affairs teams, and they were not given money to start immediate repairs to fix anything.

*On May 1, 2003, the Iraqi dinar was 3000 to a dollar. By September 2004, the exchange rate was 1460 to a dollar.

†It was a common belief that the sunglasses could allow the soldiers to see through clothing and that the soldiers were staring at the women.

Brigadier General Jack Kerns (front) was charged with all Civil Affairs activity in Iraq. Early on he lost a battle with the maneuver commanders for control of the civil affairs units, and thus there was no nationwide strategy concerning their use. At the same time he was instructing units to limit their support to CPA, fearing an unsustainable dependency upon the civil affairs units. Thus CPA was often starved for workers and hampered as civilian help failed to arrive in a timely manner. Behind him is Major General Altshuler, commander of all army Civil Affairs and Psychological Operations forces. Having sent nearly half of all the forces he had available in the first wave, he was eager to keep down the commitment as well.

The money problem would later be corrected but by then, they had already lost the trust of many in Fallujah. For now, the U.S. military came armed only with guns and promises, which were not acted upon in any meaningful way. The Baa'thists had no difficulty in keeping a separation between the people of Fallujah and the U.S. military.

In the meantime, there was a power struggle in the inner circles of CJTF-7 (Combined Joint Task Force Seven), the military high command of Iraq. The chief of Civil Military Operations, Brigadier General John ("Jack") Kern, wanted to gather all of the civil affairs teams under his command to dispatch them according to a nationwide strategy.

The two-star generals charged with commanding the divisions, and who had control of the vast majority of the civil affairs teams, objected vehemently. The reserve general, Brigadier Kern of the 352nd Civil Affairs Command, lost out in that bid to gain centralized control. Thus, each of the divisions developed its own personalized strategy on how to guide the country from war to recovery. The disparities between the approaches of the five divisions soon became so pronounced that there was no nation-wide strategy put into affect at all.

Within each military command there was a subtle debate reflecting the personality of its commanding general, swirling around whether the operations in Iraq were a matter of "winning hearts and minds" or "removing the security threats." Officers whose background led them to the application of force pointed out that the believers could never be persuaded, and those agnostics who fought for profit would cease only when it was too dangerous for them to continue. No amount of civic action projects or preaching of freedom and democracy would change that. And, so long as these security threats existed, neither democracy nor prosperity was possible.

Those officers with mostly diplomatic or civil military operations experience argued that the population was in fact the prize for both sides to win, and without their cooperation, success against the security threats would be impossible. The highly intrusive methods of searching out these security threats would likely not only alienate the population but also add to the numbers of the security threat. Kicking in doors by foreign-speaking troops, constantly threatening the population by pointing guns at them, would not likely result in their providing intelligence, which was the primary tool needed to remove the insurgents. Killing or injuring civilians through collateral damage or mistaken identity turned all the friends and relatives of the victim into enemies for life that could not be later converted. Thus, heavy-handed or insensitive security operations only increased the numbers of insurgents regardless of the body count tallied.

This academic argument as to whether the continued military operations in Iraq was a "war of ideas" or a "test of wills" had real on-the-ground consequences. Soldiers varied in their behavior according to their leadership's personality, with some units reaching out and taking extraordinary steps for cultural sensitivity, while others were indifferent, rude, and in some cases, hostile towards the population.

With the civilian occupational government undermanned and ill prepared, in practical affect the civilians in Baghdad had control of only the capital city. The military divisional commanders, each ruling as a military governor, often overruled or contradicted the Coalition Provisional Authority. One almost never saw a CPA official in Fallujah. Any civil affairs team from higher headquarters moving outside of the Green Zone needed permission from the local divisional commander to conduct reconstruction projects. Therefore, there was no independent oversight or buffer between the local commanders to work out differences. Generals used to having their commands instantly obeyed were often intolerant to local sensibilities and needs.

To the soldier, life was hardly any better than it was for the people of Fallujah. First, it was hot, unbearably hot and getting hotter. Soldiers traveling through the constant dust sipped on warm water from their camelbacks to keep up the quart and a half an hour they needed to avoid dehydration. They stood or sat in the sun for hours at a time. Often suffering with a headache from the heavy helmet and body armor, their lives were twelve hours a day of watching people there was no way they could trust. Their command trained them to take no chances. The war was over and casualties were not acceptable. When dealing with the Iraqis, keeping always at the ready to return fire was the standard even if it did offend the locals.

The attitude of many of the junior officers also reflected a "kick ass and take names" approach. A common statement heard at the unit level was, "These people are used to force and don't understand much else." Many were veterans of six months in Afghanistan and took pride in the combat history of the unit. There was an assumption by many that this would be at most six months, and then this peace business would be someone else's problem.

Early on, showers were a rarity and anything at all from home, a packet of Kool-Aid, candy, a meal other than field rations called MREs* was a luxury. The alien character of the surroundings was unnerving. Five times a day, loudspeakers from the mosques would start caterwauling in competing unintelligible syllables.

The soldiers themselves felt they were bringing something of value and could not understand the lack of enthusiasm by the Iraqis. Democracy was a given good, and the Americans resented the lack of acceptance and gratitude. Equally frustrating to the soldiers was their inability to talk to the people around them. The military had spent hundreds of billions on high-tech equipment and planes but relatively little on language skills. Thus, the military was forced to hire local translators, often with doubtful skills and sometimes with political agendas of their own. A company commander with a hired unvetted local translator was no longer the most powerful person on the battlefield, left isolated from the populace for which he was responsible.

Even with the few translators they had, speaking through an interpreter was painfully difficult. Lack of cultural understandings compounded the problem. Most of the soldiers meant well to the Iraqis and

*MRE (meal ready to eat).

felt sympathy towards them. The frustration of not being able to get across that good will exasperated them.

In the meantime, the military was hiring back as many police as were willing to return to work. There was no vetting as to who was loyal, honest, or reliable. Not comfortable with these new allies, military policemen (MPs) went on joint patrols. This marriage was not a happy one. The police saw themselves as crime fighters, not as part of the security apparatus of the central government. Soldiers would go on joint patrols and the Iraqi police understood that the soldier next to him was likely to draw fire from insurgents. Their concerns were justified. In an apparent intimidation attempt, on June 24, a rocket-propelled grenade (RPG) attack came on the mayor's office for his cooperation with the Americans.

Then, there was the matter of the bribes. Like all civil servants in Iraq, the police were not paid enough for a decent living. The society expected every Iraqi living on a government salary to take a little, but only a little, from each person on the side to make ends meet. To Americans, such was heresy and not tolerated. The presence of the puritanical Americans made life as a police officer impossible.

By mid–June, relations became so strained that the police sought to separate themselves from the Iraqi government and the military. Because of the complaints of the police in Fallujah, the MPs supporting the police moved out in July. The police said they were willing to work with the Americans, but did not want them using the station as a base. They feared it would make the Iraqi officers the target of what was seen within the city, to an increasing degree, as a legitimate resistance.

"We feel more comfortable because of this withdrawal. We can solve the problems here better than the Americans and communicate better with the people," the police commander said. "We have told the Americans many times that we have the capability. We asked them to give us a chance and see our work. If they don't like how we perform, they can come back."[2]

The city's people had a slightly different view. "We are happy they left the station, but we will be happier if they leave the entire town," said a shopkeeper nearby. "Nobody wants them here because they are occupiers and infidels."[3]

By the close of July, the Americans reduced by half the troops in Fallujah as forces long overdue for rotation left for home. That changed after a month with the return of the 82nd Airborne. Their start was not a smooth one. On September 12, about twenty-five uniformed police officers in two blue and white marked police pickup trucks and a sedan chased a white BMW that was known to have been used by highway bandits. When the police rushed up in the dark to a checkpoint manned by 82nd soldiers outside of Fallujah, the Americans opened fire.

The paratroopers killed twelve local police. In the confusion of the night, a Jordanian contingent of Special Forces guarding a nearby hospital believed they were under attack and fired on both the Americans and the police. The American patrol, thinking they were taking fire from the hospital, turned loose their Mark 19 grenade launchers and 50-caliber machine guns on the hospital building. The result was devastating on the hospital building and Jordanian guard, killing some of them. Among the city's inhabitants, the incident reaffirmed the reputation which the 82nd had as a trigger-happy, undisciplined unit.

The religious leadership of the city became open in supporting violence against the Americans. One Sunni Muslim cleric characterized the people fighting the U.S. troops as holy warriors who looked to Osama bin-Laden. "Although unorganized and without leadership, the Iraqi resistance is a ball of fire in America's face that will bring its end in Iraq," said the cleric, whose sermons drew thousands in the main Badawi mosque, one of over seventy mosques in the center of Fallujah. "We have made the Americans dizzy," said the cleric.[4]

Pro-Saddam graffiti was appearing all over the city. To the soldiers driving by, it all looked like chicken scratches, but in fact, it was encouraging citizens to kill American troops. Posters were common, warning residents to stay far from U.S. convoys to avoid being hit. One slogan scrawled on the wall of the busy open market read, "Our leader Saddam Hussein will return."

"They are moved by national pride and honor to protect their homes," said one religious teacher who managed a religious school for mullahs.[5]

The religious influence of anti–American teachers went unanswered. Indeed, intelligence contacts confirmed that Wahabi missionaries were circulating in the area, preaching in increasing numbers. Seeded in their own brand of fundamentalist Islam was a call to expel the infidels. This was not a new development. Hussein invited clerics who preached the austere form of Islam that was prevalent in Saudi Arabia. Less spoken but understood was the Wahabis' opposition to the Shi'a clerics in the south, whom they saw as heretics and feared that with a democracy would take power.

There had always been a tension between the Shi'a and the Sunni. The Shi'a resented their long history of political domination by the Sunni. The Sunni feared the Shi'a's numbers, perhaps 60 percent of the population. The Wahabi view of religion saw the Shi'ite reverence of great Islamic saints as anti–Muslim bordering on paganism. The Wahabi teachers exasperated the tension between the two groups.

At the same time, foreigners were filtering across the nearly unguarded border of Syria, answering the call of Salafi* jihadists. They

*Islam pure and free from any additions, deletions or alterations.

began trickling into Iraq in the mid–1990s, during the international sanctions for Saddam's invasion of Kuwait. These Salafi groups were organizing under the banner of Ansar al-Islam, which had ties with Osama bin Laden's al-Qaeda. Intelligence also noted the presence of Jordanian militant leader Abu-Musab al-Zarqawi, whom Saddam Hussein's secret police allowed refuge in Iraq.

Civil affairs and PSYOPS teams, made up mostly of reservists, noticed this radical religious preaching and made references to it in their reports. Nevertheless, the regular officers dismissed these references as not relevant. The professional soldiers believed religious attitudes were beyond the ability of the military to manage. They cleansed these aspects out of the reports and sent them higher.

"Mission creep" had become a byword for many military leaders as a reason to avoid further entanglements. To many soldiers, the idea that the military should take on responsibilities that civilian authorities should manage was a major pitfall. There was a genuine feeling by military officials that the military should avoid such civilian chores as managing public attitudes. If the civilians were not forced to do so, they would not come forth and do their job. The commander of Civil Military Operations, Brigadier Kern, specifically warned his civil affairs units not to take on civilian posts, citing his experience in Bosnia and Kosovo. He told the incoming units that he would force the civilians in Washington to step up to the plate.

There also was the army civil affairs principle that any military support should be temporary, and there was intense pressure to reduce the civil affairs entanglement for fear that there would not be follow-on units to carry on when the reservists went home. Nearly all of the civil affairs, as well as a great number of military police and other non-combat units, were reservists. Any excuse that could be found not to accept a mission was used. In contrast, combat units that otherwise would be standing around at checkpoints looked for any opportunity to reach out and conduct combat operations.

The commander of the 308th Civil Affairs Brigade, Colonel Tim Regan, ran into this resistance when he offered to commit his headquarters first to staffing CPA, then the regional provincial civilian governments, and then to conduct operations in the Sunni Triangle to restart the businesses in order to revive the economy. The answer was a consistent "no."

The original plan to staff CPA was for about 450 civilians who would act as senior advisors to the Iraqi bureaucracy. That was later upped to about eighteen hundred. The plan had been made assuming the bureaucracy would be intact upon the fall of the regime and without thought of how difficult it was to deal with civilian employees in a wartime

environment. The occupational government never in fact had the eighteen hundred employees as they either refused to appear or would leave
as soon as they realized the danger and saw the working conditions. The
plan anticipated a short hand-over period, but the truth on the ground
was so bad that the meager staff was inadequate. If they were bad in
Baghdad they were far worse in the countryside.

Finally, after pleas from Bremer's office, fourteen civil affairs soldiers
were sent to regional offices of CPA as the local governments were failing. The colonel in charge of the regional governments, Terry Callahan,
realized that nearly none of the civilian posts were being filled. He asked
for more military personnel to keep afloat the effort, but the request was
flatly denied. "We will never get out of here if we start taking on these
kind of jobs," said one staff officer.[6] One entire headquarters of a civil
affairs brigade sat through most of its deployment in Kuwait while the
people charged with establishing the government crossed off project after
project as unattainable because of lack of staffing.

The difficulty in such a point of view lay in that if the civilian authorities did not come forth, no one would do the job of actually running
the country, turning the military attitude into a "failure is an option"
strategy. Back at CPA headquarters in Baghdad, repeated calls to Washington for staffing by the civilian departments of the U.S. government
were ignored or delayed. The military, as the major stakeholder when
the civilian authorities failed, was left holding a bag it refused to carry.

In the meantime the job of meeting the personnel requirements of
CPA was left to a senior Pentagon official who accomplished what in government terms was lightning-fast action, but for the staff in Iraq seemed
intolerably delayed. Allen Kaupinen, who was known for his strong
reliance on the private sector over government service, by pure force of
will was able to staff CPA with people from outside of civil service, as
well as browbeat other federal agencies to meet their commitments in a
timely fashion. The problem lay in that he was not given the assignment
to even start the staff planning and hiring until the war was well underway. Thus, for months CPA was regularly understaffed and when people arrived, they had precious little time to accomplish their tasks.

In the beginning of November, the most deadly incident of the war
up to that time for the Americans occurred close to Fallujah. A CH-47
Chinook helicopter took off and headed towards Baghdad. Many of the
passengers were headed home to enjoy a well-deserved rest back in the
States in the newly created leave program. Soldiers called families saying that they would soon be home for two weeks. While the chopper was
flying low to the ground over the desert, a streak of smoke sprang forth
and headed with startling speed at the twin rotor helicopter, then
exploded. Hit by a shoulder-fired missile, the large helicopter slammed

into the ground. Sixteen soldiers died* in a single attack. Shortly after, insurgents wounded twenty soldiers outside the nearby town of Amiryah.

There was now a cycle of increasing outrages as viewed by the two sides. Ambushes and roadside bombs provoked the Americans. At the same time, "cordon and search operations," and frightened soldiers firing at people they suspected of ambushing them, made life in the presence of the Americans seemingly unbearable.

Part of the problem lay with the rules of engagement, which were unclear and had two possible interpretations. Perhaps because of political considerations, the command could not say to the soldiers that some personal risks needed to be taken to maintain the good will of the people. After the first shot in a battle, soldiers would often resort to suppressive fire, a lawful act but one that was likely to lead to civilian casualties.

Insurgents quickly realized that American combat units would not withdraw from a fight and would bring to bear their massive firepower. Thus, they would always spring their attacks in an area likely to cause civilian casualties. Explaining to the American public that young soldiers had to take such risks, or sometimes just yield the battleground to work it out later, was a step beyond for the Defense Department.

"The Americans hit a roadside bomb and then instead of catching the culprits they just open fire on everyone in sight," said an Iraqi policeman. "That's why Fallujah is boiling." It was not just the deaths of civilians that provoked the Fallujans. "American soldiers conducted humiliating house searches, breaking furniture, frisking men and women and stealing cash and jewelry," he said.[7]

"Saddam's people were terrible but they never humiliated us like this. We are a tribal society. We are hot blooded. What do you expect?" said a shop employee.[8]

There was generally a realization that for every innocent Iraqi killed or wounded by an American, ten new insurgents were recruited. General Sanchez had sent out reminders to stay with the already confusing rules of engagement as reports came in that they were being violated by frightened U.S. troops. But hardly anyone within the staff was willing to voice the opinion that American soldiers would have to take increased casualties to avoid Iraqi civilian deaths. There too was a sense that it all didn't matter as far as the Iraqis were concerned. The insurgency was quick to inflate the numbers of Iraqis killed by Coalition soldiers and the

*KIA: Staff Sgt. Daniel A. Bader, Sgt. Ernest G. Bucklew, Sgt. Steven D. Conover, Pfc. Anthony D. D'Agostino, Specialist Darius T. Jennings, Pfc. Karina S. Lau, Sgt. Keelan L. Moss, Spc. Brian H. Penisten, Sgt. Ross A. Pennanen, Sgt. Joel Perez, 1st Lt. Brian D. Slavenas, Chief Warrant Officer Bruce A. Smith, Spc. Frances M. Vega, Staff Sgt. Paul A. Velazquez, Staff Sgt. Joe N. Wilson

08/10/2003

Life on the road for many U.S. Army Civil Affairs teams was often dangerous. Short on troops for escort, they often went into remote areas in soft-skinned vehicles lightly armed.

Arab satellite networks were eager to publish and dwell upon each Iraqi killed by American fire. With no counter to show American restraint, there was a sense through the military that there was no benefit to taking on such restraints with the risks of increased American casualties. Great harm both politically at home and for a commander's career could result from withholding fire in an ambush until an identified legitimate target could be found.

General Swannack, the commander of the 82nd Airborne, asked for additional funds with fewer strings attached. He intended to spend more on civic projects and asked for more civil affairs forces to provide more carrot with the stick. The division had part of the 432nd Civil Affairs battalion, which could provide only two teams totaling ten people for all of Fallujah. The money was only marginally increased. Dozens of project nominations for large reconstruction projects were sent to Baghdad, only to never be heard of again. The headquarters of the 304th Civil Affairs Brigade under Colonel Gary Beard was held over from their original plan of mustering out. The reserve unit from Philadelphia did good work in ar-Ramadi but was too understaffed to provide the needed support for an area as large as the al-Anbar desert. There simply were not more such forces available.

The impact of these tactics and the shortfalls provided the insurgents with the tools they needed to help turn the already upset population into one willing to support the insurgency.

By February, it was clear that the insurgency was no longer an unorganized grassroots resistance but was capable of launching commando-style attacks indicative of careful planning, training, and rehearsals. On February 12, insurgents lying in wait on a rooftop ambushed General John Abizaid, commander of all U.S. forces in the Middle East, and Major General Charles Swannack, commander of the 82nd Airborne Division in Fallujah.

Two days later twenty-five guerrillas shouting "God is great!" launched a daylight assault on an Iraqi police station and security compound, freeing prisoners and sparking a gun battle that killed twenty-one people and wounded thirty-three.

CHAPTER 2

The First Battle of Fallujah

On March 24, the Marines took over from the 82nd Airborne, changing its strategy. The Army's 82nd Airborne Division had given up efforts to maintain a major presence in Fallujah, instead retreating to the perimeters of the city and mounting patrols from there.

The Marines were using a two-track approach. The first track involved 24-hour patrols to hunt down insurgents and those making and planting roadside bombs. Even more important, they were making a presence, and thus a statement that the Marines were not going away until the security improved. The second track was to help improve schools, clinics, and other government services by pumping in money and expertise.

This was all within the national strategy. CPA and the occupation were to end by July 1, 2004, but a few months away. Iraqis would be taking over control of local security, and the Americans saw themselves as only in a supporting role. The Marines saw themselves as in the process of handing over sovereignty to a local government that was a part of a central Iraqi government. This would work only if they had the support of Fallujans.

Within 48 hours, it was off to a shaky start. Marines engaged local insurgents in a long battle that left at least eighteen Iraqis, including five civilians, and one Marine dead.* The civilian dead included an eleven-year-old boy and an ABC television network cameraman.

Throughout Iraq, a new phenomenon had taken hold: answering the shortage of troops for security with privately contracted security guards. After the over 130,000 American troops, the nearly 20,000 people employed by private security firms now formed the second-largest armed force in Iraq. These guard services could cost as much as $1,500 a day.

They were everywhere. Some were Gurkas dressed in military-style uniforms. Others were clearly Western, garbed like action-movie heroes,

*KIA: Pfc. Leroy J. Sandoval

20

low-hanging pistols strapped to their legs, and exotic brands of assault weapons dangling on straps from their shoulders.

Blackwater was one of several contractor companies that provided security consulting, bodyguards, and training for police and military. A majority of the contractors were former military Special Forces, but some were from a variety of fields. It was common for contractors to go into the field in unarmored cars. It was rare that they coordinated with the military for security, but they did have access to CPA threat assessments. It was widely understood that Fallujah was a dangerous place. On March 31, four Blackwater contractors left for Fallujah without arranging for military security or informing them of their destination.

The contractors' two vehicles turned onto a Fallujan street. Men, faces covered by headscarves, split into two groups and threw hand grenades at the cars. The assailants then sprayed the burning cars with their AK47s. The passengers, their windows rolled up, could not maneuver their weapons to return fire. One American, shot in the chest, survived the gunfire, but the attackers pulled him from his disabled vehicle. A gathering mob of people killed him by throwing bricks and jumping on him. They cut off his arm, leg, and head as they cheered and danced. The bodies were beaten, burned, and dismembered. Locals cheered as one corpse was attached to a car towrope and pulled up and down the main road, while filmed by a TV news camera crew. The remains of two charred and defaced corpses were hung from a green iron bridge across the Euphrates River.

"The people of Fallujah hung some of the bodies on the old bridge like slaughtered sheep," one local said gleefully to a news reporter.[9] Another man standing near the corpses held up a printed sign with a skull and crossbones reading, "Fallujah is the cemetery for Americans." Police stayed away. No one dared make an arrest.

Attacks in Fallujah were not unusual. For weeks, there were two or three attacks every day, usually roadside bombs or mortar attacks. It was widely known that Fallujah was the most dangerous place in Iraq. However, this was different in character, sanctioned by the people themselves. It flew in the face of what the leadership of CPA and the military said, that the insurgency was not the will of the people of Iraq but some shadowy group outside the fringes of society.

There was a sense of shock as word spread from the press reports about the four Blackwater contractors. There were other killings of contractors, but the brutality and descriptions of a mob celebrating over the killings placed a pall over the Green Zone. Suddenly the civilians felt more than ever that they were the targets. There was also a deep sense of anger by the leadership over the mutilation and public display after the ambush.

There too was a sense of embarrassment among some in the Muslim intellectual elite, many who were supporting the insurgency. The senior

Fallujah cleric said Muslim preachers would tell their followers that the mutilation of the bodies was wrong. The Prophet Muhammad prohibited even the mutilation of a dead mad dog, and he considered such a thing as religiously forbidden. In the meantime, however, press reports from Fallujah found the people defiant and daring the Americans to enter the city.

On April 1, Brigadier General Mark Kimmitt, deputy director of operations for the U.S. military in Iraq, promised an overwhelming response. "We will pacify that city."

The Marines preferred a different approach. They felt that their "No better friend or worse enemy" campaign had not been given a chance to gel. Early in the campaign, due to a lack of forces, the entire western half of the country was short staffed as an economy of force measure. This undermanned force, with a scarcity of civil affairs assets and not much money, struggled to keep a semblance of security and to meet what were already unrealistic expectations of economic progress.

The Marines saw the military approach of the Third Armored Cavalry Regiment and the 82nd Airborne as too harsh and one-dimensional. Fallujah had always been a problem. Fallujans often spurned efforts to reach out, such as with gifts of frozen chickens taken door to door by civil affairs soldiers. But with the Iraqis taking on a greater role in local governance, the Marines felt they needed a more targeted approach. Plans were in the works for increased civic action projects for friends, while combat forces conducted precise raids against small neighborhoods and pockets of identified resistance.

The Marines were overruled. On April 4, Operation Vigilant Resolve began as over 2,000 troops from the 1st Marine Expeditionary Force began encircling Fallujah. Roughly, one brigade of Marines was all that was available for the expected quick fight.

One witness in the city described the start of operations in Fallujah, and the response of the town's people. "On the Sunday night we had heard the sounds of helicopters and tanks, and we knew something big was happening but we didn't expect them to seize the city," he said. " It was quiet and then at 9 P.M. the Americans tried to get inside the city. Every neighborhood started fighting against the Americans to defeat them." Helicopters and combat jets now circled over the city.

"Four houses in my block were destroyed. The house behind mine was hit with two rockets," he said. "We didn't go out, but from my gate I could see fighters carrying their weapons in the street, and fighting the Americans. I saw them being killed, and I saw their bodies in the street."[10]

Cpl. Christopher Ebert,* a Marine at the front of the force, later recounted that his unit went a few blocks into the city before coming

*Later KIA September 2004.

under fire from a house. Two of the Marines were wounded. Trapped in a narrow alley, unable to see the source of fire, the Marines put up red smoke to call for help. A tank and an armored Humvee moved up. The tank fired into the houses with a 50-caliber machine gun. The patrol withdrew under the cover of the armored force.

Soon afterward, insurgents opened fire with rocket-propelled grenades and automatic weapons on the Marines just outside the city. The Americans dove for cover and started the battle. Troops crawled forward, firing, and advancing across the open desert between them and the first line of buildings. From behind, Abrams tanks pounded the neighborhood with shells, setting at least five houses on fire. Helicopters swirled overhead, firing at any gunmen they saw.

Now mortar fire came in from the city, exploding near the Marines. The insurgents usually fired and ran. This time, they were standing to fight, moving from one building to the next from which to fire.

Marines moved into the neighborhood en masse now, seizing buildings to use as positions against the insurgents and climbing to the rooftops to get better fields of fire. The Marines were finding it difficult to fight against hit-and-run tactics in the city, when they had to try to avoid civilian casualties. The helicopters started getting fire now but none of the fire shot down its target. The Marines called in their most lethal weapon, the AC-130 gunship, a cargo plane armed with a heavy 105mm cannon, two 40mm "pom pom" guns, and a Gatling gun. By nightfall, the Marines held a penetration several blocks deep into the city. To everyone on either side, this was not the usual tactics of a guerilla war but a set-piece battle.

That night U.S. planes firing rockets destroyed four houses in two neighborhoods. The strike killed twenty-six Iraqis, including women and children, and wounded thirty others, according to the Fallujah General Hospital, where the casualties were taken. The deaths brought the total number of Iraqi dead to thirty-four, according to the hospital's count.

The next day, U.S. forces pushed further. Troops in Humvees and on foot pushed into central neighborhoods, trading fire with gunmen, but thought it best to pull back at nightfall.

April 6 was the bloodiest day of the war to date for the Marines, but it was several miles away in ar-Ramadi, where they were supporting a brigade of the army's 1st Armored Division. It started with a rattle of fire and a call for help. One of the Marines' sniper teams was taking fire. The commander of the Marine Echo Company, Capt. Kelly D. Royer, led out a QRF (Quick Reaction Force) in Humvees into Ramadi's narrow streets toward the sound of the guns pinning down one of their sniper teams. There was no time to plan, only to react as they had practiced.

It turned out that they were not needed. A radio message came in saying that the snipers fought off the ambush. But now the small group of Marines heard new fire from a different place. The platoon, sent out earlier to patrol the main supply route through ar-Ramadi, was taking fire. They were pinned down and called for help on their radio.

The company commander radioed 2nd Lt. John Wroblewski. Lieutenant "Ski" was leading another relief force in Humvees that he gathered to help the rest of his company. The company commander told the relief team to join him at the intersection at the marketplace.

The Marines noticed the day before that the residents didn't wave, and the children didn't flock to the Marines, as they did in other parts of the city. Although the Marines did not know it, earlier that morning insurgents came to the marketplace, telling shopkeepers to close their stores and stands, telling the merchants that there would be an ambush. No one came to warn the Marines.

Suddenly gunfire rattled where Royer's QRF had just been. Marines appeared to be under attack everywhere. The company commander and his Marines started running to reinforce their comrades in the 1st Platoon. The insurgents had already killed two Marines from the 1st Platoon.

As the first force ran to help the 1st Platoon, Wroblewski rolled past with his convoy. The QRF under the command of the company commander called him to stop and pick them up. They heard Wroblewski's Humvees and trucks slow as they approached the marketplace. Then they heard the rattle of AK47 fire, the deeper pounding of a machine gun, and the explosions of RPGs.

Lieutenant Ski came up to the marketplace with three Humvees and slowed as he entered the intersection. At the wheel of the first vehicle was Lance Cpl. Kyle Crowley. With him in the unarmored Humvee was Lance Cpl. Travis J. Layfield, Pfc. Christopher R. Cobb, Lance Cpl. Anthony Roberts, Navy Petty Officer 3rd Class Fernando A. Mendez-Aceves, a medic, Staff Sgt. Allan K. Walker, and Lance Cpl. Deshon E. Otey. In the back, manning the machine gun, was Pfc. Ryan Jerabek.

In the al-Ramadi marketplace on all sides of the intersection, fifty insurgents with AK47s and rocket-propelled grenade launchers had taken positions on the roofs of the one-story buildings. A heavy Russian-made machine gun was on one rooftop. Other fighters hid behind trees just beyond the market stalls.

As the Humvee, still not repainted from its original green, neared the T-intersection the insurgents hidden on the rooftops opened fire. Bullets shattered through the windshield and the metal doors, killing Crowley, the driver. The truck skidded sideways. Jerabek opened up with his machine gun but he too was quickly killed.

Otey leapt out of the Humvee and ducked behind a low wall, popping up to fire to cover the others. It was already too late. As far as he could tell, the others in the truck were already gunned down.* But those in the other two vehicles dove for cover. Firing came from every direction from AKs and machine guns as well as the shattering explosions of the rocket-propelled grenades.

Sergeant Walker was down, and the corpsman was frantically trying to tend to him. As Fernando Mendez-Aceves tried to revive his comrade, a bullet ended his life. Lieutenant Ski in the second vehicle was calling on the radio, trying to report. A bullet smashed into his face.

Now Captain Royer was coming up to help the Marines in the kill zone of the ambush. But as soon as he appeared, fire rained down on his little unit. The commander ran to the cover of some nearby houses. Looking back, he saw his radioman lagging. He shouted at the struggling Marine to find the strength to keep up. Along with him was the translator. Royer saw that he was smiling as he ran. He came panting in a sleeveless jogging outfit, tan sandals, and a navy blue T-shirt that said "Operation Iraqi Freedom" across the front. He was not even wearing a helmet or a protective vest.

Several of Wroblewski's Marines had ducked into a cinder block house. The gunfire rattled with such savagery that to stick one's head out a window seemed sure suicide. Huddled in the first room was an Iraqi family, clearly terrified. The Marines heard footsteps rushing up to the door, and one instinctively pointed his M16 at the entrance. In rushed Captain Royer followed by some of his men. Bullets now slammed into the side of the house. They ducked and wondered whether the cinder block would stop the bullets. The RPK machine gun they heard pounding would surely drill through the brittle concrete.

Royer led his small force up a flight of stairs to the roof where they could shoot back. From there they could see only shadows, muzzle flashes, glimpses of the insurgents. Now they turned their M16s on the ambushers. The aimed fire of three-round bursts immediately changed the momentum of the firefight.

Royer called for attack choppers. But there were firefights elsewhere in the city of half a million, and they were supporting those Marines.

The heavy machine gun was the most dangerous, so the young Marine commander sent his men to take out the pounding killer. By the time the Marines dodged through the courtyards and backstreets, the machine gunners were gone with their gun.

One of the Marines said they saw five Iraqis coming down the street. "Do they have weapons? Do they have weapons?" Royer called out. The

---

Lance Cpl. Deshon E. Otey and three other Marines in his company were killed in action several months later.

Marines started shooting and the five scattered. A van and some cars came up and started picking men up. There was no way to tell if they were picking up the insurgents or others. The Marines could not see any weapons.

The shooting was over. The Marines went up to the first Humvee in the ambush. There was blood, shell casings, pieces of broken weapons, the cotton and gauze of aid packs torn open and water bottles scattered about. Beside an orange and white taxi were four bodies of Iraqis. That was how fighting was for most in Iraq, a sudden flurry of fire and confusion. Then, it was all over just as suddenly.* But in the distance the shooting continued.

In the meantime, the high headquarters was reacting to the news of the attacks across the city. Sgt. Maj. Ron Riling organized an armored relief force and rolled out with Colonel Buck Connor, the brigade commander, towards ar-Ramadi. As they entered the main town of Ramadi, they immediately came under direct fire coming from every direction with small arms and RPGs. They pushed through to come to the aid of a hardpressed Marine sniper team. The squad leader was dead, lying in the middle of the street, and three of the seven Marines were seriously wounded. The senior Marine remaining was a corporal.

Riling, Connor, and their team evacuated the injured Marines and recovered the Marine squad leader's body, as well as another Marine platoon in the area. The unarmored Marine vehicles were being fired on by an Iraqi insurgent armed with rocket-propelled grenades. Riling directed two army Bradley Fighting Vehicles from the brigade's reserve into the fight to stop the attacks. He saw an insurgent run into a home. The building was heavily reinforced and had high brick and metal walls. Riling had one of the Bradleys knock down a fence surrounding the house.

The lead soldier on the door, who was in charge of the colonel's physical security detachment, attempted to kick the door down but it wouldn't budge. The 6-feet, 2-inch Riling yelled at him to move out of the way. He crashed through that door with his left shoulder, and knocked the door off its hinges. Then he opened fire, killing the insurgent in the room.†

Before the battle was over twelve‡ Marines died, and twenty-five were wounded, and an M1-A1 Abrams tank and a Bradley Fighting Vehi-

---

*In Iraq, Echo Company lost 23 KIA and more than 40 wounded of its 185 men.
†Sgt. Maj. Ron Riling was awarded the silver star for his actions on April 6, 2003.
‡KIA: Pfc. Deryk L. Hallal, Pfc. Christopher R. Cobb, Pfc. Ryan M. Jerabek, Lance Cpl. Travis J. Layfield, Lance Cpl. Anthony P. Roberts, Lance Cpl. Kyle D. Crowley, Staff Sgt. Allan K. Walker, Lance Cpl. Marcus M. Cherry, Pfc. Benjamin R. Carman, 2nd Lt. John T. Wroblewski, Pfc. Christopher D. Mabry

cle were hit. At four different locations in the city, coordinated guerrilla attacks showed a skill never before seen in Iraq.*

Back in Fallujah, the Marines were also finding that the usual rules did not apply. Said a humanitarian worker trying to bring in aid, "There are young children involved in the fighting. I saw boys, about eleven years old, masked up and holding AK47s."[11]

The fighting on April 7, became particularly heavy but with only two Marines[†] killed and five more wounded. Ninety insurgents were thought to have been killed in the exchanges. That same day, troops saw armed men firing from a mosque. They called in a laser-guided bomb during what would have been afternoon prayers. Forty Iraqis were claimed to have died, which was given wide coverage by the Arab press.

While these networks reported that the Coalition dropped a JDAM (a laser-guided bomb) on the mosque, many in the media failed to report why the bomb was dropped or stated that the action was unprovoked. In reality, the insurgents had overtaken the mosque and were using the minarets to fire on the Marines. By omitting any reference to the gunmen in the mosque, the outlets turned an act of self-defense into a purported violation of the Geneva Convention. The Arab press also reported the bombing of four houses with sixteen children and eight women as victims.

The Marines were discovering large quantities of weapons from the industrial area they now controlled. Found were large quantities of rockets and mortars, plastic explosives, bomb-making equipment, and a variety of exploding vests and belts. One was a money belt sewn full of explosives with a detonator and lead fishing weights inside. It was clear that the months of only intermittent attention had allowed Fallujah to develop into a major base for the resistance. But the U.S. operation in Fallujah had still not moved beyond the industrial zone and into the densely crowded residential areas. That would be a far more difficult task because insurgents could hide there easily with civilians as shields.

The shortage of troops was making itself felt. One platoon leader waiting for the corpsmen to treat his shrapnel wound complained that he didn't have enough men to seal the area they retreated to as they shot and fell back. The casualties were taking their toll on the offense, for each wounded required several others to carry him back to the aid station.

Nor were the defenders awed at the Marine assault or firepower. Despite the bombing of the mosque, the insurgents had returned undeterred by the prospect of a further American assault.

---

*Another platoon was also trapped and its platoon leader had to expose himself in the open in a crossfire to direct his troops. U.S.M.C. Lt Thomas E. Cogan was awarded the Silver Star for his gallantry for leading his platoon out of the ambush in al-Ramadi.
†KIA: Capt. Brent L. Morel, Lance Cpl. Phillip E. Frank

CJTF-7 estimated there to be 2,000 hard-core insurgents, including about 200 foreign fighters, under the loose control of Salafi terrorist al-Zarqawi inside Fallujah. The insurgents, gathering in units of 20 to 40 people, lacked a unified command but showed tenacity and skills that indicated military training.

"It takes a lot of military expertise to develop a block-by-block defense," one senior officer said.[12] They were covering their infantry advances with mortar supporting fire. That was a sophisticated small-unit tactic.

If things were not going as planned in the assault they were going disastrously on the publicity and thus the political front. Doctors at Fallujah's main hospital told journalists that the operation killed up to 280 civilians.

The Marines denied this, saying any bodies were those of insurgents. The Marines estimated that 80 percent of Fallujah's populace was neutral or in favor of the American military presence. Even so, in a city of over 250,000, that would leave 50,000 people ready to fight or help others who would. There too were reports that members of the Iraqi civilian defense forces in Fallujah had joined with the insurgents. The Marines watched first-hand as the insurgents used ambulances as well as police cars to carry weapons and ammunition to the fighting positions.

Back in Baghdad, the Interim Governing Council* was threatening a mass walkout. Scenes of the battle and commentaries on the plight of the civilians in Fallujah were everywhere on the airwaves and in print.

A caravan of medical and food supplies collected by mosques in Baghdad approached the sealed-off city, along with several thousand marchers. Shouting anti–American slogans and carrying banners sympathetic to the insurgents, they were accompanied by both al-Jazeera and al-Arabiya cameramen. The Marines tried to calm public anger over the scenes broadcasted on Arab satellite news by letting the caravan enter the city. The caravan was mostly peaceful, and a number of supply trucks and ambulances entered the city after they were searched. But the crowd of about 1,500 marchers was turned back at a roadblock. Some shouted insults. When several mortar rounds landed nearby the crowd cheered.

As the Marines contemplated how to continue the attacks on the enemy without alienating the general populace, several officers said they were keenly aware of their public relations dilemma. Coming under constant fire could cause a lapse in the discipline of the troops. The Marines on the line were getting frustrated.

---

*The IGC was the group of Iraqis selected by Bremer to provide advice. While they had no legal authority no CPA action was politically possible without their concurrence. A widespread walkout would have torn away any Iraqi participation in the government and could have resulted in a nationwide uprising.

Some staff officers were expressing concern about the stress being put on their Marines. Some of the complaints were ringing true enough to believe that the line troops were losing fire discipline. But in the middle of a battle it was too late to correct the behavior.

One thing was clear: with all civil affairs programs planned by the Marines suspended until the city was secure, the only vision on TV was the sight of Marines killing Iraqis.

The commander of the civil affairs unit supporting the Marines had planned to contact local religious and tribal leaders, find out what Fallujah's residents needed most and arrange for money to be spent on local projects. Now, all that was on indefinite hold. "It's hard to do civil affairs until the area becomes stable and secure," he said amidst the mortar fire. "The enemy seems determined, but I like to think this is one last gasp for breath before their day is ended."[13] He was not aware of the political uproar in Baghdad.

On April 9, the U.S. military announced a unilateral suspension of offensive operations. With the offensive stopped, a delegation of politicians from the Iraqi Islamic Party (IIP), a Sunni group on the governing council, entered Fallujah for talks. This stopped the forward motion but did not stop the fighting.

The Marines came under constant fire as they held their lines, often pressing slightly forward to remove themselves from positions that were under fire. This required even more troops and the application of air power, which brought on new stories claiming civilian dead.

In a tension-filled meeting with Iraq's civilian administrator, L. Paul Bremer, council members criticized Bremer for not involving them in discussions about U.S. military operations and for failing to pursue less violent ways to control Fallujah. There too was the ongoing confrontation with Moqtada al-Sadr, a junior Shi'ite Muslim cleric whose militia was also fighting Coalition forces in Baghdad and in cities across southern Iraq.

Al-Sadr had taken refuge in Najaf. His militia, called the Mahdi Army, maintained control over the city while U.S. forces remained outside. In Kut, another southern city held by insurgents since Ukrainian troops retreated earlier in the week, about 1,000 U.S. troops fought to reassert Coalition control. There was fighting between insurgents and coalition forces in the cities of Mosul, Baqubah, and Muqdadiya, as well as Karbala, the holy city where Shi'ite pilgrims had been gathering for a religious observance that weekend.

At the time, most military and political figures considered al-Sadr an even greater threat to the Coalition's plan to transition to an interim Iraqi government. In a sermon delivered by one of his deputies at the Imam Ali Shrine in the Shi'ite holy city of Najaf, al-Sadr wrote, "I direct my speech to my enemy Bush, and I tell him that, if your excuse was that

One of the unqualified successes for CPA was the creation of the Baghdad City Council. To create this first democratic institution in Iraq, CPA and the military turned to Lt. Colonel Joseph Rice, whose work drew regular positive mention from the international media. Here, Lt. Colonel Rice (left) is awarded the Bronze Star by Ambassador Bremer.

you are fighting Saddam, then this thing is past and now you are fighting the entire Iraqi people."[14] Until now, the Coalition saw the insurgency as two separate movements among the Sunnis and among the Shi'a, with incompatible goals. Now they were tag-teaming the Americans.

The Coalition was also trying to deal with two Iraqi ICDC (Iraqi Civil Defense Corps, Iraqi military working for the Coalition) battalions ordered to fight in Fallujah. One simply refused. When the soldiers, who had just finished basic training, were told where they were being sent, they staged a mutiny and refused to board their transport. The Defense Department used private contractors to conduct basic training. Once the soldiers finished boot camp, they were put under the command of U.S. officers whom they had never met.

As CPA was struggling with Fallujah and al-Sadr, the Marines were having trouble again in ar-Ramadi. In an intense firefight that included another ambush with a roadside bomb at the same intersection it was ambushed before, Echo Company lost four more Marines.*

*KIA: Lance Cpl. Elias Torrez III, Cpl. Matthew E. Matula, 1st Lt. Joshua M. Palmer, Pfc. Eric Ayon

Politically, things only got worse. The next day medical officials in Fallujah said the number of Iraqis killed had reached 450, with 1,000 wounded. More than 70,000 women, children, and elderly residents were said to have left the besieged city. Now, with a temporary cease-fire, civilians were allowed to return. At the same time, carloads of families began to pour out of the city along back roads. This humanitarian gesture often resulted in a nightmare of bad publicity as reporters eager for first-hand accounts printed their stories.

Most of those in Fallujah during the fighting described the Mujahadeen in heroic terms. "There are a lot of people who don't want the Mujahadeen to fight because they have been forced out of their houses and their jobs," said a retired architect who fled Fallujah after the first week and then spoke to the press. "But it is the fault of the Americans: it is the people's right to fight against occupation."[15]

"The Mujahadeen are brave and fear nothing," he said. The speaker was jailed under Saddam as a political prisoner for supporting an Arab nationalist party. He welcomed the fall of Saddam, but like many educated professionals in the Sunni community, he had seen little reward from the occupation.

"We fought for this country. Is this what we are fighting for?" he said. His family was now living in a former air raid shelter in Amariya, in western Baghdad, waiting for the chance to return to Fallujah.[16]

Upon returning to his house, one resident spoke to the press of finding by the front gate of his home the body of his sixteen-year-old son. The boy had the back of his skull torn away. It was said that he was standing by the gate when a bomb landed nearby. At the house was the owner's missing and now confirmed dead nephew. He had left his own home to check on his fiancée's family. The family retrieved the young man's body from where it lay in the street. He had been hit once a bullet through the heart. Since it was too dangerous to go to the cemetery, they buried him in a patch of ground. Later they would take out his body and bury him properly.

From his driveway, the resident described seeing an eighteen-year-old girl shot dead. Her brother-in-law rushed to help her and was reported to have been shot too. A house at the end of his street suffered a direct hit from a bomb. In the garden of his neighbor's house, he saw three men who had been sitting on a bench all dead, cut in half by the bomb. He blamed the killing on the Marines.

The Iraqi medical personnel in Fallujah eagerly complained. Inside Fallujah, the fighting made it impossible to seek help from the hospital and that was blamed on the Marines. Dozens of houses were destroyed, mosques were bombed, and the clerics turned a football ground beside the Euphrates into a crude cemetery. Said one doctor, "You didn't see any cars; you didn't see anything except the Mujahadeen."

"We had a clinic with two operating rooms. It was the worst place in Iraq to deal with a patient," he said. "There were many civilians, there were women. I saw one woman who was pregnant, and there was shrapnel in her abdomen from a shell. Her baby died. The city's main hospital, on the western bank of the Euphrates, was closed by the Marines."[17]

Ibrahim Younis, the Iraq emergency coordinator for Doctors Without Borders, said that the isolation caused many wounded to die because of inadequate care. The hospital had four operating theaters, which could no longer be used. "If they had been working, it would have saved many lives."[18]

"The Americans put a sniper position on top of the hospital's water tower and had troops in the single-story building," said Mr. Younis,[19] who visited Fallujah during the fighting. He called for an independent inquiry to determine why the U.S. military used the hospital as a military position, a violation of the Geneva Convention.

"Using force in the way they used it in Fallujah made people fight," said, a senior member of the interim council. "It isn't like these people were terrorists. They were normal people, and they had children who were dying and so everybody started to fight."[20]

These were only samples of the personal stories broadcast into Iraqi homes or picked up by the some 200 newspapers that sprung up after the fall of Saddam Hussein.

Since the siege started, the wounded from the city had not been able to pick their way through the lines to the hospital. On April 17, the Marines adjusted lines to allow for a corridor to the facility. The Marines challenged the assertion that they prevented medical and humanitarian aid from entering the city during the fighting.

CJTF-7, the military command in Iraq, read these accounts and fumed. The *Baghdad Mosquito*, a compilation of stories from Baghdad newspapers, gave a clear picture of the distorted view given to Iraqis, but the military could not devise a counter. There was no embedded reporter program for Iraqi correspondents to allow them to travel with U.S. units to give the view from the American soldier's vantage. The reporters for the Arab satellite media were aware of the violations of Islamic law and the law of warfare by the insurgents but simply did not report it. Each day, Iraqis working for CPA and the military who were sympathetic to the Coalition goals came in upset from the stories believed to be true of atrocities committed by America.

Iraqi journalists began grilling Coalition officials at nearly every briefing as to why Americans were targeting women and children, and why the Americans were punishing so many innocent Iraqis for the wrongs committed by the few who desecrated the bodies in Fallujah. Stung by the statements, Lieutenant Colonel Brennan Byrne of the U.S.

Marines said during the fighting, "What I think you will find is 95 percent of those were military age males that were killed in the fighting. The Marines are trained to be precise in their firepower." But these assurances fell on deaf ears. The journalists had seen the proof of the Coalition's savagery; they had watched satellite networks like al-Jazeera and al-Arabiya.

The international press portrayed American snipers as the villains. Said one humanitarian worker, "Food and medical aid is now arriving but the problem is getting the aid around the city. A lot of it is delivered to the mosque, but then getting it to the hospitals past the American snipers is proving to be impossible. We saw two kids arriving with their grandmother, they had all been wounded by gunfire, they said by American snipers, while they were trying to leave their house to flee to Baghdad. An elderly woman with a wound to the head was still carrying the white flag she had been holding when she was shot."[21]

Local doctors, some sympathetic to the insurgents, accused the Americans of preventing medical assistance.

But the Western press was reporting much the same. Humanitarian workers would speak of U.S. gunmen firing at ambulances and civilians. British aid worker Jo Wilding described a trip in an ambulance she was in, with flashing lights, siren blaring and "ambulance" written on it in English, which was hit as it drove to collect a woman in premature labor. Wilding was sure the shots came from American troops.

Iraqi doctor Salam al-Obaidi, a member of Doctors for Iraq, worked in Fallujah for six days during the fighting. Speaking to BBC News Online, he described seeing colleagues blown up in an ambulance, also clearly marked, traveling in front of him as his team tried to enter a U.S.-controlled area. "I saw the ambulance disappear, not all of it, but the front of it, the side where the driver and paramedic were," he said.[22] Such claimed witness statements made anything officials said seem incredible.

Lt. Gen. Ricardo Sanchez, the commander of U.S. forces in Iraq, denied that troops were firing on ambulances. "If we're shooting vehicles, it's because those vehicles have shot at us," he said.

U.S. officials recounted one occasion where an insurgent gunman was seen fleeing in an ambulance and that weapons had been found in an aid convoy west of the city. The Iraqi Health Minister, Khodair Abbas, stated that 271 people died and local doctors had been pressured to give inflated figures.

But others described cases of women, children, and old men who appeared to have been shot by U.S. soldiers. Graphic descriptions of the bodies of two men, one aged about 70, the other about 50, both shot in the forehead in an area controlled by the U.S., went out over the wire.

They had been lying at the front gate of their home for two days because the family did not dare step outside to retrieve the bodies.

In the meantime, the Marines sought to get humanitarian aid to the beleaguered populace, but their very presence placed the relief workers in danger. On April 12, an escorted convoy carrying food, water, and blood was delayed and rerouted when the Marines escorting the convoy discovered improvised explosive devices (IEDs) along its route. IEDs and small arms fire hit a second humanitarian convoy before it reached the city. The Marines returned fire and called in a helicopter gunship.

April 15th, Marines and Iraqi Civil Defense Corps searched what was disguised as a humanitarian convoy to find weapons and ammunition hidden in bags of grain, rice, and tea. This was not the first time. Other convoys had attempted to bring in arms as well. There was a bus with a false bottom filled with assault rifles and rocket-propelled grenade launchers. An anti-aircraft gun hidden in another truckload of aid also slipped through the cordon but was discovered in the city later. There too were reports of ambulances being used to gather weapons off the battlefield. Marines watched an ambulance wheel up and a man get out, collecting the machine gun, leaving the gunner, who had been shot. The U.S. military was quick to publicize the attempts to use the Red Crescent for military purposes but it was lost in the scenes of wounded women and children.

The insurgents of Fallujah were well aware of the restraint the civilians were having upon the American forces: "people fear that once a large proportion of women and children leave, the Americans will destroy the city," said one aid worker.[23] Still, nearly a third of the people had fled the city.

Far more nimble than the Coalition, the insurgents were also finding new ways to get out their message. The Americans, with their tradition of a free press, were having difficulty in fighting the propaganda. CDs were coming out in the Baghdad markets showing battle scenes and the destruction in Fallujah.

For a vast majority of the Marines who were not in Fallujah, the slaughter and agony of the battle was not their first concern. Just a mile from Fallujah, other American troops were getting on with locals, making medical house calls and sharing hospitality. While others were engaged in fighting in Fallujah, they were with farmers more interested in their own lives than the resistance.

Life among most Iraqis was much more complicated and more personal. Among most Iraqis personal relationships were what defined life, and a single reaching out on a one-to-one basis usually overcame group prejudices. For most Iraqis as well, getting along with the strange foreign men who stopped them to search their cars was not just a matter of necessity but of cultural hospitality.

"It's like another world," one officer working outside of Fallujah said. "We're doing more of the SASO (security and stabilization operations) stuff. It's more hearts and minds over here."

"We feel pretty comfortable here," said a Marine sergeant who ran a checkpoint searching cars with passengers who wanted to carry food and supplies through the military lines into Fallujah.

"Neighbors bring us food," the Marine said. "We help them get their animals across, carry food and fuel, and stuff, basically help with anything we can do within our power. It's more hearts and minds here, but still you have to be on guard. You never know."[24]

The Marines paid local farmers for damage done to their fields and were a particular favorite with the children. The Marines working with those outside of Fallujah and ar-Ramadi quickly made a connection with the Iraqis.

"I feel guilty because we've had such an impact on their lives," he said. "They say they had more freedom under Saddam Hussein. I just try to tell them that when we get this whole thing straightened out, they can get back to their normal lives. But this just isn't a place [Fallujah] you want to take your family, at least not yet."[25]

Before coming to Iraq, the Marines trained for several months on how to win over Iraqis to the Coalition cause by politely inspecting vehicles, smiling, and waving. In their original planning, this was how they envisioned their tour in Iraq. Close interaction and being able to help Iraqis was more of what they expected to be doing when they deployed to Iraq.

Nevertheless, at the same time groups of insurgents would filter through many of the same people who in turn treated them much the same. For the most part, soldiers and Marines, when they reached out to the populace, found people willing to reach back on a personal level. As long as the topic was kept on a personal level, U.S. servicemen got along well. When the topic turned to politics or religion there was resistance.

In the wake of the fighting, military officials desperately tried to plead their case to those Fallujans they had under their control using PSYOPS teams. Marines and soldiers distributed leaflets in farming villages outside the encircled city of Fallujah asking residents to keep insurgents from using the local mosque for meetings or to store weapons. Included in the message was a warning: If insurgents shoot at U.S. forces from mosques, the buildings will lose their protected status and will be fired on.

As the possibility loomed of a full assault on Fallujah, the U.S. redoubled its efforts to deal with the sensitive political and cultural dilemmas of insurgents operating out of mosques. "We want to respect their

The early reception for American troops was widely positive. Scenes like this faded as the population became impatient with a lack of progress in rebuilding and American responses to insurgent ambushes led to cordon and search operations.

culture, and we don't want to interfere with their religion, but the mosques have become safe-havens for terrorists," said one young Marine officer.[26]

Convincing Iraqis not to allow insurgents to use mosques was proving difficult. Persuading them that damage to the mosques would be the fault of insurgents was equally challenging.

"The people don't seem to like our message," said one psyoper handing out the 3-by-5 flyers. "They read it and shake their heads."[27]

By now, the talk was all about negotiations and how to stop the fighting. The Marines who were against the assault in the first place now felt they had no choice and wanted to finish the job. General Sanchez also wanted nothing to do with any cease-fire. There was a clear understanding that now the insurgents were entrenched, it was past the point of winning them over. When briefed about possible walkouts in the Interim Iraqi Governing Council and peace negotiations, he turned to his staff and said, "We have to get our minds around this political stuff to prevent anything from stopping us from killing these guys."[28]

For the Marines this was a heartbreaking time, unable to fight it out and stuck on a battle line. This was dangerous business as one supply column found out. The Marines were on a supply mission to other units in Fallujah, which had been there for more than a week. They approached the city in unarmored Humvees, but came under small-arms fire and turned back to transfer the supplies into two armored assault vehicles.

When the new convoy entered Fallujah, insurgents attacked it too. One vehicle managed to retreat but the other caught fire and stumbled deeper into the insurgent zone. They started taking RPG (rocket-propelled grenade) fire and tried to get out of the area, but lost communication with the others. Their engine was on fire. A plume of smoke rose from the vehicle.

They had run into an organized ambush. The Marines fled the blazing vehicle and ran for cover in a nearby building. Within minutes, insurgents were shooting at them from all sides, with grenades thrown over the walls that served as a courtyard of most houses. The troops saved themselves by hurling back the grenades and called for help. A helicopter rescue would have been too dangerous and likely to end in the aircraft being shot down. Instead, a force of twenty-five Marines, backed by four tanks and air support, came in.

They fought through half a mile of gunfire to reach their trapped Marines. Within the first 600 yards, they were shooting in every direction. When they got to it, the armored personnel carrier was a piece of burning metal. Insurgents were tossing grenades from the houses on either side. Small arms fire was everywhere.

Under covering fire from the tanks and planes, the rescue force was able to get the destroyed vehicle's crew into Humvees and raced to safety. During the fighting the Marines killed at least twenty insurgents.

Both sides were now developing tricks of the trade. Marines knocked down walls between rooftop terraces to allow movement from house to house without going into the street. Insurgents were digging tunnels under the houses so they could move without being targeted by U.S. snipers. Marines punched bricks out of walls to set up gun-slits, and spread shards of glass across doorsteps to alert them to approaching enemy fighters. Some Iraqi gunmen were wearing flak jackets, apparently looted from Iraqi police stores. This was not what the Marines had expected when they prepared for their tour in Iraq. But the Marines had one trump card, the AC-130 Specter gunships to fire down artillery shells on the area.

On April 13, 16, and 17, Ambassador Richard Jones, the deputy chief administrator of the Coalition, led the negotiations. They included other officials from the Coalition, working alongside representatives from the Iraqi Governing Council, Dr. Hajim, as well as a representative of Dr. Pachachi and of Sheik Ghazi, desperately looking for a way out of continued fighting in Fallujah.

On the front lines under the regular fire of the insurgents, the

Marines laid a trap. On the April 18, a platoon infiltrated some 400 yards ahead of its defensive lines to map out enemy positions and then waited in ambush for those coming up each day to shoot at them. The small force inched their way through trashed buildings and homes. They settled in near the mosque and waited all day until almost dark. "It was ghostly," said Cpl. Christopher Ebert,* who had led the way at the start of the battle in Fallujah. "We only had about three hours to go and then these six guys showed up."[29]

At about 7:30 P.M., just as expected, six armed men came sneaking up. They entered the mosque to start the next day's shooting at the Americans. The first squad opened up, killing five who were carrying a machine gun. The insurgents started to attack the squad. Insurgents fired mortars and rocket-propelled grenades, and drove three vehicles down the street with gunmen firing AK47s at the Marines.

Up came another Marine squad with a tank to support the first squad. Two of the vehicles disintegrated to the sound of Marine automatic fire, shattering glass, and the banging of bullets through sheet metal, cutting short the assault and killing another six. After an hour, the Marines went back to their lines and enjoyed a rare hot meal in place of their MREs. The Marines got away from this fight without a scratch.

On April 19, Fallujan leaders and U.S. military officials agreed to work for a cease-fire in which insurgents would give up their heavy weapons. There were threats that should the insurgents in Fallujah not comply, operations by the Marines would recommence. To the military staff, the agreement was presented only as a pause. But in the office of CPA senior officials, there was an understanding that it would be politically impossible to recommence the offense. As if to mock the agreement, that very day there was a small-arms attack coming from Fallujah. The day after, there was an RPG attack.

The announcement that the security of Fallujah, and thus its assurance of loyalty to the central government would in effect be turned over to Iraqi control, raised eyebrows in the military headquarters. There were some diplomats touting the plan. It could be a model for transition of control of all areas to the Iraqis this coming July. This was lunacy as far as many officers were concerned. The Iraqi security apparatus was not ready.

U.S. troops were now fighting to re-establish the control they relinquished prematurely. CPA was hiring 11,000 policemen a week. But of the 78,000 policemen in Iraq only 2,324 were fully trained and 59,638 untrained. The rest were still in training. The police and in large measure the ICDC (Iraqi Civil Defense Force) were unvetted recruits, whose

*KIA September 2004.

loyalty and commitment to a central government were only assumed and who were subject to intimidation.

Colonels, generals, and senior CPA staff often raised such questions, which were shrugged away as too difficult to handle. So bad was the condition of the Iraqi government that experts advised that it would take years for the Iraqis to take back control. When that turned to months, as it was clear that the insurgency would not allow for patience, the press of time made such details beyond the military and occupational government to manage.

Under the agreement, a former Saddam Hussein general would take charge of the city with the new Fallujah Brigade. Recruited locally, they would control the city and solve one of the great problems the entire Fallujah operation demonstrated. The insurgency was leaderless. Now there was someone with whom to negotiate, bribe, intimidate, or what have you. Besides, what alternative was available? Sanchez and the Marines stewed. Others looking at Moqtada al-Sadr and the other cities in the Sunni Triangle wondered aloud if they were just setting the pattern for more Fallujahs. Then there were the insurgents, who were not cooperating with any plan.

The next day things seemed only to be getting worse. There was both a small-arms attack and indirect fire from Fallujah. All told, about forty insurgents attacked, striking in the north of the city, mounting a barrage of rocket-propelled grenades and small-arms fire.

The five-hour battle wounded three Marines, one critically. Even the presence of tanks did not deter the fighters. The insurgents attacked the tanks with rocket-propelled grenades, but the weapons either missed their targets or bounced off the armored vehicles. Cobra helicopters raked buildings with gunfire, and the bombs dropped by the F-16s flattened several structures. Insurgents used grenades, machine guns, and mortar shells in continuous volleys. Marine snipers hit several attackers. The insurgents used neighborhood mosques as gathering spots, and one house of worship blared out martial music from its minaret.

From the mosque, Marines could hear broadcasted, "God is Good, God is great" and "Holy Warriors come out to fight." It seemed to be telling the people to rise up and appeared to be giving orders. The Marines chose not to target the mosque and used a public address system to answer back in Arabic. Their message: The insurgents were violating the peaceful tenets of the Koran and were a threat to Islam. The mosque switched to its morning call to prayers.

In a remarkable degree of understatement, General Conway stated in his press conference, "It is our estimate that the people of Fallujah have not responded well to the agreement that was made."

The day had another political defeat as well. The Dominican Republic

With the collapse of the Iraqi government, nearly all of the police abandoned their posts. Desperately, the military hired just about anyone willing to be a police officer; uniforms, weapons, and training were to follow. Most of these police were unvetted, with mixed loyalties, and most abandoned their posts in April 2004. Here some newly hired police come in with a few antiques they confiscated as illegal weapons.

and Honduras were pulling out of the Coalition. The Spanish had announced that they were pulling out in March. But the worst news came from the far south of the country.

In British-patrolled Basra, two police stations in the Ashar district and one in the Old City were hit in near-simultaneous attacks. A wounded Iraqi said that he heard a huge explosion as he stood at the door of his house. "I looked around and saw my neighbor lying dead on the floor, torn apart," he said. "I saw a minibus full of children on fire, fifteen of the eighteen passengers were killed and three badly wounded."

Protesters blaming the British for failing to provide security stoned the British soldiers who were trying to assist casualties. Shortly after the Basra bombings, two car bombs hit a police academy in the town of Zubair, about sixteen miles to the south. The total human toll was sixty-eight dead, including children being driven to school, and at least two hundred wounded.

In the Fallujah agreement, the insurgents were to turn in the heavy machine guns and mortars. The city's police chief informed Marine officers that the first load of weapons were ready to be collected. When the Marines arrived, they found a pickup truck loaded with rusted, antiquated, and useless arms. Among the weapons were one hundred and thirteen unusable mortar shells, a dozen rocket-propelled grenades with inert training rounds, five 57mm rockets with dud warheads, a sack of old bullets and seven rusting machine guns, including a World War II–era German MG-34.

On April 22, U.S. Marine Lieutenant General James Conway warned that the insurgents had days, not weeks, to give up their heavy weapons or face a renewed onslaught. Meanwhile the Marines held a cordon around unconquered Fallujah, and Iraqi insurgents controlled the center of the city.

Lieutenant General Conway steamed at now sitting with the job unfinished and devised a strategy that would try to move noncombatants out of the city so his Marines could pursue the insurgents with greater force.

"You've got tens of thousands of innocent people caught in the middle," he said. "If there was some simple way to remove them from the equation, it wouldn't take long."

Surprised both by the resistance and the public reaction, the Marines felt they had the way to clear out the city if only allowed to apply it. But it was in the hands of the politicians now. They stored away the lessons and wondered when they would be allowed to use them.

Without a doubt, the greatest surprise to the high command and its biggest disappointment was the Iraqi security forces. In the fighting that took place in April, one top U.S. military commander said 10 percent of Iraqi security forces worked against U.S. forces in the past three weeks. Another 40 percent of the Iraqi security forces walked off the job because they didn't want to fight fellow Iraqis, said Major General Martin Dempsey, commander of the Army's 1st Armored Division. He said it was very difficult to convince security forces that the insurgents they were fighting were not just fellow Iraqis and fellow Muslims.

The failure of Iraqi security forces to fight stunned the Americans. Washington's exit strategy depended on moving U.S. troops out of cities and handing over responsibility for security to Iraqi forces. Major General Paul Eaton, charged with establishing the new Iraqi force, characterized the failure as a command failure. Others were more blunt, saying that the entire force would have to be rebuilt from the ground up. So unprepared was the occupational government for the offensive that the newly created force, called the ICDC, was not included in the new legal code for courts marshal. In a stunning oversight, the ICDC could only be fired from their jobs, not prosecuted for failing to follow orders.

Just how weak the ICDC leadership was became apparent when one colonel on a mission in Baghdad came upon a deserter. The young man of twenty-three was a company first sergeant with only three months' military service. In the American forces, such a person would require at least ten years' experience.

The political problems were not all centered on Fallujah or fighting to the south with al-Sadr. The operation in Iraq was receiving increasing pressure from the international community, fueled by human rights advocates. Human Rights Watch criticized the U.S. for what the group said was a failure to provide clear or consistent information on the treatment of thousands of detainees from its combat operations.

"Many people have been held for months without knowing why," said Richard Dicker, director of Human Rights Watch's International Justice Program. "The U.S. military needs either to inform people promptly of charges against them if they are suspected of a crime, or to give them the right to appeal and a six-month review if they are held on security grounds."[30]

Each distraction caused by criticism from respected forums was magnified back as further evidence that America was conducting a brutal occupation and thus could not be trusted to carry out its stated goal of bringing on Iraqi independence.

On April 24, the attacks coming out of Fallujah were still serious. There were two direct fire attacks on Marines and three mortar attacks. The Marines were not idle, sending out a patrol of 30 men who ambushed and killed eleven insurgents near a mosque as they were gathering for an apparent attack.

Despite the lack of progress on the weapons turn-in, on April 26, the U.S. allowed the Iraqi police to return, promising that the Iraqi National Guard, then called the Civil Defense Corps, would do joint patrols. About 350 officers and corps members had returned to duty and several hundred were waiting in a line to re-register and thus be restored to the payroll. The returning police and soldiers said that they were eager to get back to work and arrest the thieves who were stealing from homes and businesses. The under-armed police did little to nothing to stop insurgents from gathering before the battle.

When asked to place the blame for the fighting, these security forces hedged. "The Americans came and the planes killed people," said an Iraqi police officer in Fallujah. "We want to protect our town, but too many people are dying." Added another police officer, "Since the Americans came, there is no water, nothing to eat, no electricity. Many children have died because of the airplanes."[31]

Not all Iraqis were enthused about the impending compromise. Some had genuine hopes for a democratic Iraq and feared the insurgency. There too were those who cooperated with the Coalition.

"If Fallujah can become safe, all of Iraq can become safe," said a member of the U.S.-backed Fallujah City Council. "If not, people will say we surrendered Fallujah to the terrorists."

That day, trying to replicate the success of the Marine patrol two days before, Marine Echo Company sent out a similar patrol, which moved some 200 yards into the city on foot. In the meantime 50 to 100 insurgents had sneaked around them and waited patently, watching the Marines. After one squad searched a mosque, they returned, having found it empty. They met up with the others in overwatch positions in a nearby house. "When they got back, that's when all hell broke loose," recalled Marine Lance Cpl. John Flores,[32] who was wounded in the hail of fire as the insurgents had waited for the Marines to expose themselves.

The Marine platoon was surrounded by insurgents firing from two houses, and being pelted with grenades and rifle fire. One Marine was killed* and at least 10 were wounded. "They were so close you could see their hands throwing grenades," Flores later said.

Lance Cpl. Thomas Adametz[†] braving grenade attacks and intense small-arms fire, grabbed a machine gun from a wounded Marine and fired into a squad of insurgents who had his platoon pinned inside a house. "We would have been overrun," recounted one Marine who himself was severely wounded. The machine-gun fire fended off the insurgent counterattack that came within twenty-five yards and allowed the rest of the small-unit to withdraw. As was becoming apparent, the insurgents were themselves developing small unit tactics and a degree of tactical expertise, learning from the mistakes of others.

April 28 was an intense day of fighting around the city on three separate fronts, the first in the northwest part of the city, in the Jolan neighborhood. Here, an AC-130 gunship attacked two pickup trucks carrying in weapons. After receiving fire from insurgents in the southern part of the city, Marines called in air strikes. Fighter jets dropped ten precision-guided bombs at targets on the southern flank. On the eastern part of the city, some additional bombs fell in response to fire received there.

By now, there were several different groups of Iraqis trying to negotiate. Local leaders, national political leaders, religious leaders, tribal leaders, all were trying to craft some sort of solution. The question was, did these people have influence over the insurgents?

The local leaders, who agreed to the terms of the cease-fire on April 19 with the Marines, were unable to compel the insurgents to hand over any heavy weaponry. There was skepticism by some U.S. officials that a

---

*KIA: Lance Cpl. Aaron C. Austin
†For his actions that day, Lance Cpl. Thomas Adametz was awarded the Silver Star medal.

deal would work. The people who were negotiating did not appear to be able to deliver on their promises. There also was a sense by those in uniform that in the end, the politicians would agree to just about anything, glossing over the hard details.

April 29, the news shifted dramatically from Fallujah to just a few miles east at the Abu Ghraib prison. The American media network CBS published photos taken of prisoner abuse and the impact was earthshaking. If the broadcasters had sat down with the insurgents, the timing could not have been worse as far as the officials in Iraq were concerned. There was a deep sense of embarrassment both at CPA and with the military.

Iraqi press and Arab media made the images the lead story for the next few days. In the Iraqi street there was an attitude of "I told you so." In Fallujah, it was long an accepted truth that the men rounded up in American sweeps were taken to the notorious prison where Saddam Hussein had tortured and murdered many of his victims. The Fallujans said that the only thing different was a change of management. The photos were just confirmation, although there were no deaths reported and the abuse was more mental than inflicting physical pain.

On April 30, the U.S. announced the establishment of the Fallujah Brigade to take over the city. Between 900 and 1,100 soldiers were expected to join its 1st Battalion. Many were ex–Iraqi soldiers from Fallujah and the surrounding region. Some had fought against the Marines. The brigade was to be under the command of the Marines, and it was to disarm the insurgents in Fallujah in accordance to the agreement. The Coalition provided the weapons, trucks, and radios for the new force.

Back in Baghdad, the offices of CPA and CJTF-7 (Combined Joint Task Force Seven, the headquarters for the military in Iraq) were changing focus. To the senior advisors and Bremer's office, political issues were now paramount, with the messy business of Fallujah and al-Sadr's gambit in Najaf about played out. Come hell or high water, the transition of authority from an occupied state to an interim Iraqi government would take place on or before July 1, 2004.

This was still not a sure thing, as advisors to Iraqi ministries were trying to rush through last-minute reforms hampered by the lack of staff. With few people showing up and some simply leaving as a result of the intermittent shelling of the Green Zone, some amenities had been added such as a swimming pool and nearly nightly parties, which were widely resented by the military who had to stand guard for them. More people were coming in now but with only two months to rush things through only token progress was made.

The military was changing gears as well. Commanders were being told that come July, this would be an Iraqi operation and the military would venture out only in support of local Iraqis where they needed the firepower. By now it was clear that the U.S. chose a strategy whose post-conflict goals were unrealistic and impossible to achieve, and only planned for the war it wanted to fight and not for the "peace" that was certain to follow. Now it was only in a position to have the new Iraqi government win it while the military would try to keep the wolf outside of the door.

Remarkably, the military was still saying that the insurgency could not number more than 5,000, and claimed they were a mixture of outsider elements and diehard former regime loyalists (FRLs) that had little popular support at this late date. This was largely in the face of previous warnings provided by Iraqi opinion polls published by CPA, and both CPA and the military were claiming that its political, economic, and security efforts were either successful or would soon become so. In the meantime, U.S. Army civil affairs teams in the field were reporting a bleak picture of the life of the common Iraqi. At one point a major complained of a lack of awareness as to the local situation in the Fallujah-al Ramadi area. A senior civil affairs colonel charged with compiling the statistics for General Sanchez referred to his attitude as totally unacceptable and that the higher command would inform him of what the situation was on the ground.

By the close of the fighting in Fallujah, the overflow from the cemetery was being buried in the city's football stadium. Even so, the Muslim clergy celebrated the victory over the Americans. Rumors were everywhere. One was that the Marines would resume patrolling the streets with the Iraqi police and the Iraqi Civil Defense Corps. There was a sense of defiance in the city. In accordance to the agreement, the Marines made one last patrol to demonstrate their freedom of movement into the city, but according to the Iraqis they agreed with the mayor not to return.

Once the patrol left, spontaneous celebrations erupted. An elderly Fallujan resident riding in the back of a truck waving an old Iraqi flag seemed to articulate the common theme, "Today is the first day of the war against the Americans. This is a victory for us over the Americans."[33]

Five months later....

September started the official political season for the campaign for the U.S. presidency and Iraq was center stage in the campaign. "Our differences could not be plainer and I have set them out consistently. When it comes to Iraq, it's not that I would have done one thing differently, I would have done almost everything differently," said the Democratic challenger, Senator John Kerry of Massachusetts.

The Fallujah Brigade, which the Americans organized in May to maintain security after the Marines lifted the three-week siege, had all but disappeared. Along with it vanished virtually all signs of Iraqi state authority. Local police operated under tacit control of the militants. In Fallujah, power lay with the Mujahadeen Shura Council, a body of clerics and community leaders led by Sheik Abdullah al-Janabi, spiritual leader and ruler since May.

The Mujahadeen ran their own courts, trying people suspected of spying for the Americans or other crimes, to include violations of the Islamic Sharia. Since the tacit defeat of the U.S. Marines, they put to death about thirty people convicted of spying. A laser disc making the rounds in Fallujah and elsewhere showed an Egyptian man confessing to spying for the Americans along with the scene of his beheading. Among those put to death by the insurgents was Lt. Col. Suleiman Hamad al-Marawi, the local Iraqi National Guard commander.

The entire National Guard contingent of several hundred disappeared. Insurgents also controlled most roads in and out of the city. The Fallujah Brigade for all practical purposes ceased to function as a force.

Restrained from simply removing the safe-haven, the U.S.-led Coalition was forced to sit afar and hope that it could get lucky and score a kill or at least disrupt the stream of car bombs constructed and launched from the city. Worse was the apparent planning of kidnappings and executions from the city, which the insurgents then posted on the internet. All of this was designed to destroy the support for the Iraqi interim government.

With the memories of the ill-fated commando strike in Mogadishu some ten years before and the criticism the military suffered, a direct attack was out of the question. The U.S. did however, have its old standby, strike from the air. The litany of results and bad publicity was predictable.

In the meantime, for the soldiers and particularly the Marines, life was a matter of hoping not to run into a roadside bomb, fall victim to a suicide car-bomber, or hit an ambush. However, the true effect of Fallujah was not felt in the sands of the al-Anbar desert. For the kidnapping gangs, Fallujah was the perfect place to plan an abduction and then hide a kidnap victim.

CHAPTER 3

Kidnapping As a Tool of War

By September 2004, kidnapping, assassinations, and travel restrictions so discouraged reconstruction and investment that many non–Iraqis left Iraq. Only a few of the reconstruction projects had started, and many Iraqis gave up hope that the Americans would rebuild their country. Many politicians in Washington were asking why things were not going well.

The contractors knew exactly why the reconstruction projects did not go forward: fear and corruption. A knock on the door by a stranger demanding a percentage of the contract price or threats by several strange males followed any acceptance of American money. For American or other foreign contractors, it was far too dangerous to venture away from a safe compound. Giving the contracts to civil affairs soldiers got them out where the money was needed, but when they reported the problems confronting the local Iraqi subcontractors, the commanders shrugged. They had no way to protect the Iraqis working for them. For the insurgents, kidnapping was the ideal weapon to use against a more powerful enemy.

Almost immediately upon the fall of Saddam Hussein, kidnapping as a common crime became an industry. Just prior to the invasion, Saddam granted a general amnesty for all in prison. While many were political prisoners, most were just plain criminals. With the hardened enemies of society loose and the police services collapsed, they turned to their old ways.

With the Americans not able to speak to the people and not taking police reports, they posed no threat to the kidnappers. The Iraqi police were entirely uniformed and had no detective services. The Iraqi police at first were seen as a minor part of the security mission, and largely in terms of training a police force with a respect for the rule of law and human rights. After deserting in April, many voluntarily returned to duty after the uprising. But CPA rushed them into training to get as many on the streets as quickly as possible with no real vetting or evaluation of

47

Early on, one of the most dangerous places in Iraq was the highway from the Baghdad Airport to Baghdad. Roadside bombs and snipers took a considerable toll. It was not until December 2003 that armored buses were brought in to move the troops. Even then the road remained one of the most dangerous places on earth until September 2005.

their past performance. Some were sympathetic or at least ambivalent to the insurgency and were able to undermine the work of the rest, who were hapless as a tool to fight the insurgency or the kidnapping.

By far, most of the kidnapping was criminal, but the insurgency quickly caught on. It was an ideal way to mix profit with resistance. In kidnapping, the insurgency found a way around American firepower. Nearly all of the potential victims were either wealthy collaborators or working for foreign companies with deep pockets. On September 1, seven truckers, three Kenyans, three Indians and an Egyptian, who worked for a Kuwaiti company, were freed by hostage-takers. A spokeswoman for Kuwait and Gulf Link Transport said later it had paid $500,000 ransom to the kidnappers.

There too was the Islamic tradition of ransom. Islam instructed Muslims either to free captives who could not offer ransom (in the form of money or an equivalent number of Muslim captives) or to ransom prisoners of war. But the Koran and religious law was not a guarantee for the victims.

The release of the Kuwaiti employees came one day after Iraqi militants said they had killed twelve Nepalese whom insurgents had held hostage for more than a week. The cancerous new weapon of warfare demonstrated effects far beyond the theater of war. Thousands of protesters ransacked a mosque and clashed with police in the Nepalese capital to protest the killing of the Nepalese hostages by Iraqi militants. "We want revenge," demonstrators shouted as they stormed the Jama Mosque, the only Muslim house of worship in Katmandu. They broke windows and set fire to carpets, furniture, and parts of the building.

The organization responsible for the act was Ansar al Sunna, a close ally of both al-Zarqawi and al-Qaeda. Later in September they would release a video on the internet showing the beheading of three kidnapped Iraqis.

Not all of these abductions were so bloody. On September 23, two Egyptians who worked for Iraqna, a subsidiary of the Egyptian-owned mobile telecommunications company Orascom, were thrown into a black BMW and whisked off. Armed men snatched the two Egyptians at about 10 P.M. local time from their office in the Harithiya neighborhood of Baghdad.

The Egyptian telecommunications workers were freed several days later. The freed Egyptians said their captors treated them well. "They didn't torture us. We slept well, they offered us clean food," one told Iraqi TV. "They wanted to know whether this organization belongs to Jews and we explained ... it is purely Egyptian." The Egyptian chargé d'affaires in Baghdad, Farouq Mabrouk, said the kidnapping of the Egyptians was "motivated by financial reasons." But an Orascom spokesman declined to comment on whether a ransom had been paid.

The abductions were undercutting the economic support for Iraq. Al-Jazeera broadcasted a video September 19, showing kidnappers who threatened to kill ten employees of a U.S.-Turkish company if their employer did not withdraw from Iraq within three days. The company distanced itself from the United States, saying it had no business dealings with American companies or on U.S. military bases. The top executive for the Ankara-based company was in Baghdad trying to resolve the issue, which regardless of the outcome assured the desired affect. No one would want to do business where this was a likely cost of the business arrangement. The new tool of war accomplished its goal when another Turkish shipping company said it was withdrawing from Iraq after insurgents kidnapped one of its drivers and threatened to behead him.

New groups developed around the tactic. The Islamic Army announced on the last day of September that it had captured ten hostages, including two Indonesian women. These hostages worked for an electricity company called Jibel. The hostages also included six Iraqis and two Lebanese.

Despite its lack of central control, the Iraqis showed a remarkable sophistication and sensitivity to joint political aims. If the victim had any political currency, a host of other groups could jump in to get attention. Even obscure groups could, with the promise of assistance, get notice from powerful interests. Two French journalists held captive in Iraq were announced to be transferred from the radical Islamic Army to another Sunni guerrilla group that favored their release. Three Muslim clerics from France had come to Baghdad to help gain the release of the two French hostages. The three French Moslem clerics, of Moroccan origin, met on September 2 with the Muslim Clerics Committee at the Um al-Qura Mosque in Baghdad. It did not matter that France had opposed the war. France's new law banning headscarves in its public school became the issue as local Iraqi insurgents sought to demonstrate their willingness to stand up for Muslim rights.

There were rare victories against the kidnappers. On September 7, Iraqi police conducted a successful operation to rescue a kidnapping victim. Five insurgents were captured. But on the same day, two Italian women were kidnapped along with their Iraqi colleagues from the Baghdad office of their aid agency "Un Ponte Per ..." ("A Bridge To..."). Two different groups claimed responsibility for the abductions, demanding the withdrawal of Italian troops from the country or the release of Iraqi female prisoners. The same two groups later put out Web statements saying the two Italians were killed, but the Italian government doubted the claims' authenticity. The two women, both 29-year-olds, had been working on school and water projects in Iraq. The abduction was so shocking that Italian Prime Minister Silvio Berlusconi held emergency meetings with Italian officials to discuss the abduction the next day.

By September 8, many aid agencies were so spooked that they were fleeing. Some NGO (non governmental organisation) workers had already left the morning of the kidnapping and all flights out of the country were booked. Others vowed to continue their work in Iraq and said they would keep providing funds to those organizations that chose to stay in Iraq, but they were rapidly fading. In the Sunni Triangle, the situation was so dire that the 1st Infantry Division hosted a conference over the summer. The division commander invited NGOs to go to Tikrit to work with local security forces on how to protect the humanitarian workers. The military had to fly them in by helicopter because the aid workers felt too threatened to go by car up Highway 1.

By now the campaign of kidnapping was having its desired affect of poisoning the public well and undercutting the Coalition's efforts to improve people's lives. That became obvious when four international staff of the Germany-based relief organization HELP announced it was leaving Iraq in late September. "Until yesterday, we were convinced that we can continue our work with enhanced security measures," said Frank McAreavey, leader of HELP's humanitarian de-mining team in Iraq. "But the recent incidents, especially the increasing number of kidnappings and executions, indicate an escalation of violence and do no more allow us to assess the impact on our security. Extra bodyguards and electronic monitoring are not enough to bind the risk," stated McAreavey.[34]

Some countries had more influence than did others. This was particularly true with the Turkish government and the Turkmen insurgents. Zeynep Tugrul, a Turkish journalist for Turkey's *Sabah Daily*, was abducted on September 8, in the northern Iraqi city of Tal Afar. The reporter was released three days later. She was freed and handed over to Turkmen authorities in the northern Iraqi city of Mosul after Turkmen and Turkish Foreign Ministry officials intervened for her release.

When the kidnapping got out of hand, the Muslim community's reaction seemed self-correcting. In the sermon read at Kufa, Moqtada al-Sadr also denounced the kidnapping of the French journalists as "inhumane" and added his voice for their immediate release. "You should know that such actions are not part of the Iraqi resistance. They tarnish the image of the Iraqi resistance," he said.

When the kidnapping actually went counter to the wishes of the movement leaders this was easily corrected by using the media as the means of command and control. On September 19, a previously unknown group called Mohammed ben Abdullah claimed to have captured fifteen members of the Iraqi National Guard and threatened to kill them unless a jailed aide of radical Shi'ite cleric Moqtada al-Sadr was released. A representative for the political wing of al-Sadr's office said neither the Mahdi Army militia nor any other groups allied with the cleric were linked to the kidnapping. The spokesman denounced the abductions as attempts to "tarnish" al-Sadr's image. A video was aired the next day on al-Jazeera claiming to show the release of the men, all dressed in white robes and carrying copies of the Koran.

The Coalition was not completely without success, however. On September 28, U.S. forces in Kirkuk detained Hussein Salman Mohammed al-Juburi, the alleged leader of the local cell of Ansar al-Sunna, a group blamed for killing the twelve Nepalese hostages.

Also, in a rare bit of good news, the two Italian aid workers were released on September 28, and returned home just hours later. The Italians, Simona Torretta and Simona Pari, were wearing full black veils that revealed only their eyes as they were received by the Italian Red Cross in Baghdad. Arab press was there to document the return. Simona Torretta and Simona Pari arrived in Rome late on September 28, to shouts of "Simona, Simona." The next day, Torretta told reporters outside her home in Rome that the pair's captors assured them they were not in danger. Asked if she feared she would die during her captivity, Torretta first said "Yes," but then added that their abductors "reassured us. They understood the work we did."[35] The two women worked for the aid group "Un Ponte per ..." ("A bridge to ..."), which carried out water projects. The Italian prime minister was so ecstatic, he addressed his parliament on the release. "Finally a moment of joy," Italian Prime Minister Silvio Berlusconi announced to the Parliament in Rome. To the cheers of lawmakers he said, "The two girls are well and will be able to return to their loved ones tonight."

The use of abduction was proving to be a more telling instrument of war than just about any other, putting the targeted government in a no-win situation. Speculation that they had paid a ransom, which Italian authorities denied, overshadowed the celebration. Italian intelligence officials admitted there were intensive negotiations through mediators. Those sources also indicated that "some money" may have changed hands.

With the new Iraqi security apparatus developing, a cat and mouse game ensued. Iraqi intelligence was both predator and prey as they combated the abductors. On September 29, gunmen killed five members of Iraq's intelligence agency in Basra as they were returning a civilian freed from kidnappers. As the agents approached his family's residence, the gunmen opened fire. Authorities had been able to free some fifteen hostages in Basra and capture about thirty members of kidnapping gangs in the two months before.

Near Baqubah, insurgents targeted an Iraqi National Guard officer and set fire to his home. His wife and three children were seized. Some of the people at greatest risk were the translators. Not only did they have to endure the same risk as the soldiers, but off duty they were hunted. Paid around $12 a day by the military, double what an average Iraqi made, these people were targeted with a special vengeance. Because many came from educated families they had the double value of ransom. Most, however, where simply shot.

There was one aspect of operations in Iraq which the kidnapping and attacks were not diminishing, contractors willing to work for the Coalition. While beheadings sent shock waves, they didn't shorten the lines to sign up for the $50,000 to $150,000 a year jobs for such big-dollar contractors such as Kellogg, Brown & Root, Blackwater, Triple Canopy, and others cashing in on the U.S.-funded reconstruction effort.

Of all the kidnappers in Iraq, however, one person became the master of its political theater, a shadowy figure best known as al-Zarqawi. Born in 1966 as a member of Jordan's Beni Hassan tribe, Ahmad Fadil al-Khalaylah (AKA al-Zarqawi) grew up in squalor. At seventeen he dropped out of school and became an alcoholic. A derelict, the young man turned to crime as a teenager. From a town called Zarqa, he took on the name al-Zarqawi (from Zarqa). He also was known by a number of other names including Fadel Nazzal al-Khalailah, al-Khalayleh, Fadil al-Khalaylah, and Ahmad Fadil. He also had the nickname of Habi.

Zarqawi was jailed in the 1980s for sexual assault. While in prison, al-Zarqawi turned from crime to radical Islam, drawn by its mixture of religion, politics, hatred of the Jews, and allowance of violence.

In 1989, al-Zarqawi traveled to Afghanistan to fight against the Soviet invasion, but got there too late. In Afghanistan, he met a Pakistani explosives expert named Abdel Basit, who would later be known as Ramzi Yousef. There, al-Zarqawi became an explosives expert in his own right. With the fighting over in Afghanistan, he became a writer for an Islamist newsletter and went back to Jordan. He joined Hizb ut Tahrir, a Salafi group devoted to the restoration of Islamic rule.

In 1992, Jordan arrested Zarqawi for conspiring to overthrow the monarchy and establish an Islamic caliphate. He spent seven years in a Jordanian prison. While there, he learned the Koran by heart. Zarqawi also became a feared leader among inmates. Some branded him as a simple violent thug and not very smart at that. But he gathered a following in prison and showed the ability to lead, persuade, and bully others. A quiet person by nature, he also had a reputation for an explosive temper. Inmates remembered him as a person who saw the world in purely black and white terms, people who were infidels or believers. Even other Muslims were infidels if they did not accept his interpretation of the Koran.

On his release, he struck out on his own, traveling to Europe and helping to start the al-Tawhid ("unity") terrorist organization, a group dedicated to killing Jews and installing an Islamic regime in Jordan. In 1999, Zarqawi joined in a plot to blow up the Radisson SAS Hotel in Amman, Jordan. Some of its customers were Israeli and American tourists.

He fled Jordan and traveled to Peshawar, Pakistan, near the Afghanistan border. In Afghanistan, Zarqawi, with the permission of the Taliban, established a terrorist training camp, competing with al-Qaeda for recruits. The training camp specialized in explosives. While there, he met several times with Osama bin-Laden. He disagreed with bin-Laden as being too accommodating and willing to compromise on religious issues. Al-Zarqawi was not persuaded by bin-Laden's view of America as the great enemy of Islam, being content to drive Israel off the map and join it in a Salafi union with Jordan. Al-Zarqawi saw himself as a rival to al-Qaeda.

Zarqawi went back to Jordan, probably looking for recruits and money, when he was again arrested in 2001. But he was soon released on bail. In February 2002, a Jordanian court sentenced him in absentia to 15 years hard labor for his involvement in a failed plot to kill Israelis at the turn of the millennium, a scheme co-ordinated with Abu Zubaydah, a follower of bin-Laden. This was his first co-operative connection with al-Qaeda. Later, he was convicted in absentia and sentenced to death for murder.

After the September 11 attacks, Zarqawi again traveled to Afghanistan and was reportedly wounded in a U.S. bombardment. There was controversy as to whether he lost a leg in that attack. After receiving medical treatment in Baghdad, he moved to Iran to reorganize al-Tawhid, his former terrorist organization. Zarqawi then settled in the mostly–Kurdish regions of northern Iraq with the apparent permission of Saddam Hussein's secret police, where he joined the Islamist Ansar al-Islam group that fought against Kurdish nationalist forces in the region. Before the invasion of Iraq, Ansar al-Islam trained and operated with chemical weapons. After a short time Zarqawi left the group to work on a wider focus.

On October 28, 2002, Laurence Foley, a senior U.S. diplomat working for the U.S. Agency for International Development in Jordan, was assassinated. Under torture by Jordanian authorities, three suspects confessed that they had been armed and paid by al-Zarqawi to perform the assassination. Jordanian police claimed to have broken up a Zarqawi-financed and orchestrated plot to detonate tons of chemicals in central Amman. Such as blast could have killed tens of thousand of civilians.

After the Twin Towers attack in New York, German authorities came across an al-Tawhid cell, made up mainly of Palestinians trained in Zarqawi's Afghan camps. Zarqawi, though impressed by the September 11 attacks, still did not count himself as affiliated with bin-Laden. Shortly after 9/11, a fleeing Ramzi bin al-Shibh, one of the plotters of the attacks, appealed to Tawhid operatives for a forged visa. He could not come up with the cash. He was eventually captured as a result.

Until the invasion of Iraq, Zarqawi and bin-Laden disagreed not just over strategy but on religious principles. The issue of the Shi'as was a principal disagreement between Zarqawi and bin-Laden. While both men followed the strict code of Salafi Islam, which reckons Shi'as as apostates, bin-Laden saw himself as being a unifying figure. He made tactical alliances with Shi'a groups, meeting several times with Shi'a militants. Zarqawi referred to the Shi'ites as "the most evil of mankind...."

Now, that was changed. Zarqawi was willing to join forces with the more accommodating bin-Laden to fight a great foe, although he was not willing to let go of his hatred of the Shi'a. Zarqawi was linked with a lesser-known al-Qaeda splinter group, Beyyiat el-Imam, implicated in attacks in Israel as well as the November 2003 attack on a synagogue in

Turkey. Zarqawi had ties also to Chechen jihadis, and to Sipah-e-Sahaba Pakistan (SSP), a Pakistani Sunni group who targeted Shi'ites. Operatives of those groups met him in Afghanistan.

With the invasion of Iraq, he saw the war as America combining with the Jews and the Shi'a to destroy the Sunni true religion. Zarqawi saw America's willingness to offer democracy to Iraq, which by definition would turn over power to the Shi'a majority, as a demonstration of Shi'ite complicity with the infidels. Zarqawi justified killing non-combatants, saying, "Religion is more precious than anything and has priority over lives, wealth, and children." He considered Iraq the start of the great jihad since, "it is a stone's throw from the lands of the two Holy Precincts and the al Aqsa. We know from God's religion that the true, decisive battle between infidelity and Islam is in this land...."

Upon the outbreak of war in Iraq, al-Zarqawi teamed up with a fellow Salafi, Omar Hadid from Fallujah. The al-Zarqawi associate conducted what amounted to a coup of one of the major religious orders in Fallujah. In a city known for its Sufi tradition but with Tawhid's money and offers of support, Omar Hadid and Sheik Abdullah al-Janabi orchestrated the expulsion of a prominent Sufi cleric, Sheik Dhafer al-Obeidi, from the Fallujah Shura Council. Though a Sufi himself, al-Janabi was willing to enter into an alliance with the foreigners to oppose the Americans. Al-Janabi went to the pulpit of Fallujah's Saad Bin Abi Waqas Mosque, devoting most of his sermons to calling on Iraqis to join in a holy war against the Americans. He also worked tirelessly with other clergy to accept al-Zarqawi's foreign fighters.

They in turn joined up with Sheik Zafir al-Ubaidi, a prominent Fallujah cleric. A firebrand and Wahabi, he established a religious court and sought to establish Sharia law in Fallujah. Once the Americans were kicked out he would later start issuing religious edicts that were enforced with public floggings and in a few instances death. With the vestiges of moderation gone, the stage was set to win over at least the tacit consent if not out right support of Fallujah's clerics and other city leaders to allow al-Zarqawi to use the city as a forward operating base.

Tawhid converted its alien smuggling and document forgery operations into an underground railroad between Western Europe and Iraq, supplying foreign fighters.

Realizing the need for co-operation over a wider spectrum but still venomously anti–Shi'ite, Zarqawi reached out, helping any Sunni jihadist willing to kill Americans, their allies, Jews, or Shi'ites. In particular he provided support to his old friend, Abu Abdullah Hassan bin Mahmud, the leader of Ansar al Sunnah, a subsidiary to Ansar al-Islam. He was even willing to reach out to old Baa'thist elements such as Moayed Ahmed Yasseen, also known as Abu Ahmed, a leader of Mohammed's Army.

This group of former intelligence agents, army, and ranking Baa'thists brought immediate benefits. They had developed strong ties with Syrian intelligence, a benefactor of training, supplies, and a safe-haven in the next-door country. They also brought tens of millions of dollars squir-reled away from the graft of the Oil for Food program and other Baa'thist money-making schemes.

Meanwhile, the Tawhid cell in Germany cataloged Jewish businesses and synagogues. Zarqawi's organization was implicated in an attack on a Mombasa, Kenya, hotel frequented by Israeli tourists and an attempt to shoot down an Israeli jet liner. Tawhid was also busy seeking ways to strike at other European nations that joined the Coalition in Iraq.

Zarqawi's associate, a 36-year-old Moroccan named Amer el Azizi, planned the Madrid attack which resulted in the Spanish pulling out of the Coalition in March 2004. He became al-Zarqawi's link to al-Qaeda. Azizi was a ranking lieutenant of bin-Laden, having organized and presided over the 2001 meeting in Spain where Mohammed Atta and al-Qaeda leaders put the finishing touches on the plan to attack the twin towers and the Pentagon.

In Iraq, Zarqawi teamed up with Sami Mohammad Said al-Jaf, also known as Abu Omar al-Kurdi, a trained bomb-maker that took charge of his suicide car-bomb operations. In August 2003, Zarqawi's organi-zation launched a car-bomb attack that killed more than 85 people, including Shi'ite Grand Ayatollah Muhammad Bakr al-Hakim, who led Iraq's largest Shi'a political party. The bombing was carried out with an explosives-laden ambulance driven by Yassin Jarad, the father of al-Zarqawi's second wife. It was the first of a series of attacks on the Shi'ites. From that point on, al-Zarqawi's group became a major figure in defining the conflict in Iraq.

With the repulsing of the American forces at Fallujah and the pub-lishing of the prisoner abuses in Abu Ghraib, a new idea became popu-lar: kidnapping and public beheadings. The first victim was Nicholas Berg.

Berg was a native of West Chester, Pennsylvania, a suburb of Phila-delphia, where he owned his own company, Prometheus Methods Tower Service. He inspected and rebuilt communication antennas and had pre-viously visited Kenya, Ghana, and Uganda on similar projects. He trav-eled to Iraq looking for contracts to repair its damaged infrastructure. He first arrived in Iraq on December 21, 2003, and sought work for his company. Not successful, Berg intended to return to the United States on March 30, 2004. But he was detained in Mosul by Iraqi police on March 24, at a checkpoint. Berg was released from custody on April 6, and advised by U.S. officials to take a flight out of Iraq. They offered to help make the arrangements. Berg refused and traveled to Baghdad, where he stayed at the Al Fanar Hotel. Berg's family became concerned after not hearing from him for several days. Although a U.S. State Department investigator looked into Berg's disappearance, inquiries produced no leads. Berg's body was found decapitated on May 8, 2004, on a Baghdad overpass by a U.S. military patrol. What happened next stunned Iraq and the world. On May 11, the businessman's murder was viewed on the internet. Berg was beheaded by al-Zarqawi himself.

The full-length video of the beheading of Nick Berg circulated on the internet. U.S. media outlets that broadcasted the video halted the tape just after the center terrorist pulled a long knife from his shirt. The remaining footage showed the process of wrestling Nick Berg to the ground, decapitating him, then holding his head at arm's length. Voice analysis established that al-Zarqawi was the killer. Despite the poor quality of the digitized audio and video, the graphic nature of the act sent shock waves.

Some Muslims leaders within the insurgency were horrified and disgusted. But others were drawn to the practice, willing to volunteer for suicide car-bombings in response. To the leadership of Fallujah this was a troubling sign as Zarqawi was becoming a polarizing figure. Zarqawi apparently took careful notes on the response. The next time, far more attention was taken to draw out the drama.

By August, many Iraqis were drawing a distinction between Zarqawi's movement and nationalist insurgents. One respected newspaper referred to the two groups thus: "The Iraqi resistance believes in ending the occupation using armed resistance, while the goal of terrorism is the failure of the entire political process in Iraq. The dialogue with the Iraqi resistance is an urgent necessity to heal the wounds...." But now, al-Zarqawi was entrenched with a save-haven in Fallujah. In September, al-Zarqawi took his past experience and polished it to a new, more horrific theater.

On September 2, in the upscale al-Mansur district of central Baghdad, American citizens Jack Hensley and Eugene "Jack" Armstrong and a Briton, Kenneth John Bigley, all contracted civil engineers, were at their home, which also served as the offices of al-Khaleej Services Company. The security guard that was usually on duty did not show up the night before. One of the occupants of the house came out to turn on the electric generator, something he did at the same time every day. Abductors moved in. Eleven kidnappers in all, dressed in civilian clothing, drove up to the residence in a minibus and a sedan. The six abductors in the minivan entered the offices and seized the Westerners. No shots were fired. The abductors also stole a Nissan parked outside the house.

On September 18, al-Jazeera aired a video showing the three victims. "The Jihad and Unification Group" threatened to kill the hostages if female Iraqi prisoners were not released. By now this organization, under the control of al-Zarqawi, already had a grisly history with the beheading not only Nicholas Berg but a South Korean translator, Kim Sun-il, and a Bulgarian hostage. With each of the two beheadings after Berg, al-Zarqawi became more polished and practiced in how to manipulate the press.

The Americans found themselves now responding to the demands of al-Zarqawi through the questions from the press. A U.S. official said no women were in the two jails, Umm Qasr and Abu Ghraib. But, it did hold two female "high-value detainees," former members of Saddam Hussein's regime, at undisclosed locations. The distinction may have made sense to Americans, but was lost on most Arabs.

The wife of Jack Hensley, one of the three Westerners, pleaded for their safety.

"Please let them go," Patty Hensley said from her home near Atlanta, Georgia. "They need to come home."

On September 20, an Islamist Web site showed a video of American Eugene Armstrong sitting in front of five masked insurgents, four of them armed with assault rifles. The one in the center read from a paper.

"You, sister, rejoice. God's soldiers are coming to get you out of your chains and restore your purity by returning you to your mother and father," read the man.

"We will apply God's law on them," the masked man continued. Armstrong, wearing an orange jumpsuit and blindfolded, rocked nervously back and forth, his arms bound behind him as the statement was read. "Since you didn't release our sisters, here's the first infidel," the man said. He then pulled out a knife. Armstrong was shoved to the ground and gasped as his head was severed, blood gushing out. The killer held up the head and placed it on the body.

"The fate of the first infidel was cutting off the head before your eyes and ears. You have a 24-hour opportunity to meet our demand in full and release all Muslim women, otherwise the head of the other will follow this one."

By now the affair was becoming a political problem for the British Prime Minister. The family of British hostage Kenneth Bigley publicly urged Tony Blair to meet the demands of his kidnappers and save his life.

On September 22, a headless body was discovered by Iraqi police and turned over to U.S. representatives in Baghdad. It was the body of Jack Hensley. Along with it was a message reading, "The Muslim blood is not water and the honor of Muslim women won't go to waste. Bush, eat your heart out, and Blair, may you cry with tears of blood. God is great. Glory be to him, his prophet, and the faithful."

That day, an Iraqi Ministry of Justice spokesman said the Iraqi

Council of Ministers planed to release a female prisoner "on bail" from U.S. custody. The spokesman did not say whether the ministry was responding to recent terrorist demands that women prisoners be freed.

However, a spokesman for the deputy commander for Detainee Operations in Iraq, Lt. Col. Barry Johnson, said the status of Dr. Rihab Rashid Taha al-Azawi, as well as another female Iraqi prisoner, was still under review. Taha, who once headed Iraq's bacterial-biological program under Hussein, was taken into coalition custody in May 2003. A British-educated Iraqi, she was known as "Dr. Germ."

The other female prisoner was Dr. Huda Salih Mahdi Ammash, a weapons scientist like Taha. The U.S. regarded both women as "high-value" detainees (HVDs).

The al-Zarqawi terror group said it killed Hensley after a 24-hour deadline passed without its demands being met. It said the Web site would soon post the video of the killing, "God willing."

"Thank God, the lions of the Tawhid and Jihad have slaughtered the second American hostage at the expiration of the set deadline," the message said. "The British hostage will face the same fate unless the British government does what's necessary to free him."

Hensley's wife, Pati, had made repeated pleas for her husband's life and the lives of his two colleagues.

"These were three gentlemen who had absolutely no agenda other than to enrich the lives of the people they were there to help, and to take their lives would serve no real purpose," she said in an interview two days before. The men were working on Iraqi reconstruction projects for Gulf Supplies and Commercial Services, a company based in the Middle East. Before the report of the second killing, Bush, meeting with interim Iraqi Prime Minister Ayad Allawi, said, "We all stand in solidarity with the American that is now being held captive."

Allawi, sitting next to Bush, said, "The barbaric action of yesterday is really unbelievable."

In London, Bigley's brother, Philip Bigley, asked Blair to take action. "We feel absolutely helpless," Philip Bigley said.

"We do not have the power to save Ken's life.... The only person we can now beg to help us is the Prime Minister. Who else can we ask? There is nobody." Foreign Secretary Jack Straw had spoken with the Bigley family "three or four times, once this morning."

Asked about the family's plea for government intervention, a British government spokesman said that "the government would not change its stance. We do not negotiate with terrorists."

Speaking earlier, U.S. Secretary of State Colin Powell said Armstrong's death "shows you the nature of the people we are dealing with."

Said Powell, "They are murderers, terrorists who don't want to see the Iraqi people live in peace and freedom and don't want to see their country rebuilt on a democratic base."

By now, Muslim and Christian religious leaders in the hometown of the Briton were appealing for his captors to free him.

"In the name of God, the merciful one, we as Muslim and Christian leaders in Liverpool appeal to you as believers to have mercy on Kenneth Bigley," said Akbar Ali, the chairman of Liverpool Mosque and Islamic Institute.

Joining Ali at the news conference on was James Jones, Liverpool's Anglican Bishop.

"We're appealing to them on the grounds of their own faith in the God of mercy to be merciful, to have compassion in this situation and to release Mr. Bigley," Jones said.

The interim Iraqi government repeated that it had no imminent plans to release any detainees.

Bigley's brother criticized the U.S. government. He said the initial report that the prisoners would be released was "a shadow of light in a big, long, dark, damp, filthy, cold tunnel."

"Now this has been sabotaged," Mr. Bigley told BBC radio.

Alberto Fernandez, spokesman for the U.S. Embassy in Baghdad, said the release of the two female HVDs was not pending, despite earlier reports that Dr. Rihab Rashid Taha al-Azawi may be conditionally released.

Bigley pleaded for his life in a video that was posted on an Islamic Web site. Bigley, wearing an orange jumpsuit, was sitting down in front of a flag bearing the Arabic name of the Unification and Jihad group and the message "In the name of God, the Merciful."

At times, the video zoomed in on Bigley's hands, which he clasped together as he spoke. A few minutes into the video, Bigley broke down in sobs as he talked about his family.

He also said the Iraqi people have suffered greatly and that his captors weren't "asking for the world."

"Please, please release the female prisoners that are held in Iraqi prisons."

Kenneth Bigley tearfully called upon British Prime Minister Tony Blair to help spare his life, saying, "Please, please help me."

"I think this is possibly my last chance to speak to somebody who will listen," Bigley pleaded in the video. "I don't want to die here."

He added, "I need you to help me, Mr. Blair, because you are the only person now on God's earth that I can speak to."

At the end of the video, the screen went dark and in a white font a message said: "Do leaders really care about these people?"

Later, his family begged his Iraqi captors to "be merciful."

"We have seen and heard Ken's pleas. Thank you for letting Ken make his appeal."

"All of the family are very grateful to you for his message. They wish you to say to Ken that they love him dearly and are waiting for him to come home soon," said Craig Bigley, the hostage's son.

He was joined by his uncles, who said their 86-year-old mother also was appealing for his life.

"We have heard what you say and want to continue to listen to you. You have proved to the world that you are committed and determined. Be merciful as we know you can be," Craig Bigley said. "Release Ken back to his wife and family. We ask you, as a family, to be all merciful."

Speaking at the United Nations, British Foreign Secretary Jack Straw said, "I wish that the prime minister were in that position and so does he. The only people who can release Mr. Bigley are the terrorists who have captured Mr. Bigley."

On the twenty-sixth, Blair announced that his government was doing everything it "properly and legitimately" could to secure the release of Bigley but he warned against raising "false hopes." That day an Islamist Web site posted claims that Bigley had been killed.

On the twenty-ninth, Prime Minister Tony Blair said that if Bigley's kidnappers made contact, "it would be something we would immediately respond to." The British government expounded on the announcement, saying it was ready to listen to kidnappers holding hostage Ken Bigley in Iraq but was not prepared to negotiate with them or pay them a ransom.

A tape then appeared showing Bigley, dressed in an orange prison-style jump suit, seated in front of seven armed, hooded men. Behind them was the banner of Tawhid and Jihad. Bigley made a brief appeal, saying: "I am a simple man who wants to live a simple life." He then addressed British Prime Minister Tony Blair. "Here I am again, Mr. Blair," Bigley said, "very, very close to the end of my life. You do not appear to have done anything at all to help me." One of the hooded men then spoke, saying the kidnappers extended the deadline for Bigley's death to allow time for Coalition authorities to meet their demand to release women prisoners. "Because Britain is not serious in releasing our sisters, there is nothing further for this malicious Briton than the sword," he said. The speaker drew a knife from his belt, while three of the others grabbed Bigley. The men shoved Bigley to the floor and cut off his head, which the killer then lifted for viewers to see.

Elsewhere, as if to mock the whole affair, an agreement was announced with a militant group for the release within 48 hours of the French journalists abducted the previous month, who reportedly were close to being freed. As it later turned out they were not freed until December 21, but the headline was the goal in the first place.

CHAPTER 4

The Decline in Credibility:
Fallout of Abu Ghraib

By September 2004, Abu Ghraib Prison was only a marginally better place to serve than it had been the November before. Then, American National Guard MPs living in the dilapidated buildings that were once one of the worst prisons in the world, were accused of mistreating the prisoners.

There was a nice mess hall now, made of thin sheet metal, with TVs tuned to the Armed Forces Channel. But, over the two hundred and eighty acres, twenty-four guard towers sprouted machine guns and the troops sat in the heat.

There was also the shelling. The shoot-and-scoot shelling was less frequent in September but still there was enough to force the soldiers to wear their heavy armor regardless of the 115-degree heat. The need for the precaution was real. On September 18, insurgents shelled the Abu Ghraib prison with eight high-explosive mortar rounds at 9:30 A.M. As usual, they caused no damage other than to the nerves of both the prisoners and the guards. Most of the prisoners lived in tents on concrete slabs and required constant observation, therefore exposing both guards and inmates. It wasn't the only shelling that month.

There had been a lot of construction and that required increased security as crews delivered materials. The U.S. government bankrolled a new hospital at a cost of twenty-six million dollars. There were more Iraqi guards now from the newly created Iraqi Correctional Service. Even with the increased Iraqi presence, there were never enough people to do the job and many soldiers openly wondered if the Iraqi guards were trustworthy.

For the U.S. soldiers and Marines, the hardest duty continued to be just outside of the fortress-like walls where the family visitors came. The women were the worst, far more emotional than the Iraqi men, who seemed more patient and willing to wait in line. This interaction point between the U.S. soldiers and civilians was where an attack was most likely to take place. All knew that everything the visitors saw would be reported back to the insurgents, who were watching and waiting. Everyone also knew that they were the center of the press's attention because of the abuses that had gone on before. They had to live down the past. So sensitive was the subject that upon return from duty, Abu Ghraib was the only subject reservists and National Guardsmen were directed not to comment upon to the press.

Abu Ghraib Prison and the treatment of prisoners would not go away as an issue. With American troops through 2003 arresting Iraqi civilians, the prison population grew to over 8000 detainees. Their numbers not only became a serious logistical problem but also posed both political and legal problems. Reporters and activists were raising human rights issues, regardless of the conditions in which they were held. Many of the prisoners were caught in the act of attacking Coalition troops or carrying illegal weapons such as explosives or RPGs. Nevertheless, sweeps on suspect intelligence brought in far more of the arrested than could be proven guilty of a crime. A typical complaint through 2003 was that an IED would explode in a community, then U.S. troops would descend and pick up every male on the street within a block of the explosion.

A panel of high-ranking officers was created to review the release of detainees. They proved reluctant to let anyone go if there was a report involving an attack on a soldier, regardless of how poorly written or how lacking in evidence. In an effort to move the prisoners into the Iraqi criminal system, military lawyers plowed through the mountains of reports. For these experienced prosecutors it was a frustrating time. There were cases where soldiers died from the roadside bombs and ambushes these prisoners were accused of setting. Time after time, it was clear that evidence was not preserved, witness statements not done, soldiers critical to any prosecution not named and redeployed out of Iraq. At one point, one of the reviewers, after reading such a report of an attack that killed a 19-year-old soldier he personally knew, wrote, "Can not prosecute for lack of evidence" and handed the form back with tears in his eyes. They found that at best, one in five of the cases involving dangerous detainees was fit to transfer to possible prosecution. The lack of investigative skills of the soldiers and their lack of skill in preserving evidence made prosecuting most detainees impossible.

Out of desperation, the military turned to the Iraqi tradition of group accountability, releasing many to tribal elders on their assurance that they would be responsible. There was no way the Americans could enforce the arrangement. All they could do was not release any further detainees should the offender break his promise and attack the Coalition again. In the Saddam days, the tribal leader would have been punished as well along with the rest of the family.

There were those too dangerous to release under any circumstances. A senior military leader in Iraq, upon looking at the detention list, put that core group at about 3000. Major General Miller put in place a plan to have the prison at least nominally under the control of Iraqi prison officials. This, the military hoped, would provide political cover, but no one was fooled.

Six hundred prisoners walked out of the old prison in the month of September. Still, in Abu Ghraib and at the second facility, Camp Bucca in southern Iraq, the Coalition had approximately 5,200 detainees. As the problems of the scandal continued, that number gave weight to the embarrassment and became a tool for the insurgency. Preached Sheikh Abdullah Al-Janabi, Fallujah's de facto ruler, "Where is the freedom? Where is the democracy? The jails are now fuller than they were in Saddam Hussein's time. Is this freedom?" This sentiment was echoed throughout the insurgency.

On the eleventh of September, the International Committee of the Red Cross (ICRC) reported findings of a U.S. investigation that determined that as many as 100 Iraqi prisoners were held secretly at Abu Ghraib Prison. The prisoners' names were not relayed to the ICRC. The Americans admitted that some persons were hidden from the ICRC and thus were not allowed to visit them. The ICRC protested.

The original prisoner abuse scandal had not dissipated. The American Army found that twenty-three uniformed military personnel were alleged to have been involved with the abuse. In addition, four contractors, people who were hired to be part of the interrogation, were also found to have violated the law. The civilian CIA-contracted interrogators implicated in the abuse, however, could not be prosecuted because of a loophole in the law.

On the same day as the Red Cross was issuing its report, Army Specialist Armin Cruz pled guilty to charges of prisoner abuse and conspiracy. While at Abu Ghraib, Cruz admitted to handcuffing three detainees and forcing them to crawl on the ground. He also participated in the forcing of prisoners into a naked pile on the prison floor. The court sentenced Cruz to eight months confinement, reduction in rank, and a bad conduct discharge. Cruz said that he knew he was abusing the detainees at the time. By September, he was the second soldier from Abu Ghraib to plead guilty. Private Jeremy Sivits pled guilty to abuse charges in May. The court sentenced him to one year in prison and a bad conduct discharge. Five other soldiers awaited courts-martial in the abuse case. Iraqi press covered the sentence, and there was widespread comment over what they viewed as light punishment.

When the Abu Ghraib scandal came to light, the Iraqi chief justice said that America's response in punishing the soldiers involved would prove to Iraqis that America had come to bring freedom. To most Iraqis, the response was not so favorable. In a society that dealt as much with collective as well as individual guilt, the investigations by military officials that resulted in the punishment of only lower enlisted personnel smacked of a cover-up. With commentaries attaching blame to American senior leadership being widely circulated in the heat of an American political campaign, the rebroadcast over Arab media brought most Iraqis to the conclusion that the courts-martial were a sham. Al-Jazeera made sure to point out, in reporting on Specialist Armin Cruz, a segment repeating that Brigadier-General Janis Karpinski had since been suspended from her post. She was reported to have said that the U.S. Secretary of Defense, Donald Rumsfeld, directly authorized Guantanamo-style interrogation tactics. This commentary was regularly made on each action the military made to deal with Abu Ghraib. In fact of the matter, at that time the general's statements were more ambiguous.*

The charges were not limited to the Americans. Nineteen British soldiers also faced allegations of murder and brutality. It was alleged that the soldiers shot and killed an Iraqi civilian who had attacked a British soldier at a checkpoint. U.K. Trooper Kevin Williams appeared in a London court on the seventh of September on murder charges relating to the killing of an Iraqi lawyer.

All of these factors were making military operations around Abu Ghraib dangerous as the now infamous prison drew insurgent activity to exploit what they saw as an advantage. Efforts to recover by releasing prisoners counted for little. A few days after hundreds of prisoners were released from Abu Ghraib the bloodletting continued just a few miles away in the western desert with two more Marines killed.†

One fallout from the prisoner abuse scandal from Abu Ghraib was that any such accusations were now taken seriously. New allegations were surfacing that U.S. soldiers in Mosul might have abused prisoners there.

The press attention focused on one detainee, an Iraqi lawyer who said he was hooded and stripped naked in a building known as the "disco." He claimed the Americans subjected him to loud music, poured cold water on his body, and threatened him with sexual abuse. He claimed that for fifteen hours they tried to break him down by taking him frequently inside and repeatedly stripping him, pouring cold water on him and playing loud music. He said as the loud music played, they interrogated him with a loudspeaker that was placed next to his ears. He claimed

---

*General Karpinski was demoted on May 5, 2005, for failing to supervise the troops at the prison.

†KIA: Lance Cpl. Drew M. Uhles, Lance Cpl. Gregory C. Howman

that other prisoners were burnt with fire and reported seeing some with bandaged broken arms.

Another detainee said that he was also taken to the "disco." He claimed he was forced to stand for hours, handcuffed and hooded, which made him disoriented. He said he was kicked in the stomach, which was followed by continuous beating with a stick and kicking with boots until he was left unconscious. He claimed to awake after they poured cold water over his head. He also claimed to have been taken to a room where "group torture" occurred. Other detainees were said to have been prevented from using bathrooms, and many soiled themselves. The press reported that prisoners were ordered to shout, "Long live the United States." He claimed he saw a fourteen-year-old Kurdish boy bleeding from his anus and lying on the floor. The accuser also said to have heard soldiers discussing the boy's situation, which they reportedly said came as a result of a metal object being inserted in his anus.

After an investigation a report later released by the U.S. Army found that detainees "were being systematically and intentionally mistreated" at a holding facility near Mosul in December 2003. The Army's 101st Airborne Division ran the lockup. "There is evidence that suggests the 311th MI personnel and/or translators engaged in physical torture of the detainees," a memo from the investigator said. The January 2004 report said the prisoners' rights under the Geneva Conventions were violated. The abuses included forcing detainees to perform exercises such as deep knee bends for hours on end, to the point of exhaustion, blowing cigarette smoke into the sandbags the prisoners were forced to wear as hoods, throwing cold water on the prisoners in a room that was between forty degrees and fifty degrees, blasting the detainees with heavy-metal music, yelling at them and banging on doors and ammunition cans.

That month al-Jazeera gave repeated mention of a claim by a woman who said she was tortured by American intelligence officers. The story had originally been published by an anti-war-leaning newspaper in Britain.

True or not, these reports were widely repeated in the local and Arab press. Human rights advocates also used the claims as evidence requiring independent review of American military detention and interrogation teams.

By September, Abu Ghraib was the perfect backdrop for protests and verbal attacks on the government. At a demonstration outside Abu Ghraib, Shaikh Abdul Salam al-Kubaisi of the Association of Muslim Scholars, a Sunni group, called on National Guardsmen to rebel against the government of Ayad Allawi. In doing so, he articulated as well as any the position of the insurgency.

"It is strange to hear someone announce that Iraq cannot achieve democracy without the Americans," he said, referring to Allawi, "who has abandoned Islamic, regional and patriotic principles, forgets that America is the one that slaughtered its native Americans and killed millions of Red Indians. He forgets that America is the first to have made mass graves by bombing Hiroshima.... We live in strange times. As practically everyone is condemning America and its conquering of Iraq, we see a small bit of scum fighting the current, calling America a liberator and friend," referring to Allawi's speech thanking the U.S. for the invasion.

"Let it be clear for everyone that the traitors ... cannot give orders. To die for the country, to be a martyr is not death. Death is for those who betray their religion, soil, honor, and country."

"Today Iraq is facing the biggest conspiracy, a conspiracy to eliminate its most faithful people, all the faithful whether Muslim or Christian, Arab or Kurd or Turkmen.... That is why the Americans have formed the Iraqi National Guard and police."

Kubaisi described the Iraqi security forces as "just a cover in order to sabotage Iraq.... Because of this I call for the leaders of the National Guard and police not to obey their orders which are meant to make them the first spear, the first arrow as the criminal of the century Bush says." Kubaisi concluded by calling on the Iraqis to unite in a peaceful resistance against "the fear and terror inflicted upon them by the U.S. invader" and to be confident of victory.

The problems of Abu Ghraib had lasted over a year as commanders struggled to confront problems for which they had not planned. In hindsight, no one had made preparations to take into custody large numbers of Iraqi citizens. The planners had simply assumed that an Iraqi criminal system would solve all of the military's problems upon the fall of the government. As with many aspects of the campaign planning, there was a failure to deal with "non-kinetic" (non-combat) dimensions of the war by senior military commanders, expecting others to do their post-conflict work.

Therefore, Abu Ghraib became a rallying point for the insurgency that otherwise had nothing else in common with their final aims.

CHAPTER 5

Just Not Enough to Do the Job

From the beginning, Army Chief of Staff General Eric Shinseki told Congress in February 2003, "hundreds of thousands" of troops would be needed to occupy Iraq. Mr. Paul Wolfowitz, the deputy defense secretary, called the estimate "wildly off the mark." Secretary of Defense Donald Rumsfeld rejected the initial call for a commitment more than what was allotted and made it very clear such requests would not be welcome. By June of 2003, the nearly 150,000 troops were seen as not enough to do the job by many on the ground and back in the United States. In an interview, former Army Secretary Thomas White said that senior defense officials were "unwilling to come to grips" with the scale of the postwar U.S. obligation in Iraq.

Iraqi citizens went upon a riotous looting spree with the collapse of the Iraqi Army. Almost immediately upon liberation, Baghdad was plundered. This became an ongoing pattern not just in Baghdad but also in slow motion in much of Iraq's state-owned industries.*

Early in the process, the newly created Coalition Provisional Authority, desperate to get a handle on the wholesale theft of state-owned property, turned to the military. Lacking much expertise in the matter and not having nearly the numbers of troops needed to occupy all of the factories and mines, it turned to two civil affairs soldiers, both investment bankers,† to survey the assets and determine what was worth saving. One

---

"U.S. troops stood by helplessly, outnumbered and unprepared, as much of Iraq's remaining physical, economic, and institutional infrastructure was systematically looted and sabotaged. And even once it became obvious that the looting was not a one-time breakdown of social order but an elaborately organized, armed, and financed resistance to the U.S. occupation, the Bush administration compounded its initial mistakes by stubbornly refusing to send in more troops." Larry Diamond, Foreign Affairs, "What Went Wrong in Iraq," September-October 2004.

†Lieutenant Colonel Brad Jackson and Specialist Glenn Corliss.

Nearly every public building in Baghdad was looted, down to the plumbing and wiring. The first job for the military was to start a massive rebuilding project to get basic governmental services working.

young soldier, Glenn Corliss,* at considerable personal risk, raced about Iraq, sometimes alone in an SUV, categorizing and reporting the wholesale looting that was ongoing. Some of his reports were heeded and assets were saved, but much of the property that could be stolen in fact disappeared or was destroyed. Local military commanders simply did not have the forces to guard the facilities, and the guards hired on the spot with no vetting were often in on the looting.

This lack of manpower was most felt at the unit level as battalions struggled to patrol the teeming streets of Baghdad and the Sunni Triangle. Sealing the borders was out of the realm of possibility. One of the first choices forced upon the commanders was whether to provide escorts, which were already in short supply, for the civil affairs teams. As the demands for patrolling and guarding became more pressing, these civil military forces had either to limit their missions or provide security for themselves, inevitably cutting down the favorable contact with the local population.

*Glenn Corliss prior to the attacks on the twin towers in New York was a vice president at Bank One. He enlisted in the Army Reserves and was activated to serve in Iraq at the lowly enlisted rank of Specialist. For his efforts he was awarded the Bronze Star Medal.

At the same time, soldiers trained to take no chances rapidly alienated local Iraqis. They would regularly not stop at intersections or at traffic accidents and used their military vehicles to push off the road cars stopped in traffic. Unfortunately, some of the training did not take into account local reactions when soldiers shoved weapons into the faces of Iraqis, shouted at them, and tracked (aimed their weapons) at people along the side of the road. This combined aggressive training, plus the scarcity of the favorable impression of the civil affairs operators, undoubtedly added to the numbers willing to support the insurgency.

At the early stages of the occupation, everyone understood that at some time an Iraqi Army would be needed. There was an assumption that the Army would be a token force at first. Such a force would only be lightly armed, a professional force along the lines of the American army made of a few volunteers. Throughout late April and May, the American army almost gleefully set about destroying all the heavy weapons it could find, on the premises that there was no use for them.

At the same time, one of the early challenges of the Coalition Provisional Authority was the numbers of weapons in Iraqi society. Saddam Hussein, in anticipation of the invasion, had armed the entire population. Nearly every household had an AK47.

One of the first proclamations signed by CPA allowed every household in Iraq to keep their AKs. The stated reason was to allow households to protect themselves from the lawlessness. In light of the looting and revenge killings, the concerns of many Iraqis were justified. As well, there was the practical side. To rid the nation of its guns would have required the U.S. Army to go searching house to house. Even with a larger force, disarming Iraq would have been beyond the military. Thus, while the U.S. military was taking steps to impede the rapid rearming of the Iraqi army, the principal tool of an insurgency, light arms, remained in place.

The most far-reaching result of this armed population was to make the size of the insurgency indeterminable. At any one time, those willing to take up arms against the Coalition in a particular area could be as few as the criminal outside fringe or as many as every able-bodied man. This made the intelligence estimates wildly inaccurate. The true strength of the insurgency depended on the local relationship between the populace with the unit of the ground and what al-Jazeera was airing at the time.

In the meantime, there was a problem with the old Iraqi army. The leadership, mostly junior and mid-level officers, wanted to report for duty. This professional corps posed a dilemma for the Coalition in that they did not trust them to come back to a new army, but were also afraid that they would become the core of a resistance. The solution was to

One of the more unusual heroes of the war was a young soldier by the name of Glenn Corliss. After 9/11 he enlisted as a private in the U.S. Army Reserves. A vice-president in a major banking firm and expert at assessing investments, he was called to active duty as a junior enlisted soldier and sent to Iraq. CPA asked for his services to report on the condition of Iraq's state-owned companies. At considerable risk to himself, he rushed about the countryside, sometimes without military escort, to determine what could be saved from looters with the desperately short-staffed military. The subject of *Wall Street Journal* coverage, he was invited by the German goverment to speak at a conference on investment in Iraq. The Army general staff was indignant at the idea of a reservist junior enlisted soldier representing the military at such a high level and would not support the appearance.

simply pay them. In short order throughout the summer of 2003, every member of the Iraqi army was paid a stipend. Because such a high percentage of the officers were Sunni and many were Baa'thist, a considerable number of the insurgents were in fact fighting the Americans while they were on the payroll.

Iraqi police and security forces demonstrated that they could be enticed to show up (at least to be paid), but their loyalty or competency was not so easy to ensure. What the Americans could never overcome was the problem that the Iraqis had to live in Iraq and thus needed some accommodation with the people with whom they shared their neighborhoods.

The town of Saqlawiya, for example, was about nine miles north of

Fallujah and a strategically important village because of the nearby bridge across the Tharthar Canal, keeping open the major highway. Supposedly, there were ninety armed members of Iraq's National Guard at the outpost, part of the 6000 Iraqi National Guard on the rolls. Like elsewhere in Iraq, the Marines depended upon these posts to set up checkpoints, conduct patrolling, or make traffic stops. This was a major part of the plan to keep insurgents from settling in to use their newfound tactics of kidnapping, roadside bombs, and car bombs.

On September 6, a Marine convoy moved along the main highway near Saqlawiya. A car bomb driven by a suicide volunteer stalked the convoy, pulled alongside and detonated. The results were devastating. Seven Marines* and three Iraqi National Guardsmen were killed.

In fact, there were only a few Iraqi troops in the nearby city and none did any patrolling. There was a similar problem throughout Iraq. A roadside bomb ambushed another such convoy that day near Qayyarah, killing one of its soldiers.[†] The guardsmen in Saqlawiya, who were from the nearby city of Fallujah, had long been disillusioned with the Americans. With the April battles in Fallujah the guardsmen were put in an untenable position. To fight alongside the Americans brought risk of violent retribution on their families. Nearly all deserted.

Throughout the Fallujah area, the National Guardsmen returned to work after the peace agreement. They supposedly operated checkpoints and conducted patrols with the former soldiers, who called themselves the Fallujah Brigade. The Marines were trying to reconstitute the two battalions, mustering members to report to outposts in such nearby towns as Saqlawiya. But it was clear that many of the deserted soldiers were simply too afraid to report for duty. All of the vehicles provided by the Marines had long been stolen. In practical effect, the Marines were left to patrol and secure the desert around the attack site, and there were just not enough to do the job.

From a general's-eye view, tragic though they may be, the casualties were not seen as a threat to the operation as a whole. Each day's briefing would start with a statement that the situation was stable. Nevertheless, with each loss there was back home a heartbreaking ritual.

In some cases, the family would get a phone call if the soldier or Marine was seriously wounded. Then, there would be an agonizing wait with little information of the seriousness of the injuries. Unit members returning to base would often have a good idea of the situation and what

---

*KIA: Lance Cpl. Michael J. Allred, Pfc. David P. Burridge, Lance Cpl. Derek L. Gardner, Lance Cpl. Quinn A. Keith, Lance Cpl. Joseph C. McCarthy, Cpl. Mick R. Nygardbekowsky, Lance Cpl. Lamont N. Wilson. McCarthy had been seriously wounded earlier and had been returned to duty.
†KIA: Spc. Brandon M. Read

had happened but were under strict orders not to e-mail relatives. Meantime, the frantic relatives would be pleading through their e-mails to the unit buddies as to what was happening. Then, there would be the knock on the door.

The death notification often came as a surprise. The sight of a sedan with government plates turning into the driveway, carrying two officers in dress uniform, was a nightmare that stalked the backs of the minds of hundreds of thousands of families in America. For the military assigned to the duty, it was particularly difficult. "She knew as soon as she saw them what had happened," recounted one officer. "It was just such a shock. I sat ... and let her cry."[36]

This required special skills, a strength that many soldiers simply did not have. "A lot of people don't have the stomach to do it," one such soldier said. "There's a lot of emotion involved. Sometimes people take the training only to back up later and say they don't want to do it."[37]

If it was bad for them, for the relatives it was worse. "I can tell you it's pretty hard for a parent to open his door and find two Marines walking out of a car in front of your home," said one Marine's father. "I'm former military, so I knew what that meant."[38]

Though with more troops per square mile, the city of Baghdad contained millions of people, so life was no safer. A division of troops was dedicated to operate in the city of over five million people but it had become the hub from which the insurgency was operating and targeting. Only multiple vehicles would move around, usually at least four at a time. This greatly decreased the coverage of the American force. The reason was aptly demonstrated the sixth of September. An army Bradley fighting vehicle in Baghdad was ambushed with small arms and grenades, killing its commander.*

The roadsides just outside of Baghdad were no safer that day. The platoon leader in charge of a convoy carrying equipment and supplies from a port in Kuwait to the Stryker Brigade guided his trucks around the huge city. He was in a gun-truck protecting the rear of the convoy. He knew from the flash that some kind of roadside bomb had gone off. This was not the first time an IED had hit one of his convoys, but before there were no casualties. This time it was different. An up-armored Humvee was the target. The driver was injured and one other soldier was killed.† The soldier who died was on top, manning the 50-caliber machine gun that protected the rest of the convoy from the front. Had it not been for the armor, likely all four in the vehicle would have died.

---

*KIA: Staff Sgt. Elvis Bourdon
†KIA: Spc. Tomas Garces. He'd been recommended for the Bronze Star medal with "V" device for his actions during an ambush in July.

Nor was it any better out in highways in the desert. An IED exploded beside a fuel truck in a convoy, killing one and wounding a second.*

Much of the problem lay in that the U.S. military was suffering the results of its own past successes. A 2004 twenty-six-year-old company commander would be able to defeat the rest of his brigade of a generation ago with likely little loss. Not only did he have a considerable advantage in a close-in fight with better-protected, faster vehicles armed with bigger guns, he was backed by an integrated support system that allowed the modern force to bring to bear pin-point fire power at any place of his choosing. The U.S. military commander was able to control individual squads, moving them just about anywhere the enemy could be found. Backed by intelligence tools that could easily find the larger enemy force, listening to nearly every word the other commander said, and with the ability to disrupt the enemy, the modern smaller army could defeat a huge force. The larger force would find all of its former advantages now its downfall as it could no longer feed, arm, and control its basic functions. No one with a modern military education was surprised by the collapse of Saddam Hussein's army.

This new super-efficient army was more expensive per unit but required fewer soldiers. This made a lot of sense in a peacetime military that expected to fight short wars. It made no sense now in Iraq. The insurgency spread out like a virus with individual actors not relying on commands from others, only inspiration. Money, fear, a few trained leaders, relatively small amounts of explosives, and playing on religious prejudices took the place of the massive convoys of rations and munitions a conventional military force required. The attacks by the insurgents were designed to kill people, not the "force" as the Americans constantly sought. The aim was to inspire and intimidate, to force the Americans to relegate their force to mundane tasks such as roadblocks and escort duty, and to separate the people from the Americans. Their aim was also to provoke the Americans into striking back at the populace, making the occupation the apparent problem and not themselves.

The insurgency also found that it could adapt almost instantly to any new technique or operation the Americans would launch. From the start, Iraqi and foreign journalists provided a sometimes inadvertent and sometimes deliberate propaganda service through media coverage of insurgent activity and attacks. It also provided a command and control network. This informal "net" gave warning, told insurgents what attacks worked and did not, and allowed them to coordinate their attacks to reinforce those of other insurgent cells and groups.

Many frustrated commanders continued to apply the only tool for

*KIA: Pfc. Devin J. Grella

which they were trained, trying to fix and destroy the enemy. Therefore America's small but super-efficient killing force, doing the chores of searching houses of angry Iraqis, conducting sweeps, manning checkpoints, and searching cars was not curbing the insurgency. Estimates continued to flow in that the numbers shooting at the Americans were increasing. The Americans, on the other hand, were stretched as far as they could be with just enough units to maintain the present level.

In the meantime, the military, downsized after the cold war, was feeling the strain. Officials said the Army's ability to recruit and retain soldiers would erode unless tours were shortened from twelve months to between six and nine months. Intentions aside, the soldiers were not going home early. There were just not enough to replace them. Other bad news was leaking out. Iraqis would not be able to take over the most demanding security roles until late 2005.

CHAPTER 6

The Routine Distant THUMP

By September, life as a Marine in the al-Anbar had long lost any sense of adventure. Each day on guard or detail was in indescribable heat. The temperature regularly rose to over 120 degrees. Some days it was hotter, going over 130. Most people had lost at least ten pounds as appetite waned. They were told that in a few weeks the weather would break, but that did not help now.

Back in the States, they were told that it would be a dry heat and not so bad, but in anything over 110 degrees Fahrenheit the lack of humidity did not help. No matter how much you drank, you were dying, losing more salts and water than you could get in. In the old days, Saddam Hussein told the Iraqis not to worry. If the Americans came, they would simply die of the heat. Even the Iraqis stopped doing work at about 11 A.M. and came back out late in the afternoon. Someone forgot to tell the Marine officers. The Marines regularly patrolled through the hottest part of the day. The Iraqis thought the Americans were crazy.

The sun would beat down on the black-colored weapons, making them too hot to touch without gloves. Even the body armor and web-gear were to hot too handle, but still worn. Those moving in their Humvees did not get any relief from the wind generated by the speed. The hot air pressed into the face of the Marines as though they were staring into a hot blow dryer. Most wore a face covering and goggles to keep from being blistered as they manned their post as top gunners on the vehicles. What was worse was trying to stay alert. At any stop, there was a compelling need to sleep in the swelter. Staying alert was a matter of life and death. Staring out at nothing, keeping the weapon pointed at upcoming cars and likely ambushes, with a headache from being heat sick, wishing that you were anywhere but here was the life of most in the al-Anbar.

Probably, nothing was worse than for those assigned to the Marines around Fallujah, helping to harden positions and other construction work. Often times Marines would hire local contractors, but Marines had to shadow them as escorts. The heavy construction, however, had

A Civil Affairs team gets ready to roll out into al-Qiem, Iraq. So effective were these small units with the community that insurgents put a bounty on them. The temperature on the day of this mission approached 140 degrees.

to be done by Engineers or Seabees. In the heat, they would operate the heavy machinery, often having to move to the construction site with the present danger of roadside bombs. The most dangerous of places to work was around Fallujah. The heavy machinery was loud enough to be heard in the city. The insurgents had both the means and the time to set up firing positions and lob mortars or rockets into the construction. This was important work for it improved the chances of survival of the Marines.

Most were used to the almost regular indirect fire. These were not barrages like those suffered in Korea or World War II. They were pinpoint shoot-and-scoot raids. The insurgents had long learned that to stay around much after the second or third round fired would invite a lethal response. The distant hollow pop with a following boom was part of life around Fallujah. For most, at first there was almost a Disneyland quality to the danger posed by these attacks. For nearly everyone, the attacks landed somewhere in the distance and there was nothing one could do other than hit the deck at the sound of the distant bang of the launch. Most would simply stop and wait to hear the thump. After a while, it was just one more stress for the people working there.

At night, everyone got used to waking at the distant hollow sound of a mortar tube or slightly sharper report of a rocket launch. It was not loud, but like tuning your ear to the cry of the baby, you woke up at that pop. A rush came and then as always, after what seemed too long, there was a "crumph" sound. It was just another round meant for somewhere else. Everyone knew that this was a form of Russian roulette.

By now, there were concrete prefabricated bunkers everywhere. To most, they seemed a futility. No one knew of anyone who ever got to a bunker before the end of an attack. In some places, like the Green Zone "Palace," there was an elaborate alarm system, which only intermittently went off. It never sounded before the attack came. Annoyingly loud, it always came after the attack had ended. People joked that the warning system was designed to tell everyone that the attack was over. Still, people were supposed to run to the shelter and wait the hour or so it would take a patrol to go to the attack site, reporting that the attackers had long gone. Most people just ignored the alarm.

On September 4, positions around Fallujah heard that distant bang of a rocket launch. Everyone stopped for that moment and adrenaline snapped them out of their heat-driven drowsiness. In one place, the explosion was not that distant thump. One Seabee of Task Force Echo was killed* and another three wounded as they were building up an entrance gate to protect the base.

Fallujah was not the only place that day to suffer a hit-and-run indirect fire attack. Balad was regularly subject to indirect fire. On some September days, there were three attacks. Said one soldier stationed there in a call back home, "We had a small [one round] mortar attack last night. It has been that way every day this week.... No one pays any attention to it anymore. Here in LSA Anaconda we are surrounded by fields and patches of reeds. Flying over it looks like the farms you see back home. There is a lot of irrigation ditches and vegetation to hide in. I see women mostly doing all the work in the fields. They come right up to our perimeter. We have guard posts every 100 yards or so.... We almost never catch the people shooting at us."

The insurgents took to burying the mortar tubes in the mud and hiding them with a mud-covered board or vegetation. They would walk up to the tube, drop the single round, cover it back over, and walk away. Responding patrols hardly ever found the hidden launcher.

In Tikrit, Saddam's hometown, the attacks were a matter of daily life. In late September, when Captain Kirk Holt, a fiscal manager for the 1st Infantry Division, was briefing his relief so he could redeploy from his reservist call-up, a mortar round landed close by. He was so accustomed to the shelling that he just continued with his briefing, not taking any

---

*KIA: Petty Officer 3rd Class Eric L. Knott. It was his 2nd tour of duty.

Gunners on top of Humvees quickly took to carrying two weapons, as the crew-served weapons could not be turned around fast enough to engage an oncoming car bomb.

notice. The new arrivals interrupted him to ask if they were under attack. He just shrugged and said, "You'll get used to it."

Artillery units that were converted to makeshift infantry protected some places, but they still brought their guns. In Baqubah, mortar attacks happened but to a lesser extent because they were so quick to return fire with their counter-battery. "I'd hear one round in and three rounds out," said one reservist assigned to the city.

The airbase near Balad called "LSA Anaconda" had an advantage other bases did not have, helicopters for a quick reaction. Following an indirect fire attack on the base, an OH-58D Kiowa helicopter followed a vehicle from the point where the attack originated and directed a patrol which detained twelve individuals. The Coalition could not celebrate the victory for long. The next day, a mortar attack in western Baghdad killed two soldiers from the Illinois National Guard and injured sixteen.*

For the Iraqis working in critical government posts, the routine was as bad as for the soldiers. Explosions went off near the former Saddam International Airport, and plumes of black smoke were seen rising from

*KIA: Spc. Charles R. Lamb and Sgt. Shawna M. Morrison

the area on September 18. It was a common occurrence with only rare damage, as the rockets were fired blindly onto the massive installation.

On September 23, insurgents fired mortar shells at a Shi'ite mosque in the Abu Dishar quarter of southern Baghdad, putting a sizeable hole in its dome and damaging the courtyard. It was not clear why the house of worship was attacked. In Iraq, much of the violence was often difficult to understand. There was always an element within both Sunni and Shi'a communities that distrusted the other and were willing to turn the resistance into a sectarian war. No one ever took credit for the attack on the mosque. In the street, a rumor spread that it was the Americans that attacked the mosque, although most did not believe it. There would be scores to be settled, but those scores would have to wait. In the meantime, the Arab media gave only passing reference to the attack, highlighting rather the plight of those killed or injured by the Americans.

The insurgents were not always careful or skilled with their fire. Indeed, many of the launchers found had no sighting mechanisms and were often homemade tubes crafted from old pipe. That left civilians at constant risk. On September 27, in Baghdad, a rocket landed in a busy shopping street in the city center, killing one person and wounding several others.

But the weapons could be deadly enough to the intended target. After nearly a year and a half, many of the insurgent groups had a detailed map of most American camps. The Americans hired local contractors to repair and improve their bases. Some of these would take careful note of facilities, concentrations of soldiers, and what parts of the bases were empty. This would be passed on to the teams of mortar men. This was particularly true in Baghdad, where there were many covered places from which to fire. Attacks around 10 P.M. to midnight and early morning attacks were particularly favored. But no time was safe. On September 30, an American soldier in Baghdad was killed following one of many repeated shoot-and-scoot raids, using a 122mm rocket.*

KIA: Staff Sgt. Darren J. Cunningham

CHAPTER 7

Living with the IEDs

On September 18, a small convoy of trucks carrying mail, a maintenance team, and a supply sergeant, escorted by two Humvees, rolled through the midday heat. The Humvees were not the standard factory-made armored vehicles, but had armored plate bolted to the sides and an amateur armored cupola welded around a machine gunner. One truck had a homemade iron box above the driver that was not even painted, which provided what protection a quarter inch of metal could to a 50-caliber machine gunner. The small convoy drove wearily past Taji and down Highway 1 towards Camp Victory, Baghdad. As they were making the turn off the main highway to the airport road, a startling boom kicked up a pillar of dirt alongside the truck with the rust-colored armor for the Ma Deuce gunner.* Those in the Humvee behind watched the gunner disappear and wondered if he was hit, and more seriously, wondered if it was a small-arms ambush or if another IED was waiting for them. They were in an unarmored Humvee with the doors off. One passenger started firing three-round bursts into some trees even though he could not see an enemy, because there were some houses behind the trees. If it was an ambush, it would likely come from there. The soldiers in the Humvee would be easy targets. The last Humvee started firing at the trees too with its SAW,† the gunner not knowing if the vehicles up front actually saw the person who triggered the roadside bomb.

As planned in the convoy brief, the small force moved forward about half a mile and stopped to check on everyone. The fifty-caliber gunner popped up unhurt. He had only ducked at the nearby explosion. The homemade cage that protected him was pockmarked with shiny gouges where shrapnel had bounced off, and the right-side door of the truck had four holes in it. Only one went through the thin sheet-metal door but missed the two soldiers inside. After taking a short roll-call to make sure

---

*Ma Deuce is the nickname soldiers call the M2 fifty-caliber machine gun.
†Squad Automatic Weapon.

The most dangerous job in Iraq was that of a gunner on a vehicle. Most gunners remained exposed with no armor for the first two years of the war.

everyone was all right, they drove on. Every soldier there had been through at least four such episodes before. This was getting to be routine for them. Still, the four soldiers in the Humvee looked at the damage done to the truck and said to one another, if it had been them, likely someone would have died.

This event repeated itself about thirty times each day throughout Iraq in September 2004. In a majority of cases, it ended as did this incident, with just shattered nerves and a little damage. In one or two attacks, a soldier would die. For each soldier that fell to these roadside bombs, eight would come away with an injury.

Roadside bombs were one of the earliest weapons of the insurgency. They were easy to make: Iraq literally had millions of them in the artillery shells left over from the old Iraqi army. The munitions depots covered hundreds of square miles and there were just not enough troops to secure them. The U.S. military did not have enough explosives experts to destroy them. Artillery units calculated that it would take ten years to dispose of all of the shells. Some effort was made to hire security guards, but many of the under-armed locals would not challenge the insurgents

Unused explosives after the first phase of the war were literally scattered about the countryside. Millions of artillery shells, mortar shells, and tank rounds were available to the new insurgency, who turned them into roadside bombs.

removing the stores of weapons. Worse, many of the security guards would remove the shells themselves to sell. Thus, improvised explosive devices (IEDs) became to Iraq what the booby trap was to the soldier in Vietnam. The Americans, bound by the highways and roads to move their supplies, personnel, and equipment, were easy targets on the main supply routes.

At first in the summer of 2003, many of the IEDs often misfired or were buried too deep. But the insurgents quickly learned to not bury the bombs and find other ways to hide the IEDs. At first, they used garage door openers and toy remote control devices, but the Americans soon caught on. The Americans made jammers, beaming signals on the same frequency from the front of their Humvees or from helicopters. Every so often, a car or building would mysteriously explode from the device prematurely triggered. The insurgents adjusted.

Now, they were planted throughout the Sunni Triangle and Baghdad as a means to ambush or as an alternative to artillery. At first, the response was to limit travel to only essential missions and to send out patrols along the approved routes. With travel limited to high-priority missions, only high-priority missions were being attacked. Limiting routes only made it easier to target the bombs. Although patrols would find hundreds of IEDs planted from the night before, the one or two missed would prove deadly. Efforts to plant snipers and ambushes along the route had some success but the sheer size of Iraq's road network and the limited numbers of forces available made the effort an ongoing cat and mouse game. Insurgents easily found new volunteers, often paid handsomely by local standards, to plant the bombs. With a short ten-minute training session on how to implant the device and following the recruit at a distance to the site to ensure the emplacement, the trap was set.

One of the most dangerous jobs in Iraq was the morning patrols to clear the IEDs planted the night before. September 2 was typical for Iraq with the dangerous job often shouldered by the Iraqi National Guard. That day, five Iraqi National Guard troops were wounded, one critically, when a roadside bomb exploded near their vehicle in the al-Faysalia neighborhood in the northern part of Mosul. Three other roadside bombs did not explode.

Every unit that owned ground had to conduct route clearance. This was simply driving at a slow rate of speed (10 to 20 mph) scanning for suspicious items along the route, and then dismounting to clear those suspicious items or areas. It was a job nobody liked and everyone knew was hot, miserable, and exceptionally dangerous work. It also did little to solve the problem. An area cleared stayed clear only for at best a day. Even four times a day did not always keep a route clear. The best times were at sunrise, mid-morning, two hours before sunset and in the evening. Doing the clearance less often saved on the numbers of troops needed but increased the danger for the clearing patrols.

Troops had to dismount to clear overpasses, bridges, signs, under bridges, culverts and guardrails. A 155mm artillery shell had an effective killing radius of 60 yards. A clearing team would often get far closer than that before they saw a well-placed IED.

Before doing so, they had to clear the area where an ambusher could hide. Because soldiers were needed in overwatch to cover the element that was clearing, the operation required a considerable force. Where commanders lacked the troops, they were forced either to leave routes uncovered or to skimp, putting the clearing force at risk. When undermanned, a number of these small groups were ambushed.

By September, Iraqi National Guardsmen (ING) were doing many of the route clearance operations. But the Iraqis were even more vulnerable than the Americans. Commanders found that they had to accompany the Iraqis to assure that they in fact conducted a real clearing. Otherwise, the Iraqis, with their old-style and not very effective flak jackets, would simply say they cleared a route, knowing that the likely preferred

With the shortage of armored vehicles, many of the soldiers supporting CPA took to riding about in unarmored SUVs without escorts. They would simply roll their windows down to shoot and hope they did not run into roadside bombs.

target would be an American supply column and not them. But that did not solve the wider problem. Where units did deliberate route clearings on a regular basis, the insurgents would simply move down the same road to a unit area that did not or could not be so thorough to plant the IEDs there.

Throughout the summer, the Marines charged with the al-Anbar, which included Fallujah, had been averaging two or three KIAs a week from IEDs, with the feeling that no progress was possible so long as what they saw as an enemy haven was within their midst. Movement in and out of Fallujah made it possible to stage and plan attacks. Those easiest to reach were the Marines nearby.

Patrolling in the desert was always dangerous. IEDs were a way a few insurgents could cause multiple casualties. The vast distances and long roadways made roadside bombs easier to place there. On September 3, three Marines were killed by a roadside bomb while securing a bridge.* A fourth Marine was also killed in action that same day in the al-Anbar.†

*KIA: Capt. Alan Rowe, 1st Lieutenant Ronald Winchester, Lance Cpl. Nicholas Wilt
†KIA: Lance Cpl. Nicholas Perez

Hitting back seemed to have no effect on the bombers. Despite the air strike on Fallujah the day before, it was business as usual on September 16. A U.S. Marine Corps Humvee hit a roadside bomb south of the city.

In Baghdad as well, an explosion went off in the Bataween residential area, behind al-Madhaq Restaurant. The bomb killed one man and injured sixteen. IEDs became a favorite way to intimidate Iraqis cooperating with the Americans. A home was attacked with an improvised bomb near Sadiyah. This was the second attack on this home since August 21. Another bomb was removed from the house, but there were no injuries. September 16 was not unusual but only illustrative of Iraq and the improvised explosive devices.

By now, most of the Humvees had at least some armor in response to the IED threat. No sooner did the roadside bombs appear in May of 2003, soldiers were slapping anything they could onto their vehicles to protect themselves. Soldiers hired local contractors to weld on "Hadji"* kits made of whatever metal plate they could find, using unit funds or money out of their own pockets. Some soldiers took to calling it "hillbilly armor" after the dilapidated automobile on *The Beverly Hillbillies,* a comedy show in the 1960s. Humvees rumbled around looking like a scene from the popular movie *The Road Warrior,* in a variety of designs. Army regulations discouraged the practice, and many commanders at first disallowed it. Regulations said that the armor had to be tested. The only authorized modification of vehicles was a combination of plywood and sandbags. This did not stir the confidence of the soldiers and Marines who had to ride in them. Soldiers thinking that even faulty armor was better than no armor often ignored the regulation.

The brass itself was slow to bring in armor. Even after seventeen months, many of the Humvees traveled the roads without the authorized armor. Some had none at all, making them and their occupants the favorite target of the roadside bombers.

Those most vulnerable were the long haulers. Most of the big trucks had no armor at all. Tragically, despite the knowledge that roadside bombs were the principal threat to the vehicles on the road, the senior leadership showed no sense of urgency in providing armor for the vehicles. A considerable number of soldiers found themselves next to an exploding bomb with only a thin piece of sheet metal—or in the case of the Humvees, with their plastic doors removed to allow the soldier to shoot out, nothing but air between them and the shrapnel.

But even heavily armored vehicles sometimes were not protection

---

Hadji was the brown-skinned childhood friend and sidekick of the principal character in the children's cartoon series Jonny Quest.

This Humvee parked along the side of the airport road in Baghdad was one of the lucky ones with the newly arrived armored doors to provide protection against roadside bombs. By November 2004, with the start of the 2nd Battle of Fallujah, most "hummers" were still not armored with other than what plate armor soldiers could get locally welded to the sides of their vehicles. This improvised armor was often referred to as hadji or "hillbilly armor." Some commands, following army regulations, forbade soldiers from armoring their own vehicles.

enough. On September 5, a tank was knocked out at the village of Khalidiya by a homemade bomb, killing one soldier.* There were some successes with military equipment. The wheeled Styker armored vehicle with its basket-like metal cage around it did well against insurgent weapons. One Stryker took five direct RPG hits without harm to the crew and fought on. However, no amount of armor could protect a Stryker crew from a lucky hit.

Life in an armored vehicle could be explosively violent. Recalled one wounded crewman, "...and all of a sudden just 'boom'—the loudest thing I've ever heard in my life. My goggles shattered and the smell of flesh and metal burning and I was like 'oh man, we got hit.' I looked down and I saw my hand hanging there from a tendon."[39] The soldier lost his arm.

On a regular basis, EOD (explosive ordnance disposal) teams would

*KIA: Staff Sgt. Gary A. Vaillant

come across roadside bombs. Where possible, the teams would try to explode the bombs or at least damage the triggering device from a distance with 50-cal fire. Most of the time, this would not work and the team would have to come up to the bomb, place another explosive nearby and explode it with a countercharge bomb at a distance. The insurgency quickly realized that these EOD teams were disrupting their tactics and set up ambushes for them or booby-trapped the devices to kill the EOD teams.

Nearly every EOD team member knew that the bomb might be rigged to explode at the slightest vibration or that at any moment, from a distance, the bomber might be waiting to explode the IED in their face. Most knew the story of Staff Sgt. Kimberly Voelz, an EOD team leader whose husband worked in the same unit in Iraq as a leader of a separate team.

After both were deployed to Iraq, it was time for Kimberly to make the choice as to whether to re-up. She talked it over with her husband Max, what it meant to continue in such a dangerous job. They had met when they both attended bomb demolition training in the army. For her, the army was a big part of both their lives and she again took the oath of re-enlistment. She was told that upon returning from Iraq, they would be stationed at Aberdeen Proving Ground, Maryland, only hours from her hometown.

A week later, in December of 2003, she came upon an IED in Iskandariyah near Baghdad. As the team leader of her group, she had a reputation of being protective of her soldiers, preferring to take the risk herself to that of the others in her team. She had been defusing between three and seven such devices a day since she arrived. It was dark and the bomb (a booby-trapped tank shell) was taped to an electrical tower. Simply destroying it from afar was not an option here. Knocking out the electrical grid would be a major victory for the insurgents. As she approached the bomb to inspect, it fell from the tower and exploded. The two soldiers with her rushed her broken body to the military hospital in the Green Zone. Still conscious, she reassured the others, although her injuries were clearly severe. Her husband Max rushed to her side from the other EOD team in the area. In one of the most tragic and touching moments of the war, she died in the arms of her husband.

If the bombs were difficult to find, the people were doubly so and were the real target of the Coalition. Few Iraqis would dare inform on the bombers. Still, the Coalition would have its successes. On September 3, near Tikrit, Coalition forces detained nine individuals during a raid. The suspects were believed to be responsible for an RPG attack the week before near Kadeysia and bombings in Tikrit. The raid took place after an Iraqi civilian provided information to the Iraqi National Guard. The

For military units, being stuck on the road while roadside bombs were being cleared was a common occurrence. Notice that some of the soldiers are armed with AK47s. For the first year there was a shortage of rifles; many officers were armed only with pistols. Many of the CPA administrators issued Iraqi AKs to allow their supporting military teams to protect themselves.

1st Infantry Division also detained three more who were suspected of attacking Coalition forces using improvised explosive devices near Duluiyah. One of the individuals, Tarik Salman Rumayed al-Faraji, was a known IED bomber. A day later, U.S. troops swooped down from a helicopter on a safe-house at Almad al Hamadi, southwest of Baghdad, catching by surprise fifteen Iraqis. The safe-house contained a large weapons cache that included multiple IEDs.

In Baghdad, IEDs were not limited to attacking vehicles. Anywhere soldiers could be predicted to turn up was likely to attract a bomb. On September 13, insurgents planted a homemade bomb near an observation post, killing two soldiers.*

The IEDs by September had become as much a threat to Iraqi security forces and police as they were to Americans. On the evening of the twentieth and the next day, a civilian was killed and ten other people wounded in two roadside bombings targeting Iraqi security forces. Members of the Iraqi police force and National Guard were among the

*KIA: Sgt. Carl Thomas and Staff Sgt. Guy S. Hagy, Jr.

casualties. The first attack came as a roadside bomb exploded as an Iraqi National Guard vehicle passed, wounding three guardsmen and a civilian. It was not the first time Iraqi security forces were targeted in September. On the second, an improvised explosive device detonated near a police patrol, killing a civilian and wounding six other people, including two Iraqi police.

The elite of the military tended to take fewer casualties because they took special pains to be in a position to strike first. They too had to travel from one place to another in Iraq and as they did so, they were as vulnerable as the common soldiers. On September 21, they took a rare casualty as one of their Humvees fell victim to an IED.*

*KIA: Pfc. Nathan E. Stahl

CHAPTER 8

The Low-Tech Cruise Missile

It is hard to describe a car bomb to someone who never was in the presence of one exploding. When you are a half-mile away, you don't just hear it, you feel it. At a quarter mile away, the air in front of you turns hard and slaps you. It always comes as a startling surprise.

To the people on the scene itself, it would be earth-shattering. On September 18, a mission to escort an Iraqi contractor to fix a security fence at an overpass on the airport road to Baghdad close to Camp Victory was waving Iraqi vehicles past its three Humvees. An orange and white Chevy Caprice, a typical Baghdad taxi, steered toward the soldiers and exploded.

The senior sergeant on the mission felt his body go up in the air and was upside down looking back at where the car had been and then landed on the ground.

The patrol was lucky: the bomber detonated too soon and the car bomb, with the explosives in the trunk, was a relatively small one. Most of the force went away from the soldiers. Wounds but no deaths resulted from the attack. The senior sergeant lost part of his hand with multiple fractures in his arms. His IBA (individual battle armor) and helmet had saved his life.

The sight of a car-bomb scene stuns with visions of fire, bloody streets, body parts, people crying hysterically, people carrying away survivors and loved ones to safety, some clearly already dead, children wandering around, a blank look of not understanding what has happened, and security forces desperately trying to get things under control. Cars packed with five hundred, a thousand pounds, or more of explosives, driven by those willing to die in order to kill, were the most feared weapons in Iraq.

Many of the drivers were jihadists believing paradise awaited with the flick of a switch detonating the bomb. As it turned out in investigations, some only thought they were delivering a car or on their way to pick someone up. Some were told that they were only to park the car

91

Car bomb attacks on convoys devastated soldiers' morale. Before the military established countermeasures, many American soldiers mistakenly killed innocent Iraqi motorists while trying to protect themselves from car bombers. This resulted in many Iraqis opposing or fighting the Americans.

close to the target, which would detonate after they left. Some came only after their family was captured and threatened with death unless the car was delivered. The planner would be waiting just out of sight with a remote control detonator in hand. Whatever the case, the insurgents had come up with their own low-tech version of an American cruise missile with much the same effect.

For the outposts, which were the favorite targets, guard duty in the sickening heat was one of constant danger. Nineteen- and twenty-year-old American soldiers knew that death could come at any moment in a flash without warning, in spite of the HESCO barriers* and concrete blast walls at every entrance, which grew more serpentine and larger with each reported attack. They had long learned to have just one or two Iraqi National Guardsmen up front to stop each car and have the driver step out. Those first people at each entrance to the Green Zone

*A HESCO barrier is a wire and cloth basket about five feet tall filled with dirt.

and American camps all knew there was no chance of survival should a car bomb come. At nearly every entrance at the beginning of the day, long lines of Iraqis who wanted into the Green Zone, or who were working as contracted help at the U.S. bases, watched warily at the cars approaching. The wait to have an ID checked and be searched was as dangerous as any soldier's duty. Regardless of the pay, being a common worker for the Americans required courage.

The people most vulnerable to the car bombs were the Iraqi police, who were favorite targets. The killing of September started early with these targets on the 4th. Twenty Iraqi police officers were killed, and thirty-four Iraqi police and two Iraqi civilians were wounded, when a car bomb exploded in front of the Kirkuk Police Academy at about 3:45 in the afternoon. The police were going home from the first shift. Iraqi police sealed off roads leading to the blast site, but by then it was already too late to control the situation. Iraqi police had to fire warning shots into the air to disperse weeping and frustrated people who were racing to the area to learn the fate of their relatives.

By September of 2004, suicide car-bombings were not new in the north. The first came on September 10, 2003, a year before, when a car bomb exploded outside of the CIA compound in Irbil. But this September was a record for the most feared of all insurgent weapons.

Compared to the other weapons the insurgents used, the car bombs dwarfed the others in their impact. On September 14, two Task Force Baghdad soldiers were killed and three others were wounded when the soldiers were attacked with an improvised explosive device and small-arms fire at approximately 4:30 in the afternoon. As bad as that was, it paled in comparison to another attack with a car bomb which killed at least forty-seven people in the Iraqi capital. Rescuers pulled injured victims of the blast from the wreckage of market stalls and amid body parts strewn across the road. The blast left a ten-foot-wide crater in front of the police station on Haifa Street, where dozens of people had lined up to apply for jobs. While a U.S. helicopter circled overhead, some among the angry crowd at the site denounced the Iraqi interim government. The crowd took to chanting, "Bush is a dog."

Nor was the south, which was relatively calm, immune to these car bombs. Two days before the September 14 attack, a car bomb exploded within fifty yards of the U.S. consular office in Basra, killing two people who were sitting in a nearby car and injuring three.

In September, downtown Baghdad became a particularly dangerous place because of car bombs. Police vehicles had been deployed to help U.S. troops seal off the area around Haifa Street, where U.S. and Iraqi forces were raiding suspected insurgent hideouts, in turn sparking a gun battle on September 17. Around 12:40 P.M. local time, police asked a driver to

A car bomb near the Baghdad city hall. One car bomb could terrorize an entire city. Following an explosion that could be heard throughout downtown Baghdad a plume of black smoke could be seen for miles. This was an everyday event once the uprising in Fallujah provided a safe haven for their production.

stop, but the car continued forward on al-Rashid Street. The car rammed into a half-dozen cars that were blocking a bridge in central Baghdad. The driver exploded his vehicle in the middle of the parked cars. The blast left a 6-foot-wide crater and littered the area with debris, including at least five artillery shells that came from the suicide car. Parts of the car, an old Chevrolet Malibu, were found more than a hundred yards away.

The street was a busy shopping area with cafes and street vendors. The blast killed at least eight Iraqis and wounded forty-one others.

Regardless of the horrific scene, the Iraqi police were not intimidated. "By attacking Iraqi police, they think that they will be sent to heaven, but by God's will, they are now melting in hell," an Iraqi police officer said.[40] The raid continued and the security forces arrested sixty-three suspects, including Syrians, Sudanese, and Egyptians, as well as seizing rockets, grenades, and machine guns. At least ten people were wounded in the gun battles.

Being in the heart of one of Baghdad's busiest commercial areas, the raid was a short distance from the famed al-Moutanabi Street. The outdoor book market attracted large numbers of shoppers that day. When police fired shots to disperse the crowds, thousands of shoppers streamed from the area.

U.S. forces had already that day intercepted another car carrying explosives as it tried to break through a checkpoint in the Haifa Street. When the vehicle refused to stop, troops opened fire, setting off the explosives. The two people inside the vehicle were killed, and an Iraqi National Guard soldier was wounded.

On September 22 in Baghdad, a blast shook a crowded street near a police recruitment center in front of an ice cream shop frequented by Iraqi police recruits. The car bomb killed at least seven people and wounded at least forty-seven others as well as damaging or destroying sixteen vehicles. The second car bomb killed another eleven people and wounded some fifty others. Bloodied bodies, shattered glass and debris littered the street in the commercial neighborhood of al-Jamiyah. The engine of the suicide car was hurled about 150 feet away. That same day another man in a black Opel car drove up near a shop and detonated the explosives.

Human remains were strewn over street. One owner of a nearby shop helped relief workers to pick up human remains and put them into plastic bags. "I found this in the back of my pickup truck," he said,[41] holding a piece of a brain in his hand.

The U.S. troops and Iraqi police were not willing to sit back and just take this level of attacks. The same day they killed four insurgents and arrested twenty-seven others in a raid along Haifa Street. Weapons were confiscated in the operation, including small arms, rocket-propelled grenades, mortars, mortar tubes, and rockets.

The Americans were not impotent, and their combined technology and intelligence skills were formidable. That became evident when the Americans killed Sheik Abu Anas al-Shami with a missile, striking the car he was traveling in the west Baghdad suburb of Abu-Ghraib. He was the spiritual leader of Tawhid and Jihad.

The next day in Baghdad, U.S. forces opened fire on a vehicle packed with explosives after it tried to break a security perimeter, again on Haifa Street. In the busy commercial district of Karrada, the rolling bomb missed its apparent target, a U.S. convoy. It hit an occupied private car, which caught fire after the bomb detonated. The two people inside were burned to death. Another car bomb exploded on the airport road, killing one Iraqi National Guardsman and wounding three U.S. soldiers. That same day, while American soldiers were responding to one of the car-bomb attacks, another car bomb exploded. Two soldiers were killed* and eight injured.

*KIA: Sgt. Thomas C. Rosenbaum and Pfc. James W. Price

By now, many convoys had placed signs on the back of their vehicles in Arabic politely asking Baghdad cars to keep their distance as they came up upon the rear of the Americans. A machine gun pointing menacingly at the driver of the upcoming car brought the request home more forcibly.

Meanwhile up north, another car approached the gate in front of the Kirkuk headquarters of the National Guard at high speed. The National Guardsmen fired on the vehicle. "I saw a speeding car crossing an open field heading toward the would-be recruits, then there was a huge explosion and a big fire," said a street vendor.[42] The suicide car bomb detonated in front of the Iraqi National Guard headquarters, killing nineteen people and wounding thirty-eight others.

That September day also saw an attack in Baqubah. A car bomb went off near the Technical Institute, injuring ten people.

A match of wits had developed between the car bombers and the base commanders on how to keep the car bombs from blowing up among the guards at the entrances of the bases. They constructed labyrinths of barriers for the protection of the guards. On the twenty-seventh, these extensive measures foiled an attempt by two car-bombers at the Marine base at Karmah. The first vehicle, a black BMW, exploded while driving through the barrier system outside the base. It was followed seconds later by a blue Kia pickup truck, which also detonated in the barrier system outside of the compound. None of the guards were injured.

Perhaps the most profound affect the car bombs had was in the separation they created between the U.S. soldiers and the population. With the threat of car bombs exploding at any moment, the approach of any vehicle required a soldier to level his weapon at the driver. This was more than just disconcerting. Car bombs stalking convoys would drive alongside or pull just ahead of the target because most of the explosives would be in the trunk. For civilians, passing a slow military convoy, or coming up to a checkpoint too quickly or at night, could be fatal. Troops on an almost regular basis fired on cars that passed or approached too quickly. There were a number of tragic cases in which families or dignitaries were killed by mistake. All of these incidents were played up in the Arab press, often with accusations of carelessness against the soldiers and Marines involved.

The principal weapon against the car bomb was the checkpoint. Setting up checkpoints, sometimes at random spots, disrupted the car bombs' travel and forced them to explode there. Though still deadly, this would not result in the mass death should they get to their intended target. This made duty at the checkpoints exceptionally dangerous and difficult. Each car coming up could be instant death for the first person at the checkpoint.

Car bombs became the weapon of choice by the foreign jihadists and became a poor man's cruise missile with much the same effect. Starting with attacks at the gates of U.S. bases, car bombers quickly set their sights on attacking convoys.

It was particularly dangerous at night, when the soldier, blinded by the oncoming headlights, could not see into the passenger compartment. Travelers at night quickly learned to turn on the inside lights to show that they were not a single Iraqi male to the nervous soldiers. There were many mistakes as confused drivers and unsure soldiers led to the death of the innocent. On the other hand there was a long list of casualties from car bombs exploded at checkpoints.

To make matters worse, there was often a lack of coordination between Iraqi police, Iraqi National Guard, and U.S. military checkpoints. It was common to see a patrol or checkpoint wave a driver through, only to have another checkpoint just down the road. In cases where they were close together, upon being waved through one checkpoint, the driver would think that he was cleared for next one as well, or the procedures would be different. The language barrier was always a severe problem with an Iraqi driver suddenly confronted with American soldiers shouting and gesturing wildly to pull over or stop. There were a number of cases where confused drivers panicked and tried to drive away only to be killed by mistake.

Part of the strategy was to provide a piece of bad news for the Coalition for each piece of good it created. On September 30, two car bombs aimed at disrupting the opening of a sewage treatment plant exploded, killing forty-two and injuring one hundred thirty-seven. Thirty of the dead were children, attracted by U.S. soldiers handing out candy at the event. Horrified, interim Iraq Deputy Prime Minister Barham Saleh said, "We are obviously seeing a major onslaught by the terrorists on Baghdad and some other Iraqi cities."

That same day, about a half-mile away, another car bomb detonated at an Iraqi National Guard checkpoint, about two miles west of Baghdad University. The suicide car-bomber hit a compound used by the U.S. military and Iraqi police in Baghdad's Abu Ghraib neighborhood around 9:40 A.M., killing a Task Force Baghdad soldier* and two Iraqi police officers. Three other soldiers were wounded. Sixty more people were wounded in that incident.

An exasperated Lt. Col. James Hutton, a 1st Cavalry Division spokesman, pointed out the obvious, not understanding the seeming lack of Iraqi outrage towards the insurgency: "This despicable act killed not only a multinational forces soldier, but Iraqis who were merely going about their business of defending this country. The terrorists offer nothing but destruction." The deaths came as U.S. military officials noted a record number of car-bomb attacks for the month of September.

An Islamist Web site with ties to the Unification and Jihad group posted a message. From the group's military wing it claimed responsibility for the suicide attacks. The message, dated September 30, said, "Three knights from the Martyrs Brigades of the Tawhid and Jihad have performed three heroic attacks." The message said the first attack "targeted the municipality of the city of Abu Ghraib west of the capital Baghdad, where its director and his band were meeting with their American masters. It resulted in the death of five U.S. soldiers and several Iraqi police." The message added, "The other two knights have carried out an attack against a U.S. convoy and thank God the attack was successful." There was no mention of the children killed in the attack.

*KIA: Spc. Rodney A. Jones

CHAPTER 9

Bloody Baghdad

Throughout Operation Iraqi Freedom the most dangerous place was Baghdad. A city of approximately five million in a country of twenty-five million, the capital suffered half of all the attacks and deaths. Planners warned that Fallujah, the defacto safe-haven, only a forty-five minute drive away, would produce more Baghdad violence. Events later justified the prediction. Throughout the summer of 2004, attacks increased. There were whole neighborhoods that challenged the Americans on nearly every appearance.

Even in "safe neighborhoods" there was a steady daily drip, drip, drip of violence. For nearly every military base, it was life with intermittent shelling from rockets and mortars. In most cases, it was one or two rounds. They usually caused no harm and in some cases missed the base altogether. But, with five million people within earshot of at least one base, these attacks had a telling impact on the popular perception of the strength of the insurgency.

But the more dangerous life was outside of the secure bases and in the "Red Zone." On September 5, a U.S. patrol came under attack with small arms fire. One soldier was killed.* But, the Americans were unwilling to simply be targets. The day before there was an assault on a known safe-house in the vicinity of Almad al Hamadi, southwest of Baghdad. The raid resulted in the capture of fifteen Iraqis and a large weapons cache that included multiple IEDs.

That day was significant for another reason as well. The Interim Iraqi Government had had enough of what was clearly cheerleading for the insurgency on the part of some foreign press. Iraqi security officers raided al-Jazeera's Baghdad offices and sealed the newsroom with red wax. The government banned the Arabic television station from broadcasting in the country. It did not stop the network, however, for all who received the station from a satellite dish.

*KIA: Pfc. Ryan M. McCauley

Business revived quickly in Baghdad after the initial war as signs of Saddam Hussein were defaced by an angry population. The newest innovation to Iraq was cars available to everyone. Automobiles flooded into the country, many stolen from Europe, and clogged the highways and created an almost immediate fuel crisis. Gas was officially priced at thirty-two cents a gallon, and the fear of a complete breakdown over lack of fuel preoccupied early military planners.

The seventh was particularly violent in Baghdad. A roadside bomb targeted the Baghdad governor's convoy as he was traveling through the capital, killing two people but leaving him uninjured. Three of his bodyguards were hurt in the attack in the east Baghdad neighborhood of Hay al-Adel. That same day, another ambush using RPGs was sprung on a patrol. One soldier was killed.[*] In a separate incident another roadside bomb struck a convoy killing another in his Humvee.[†] MPs became engaged in a firefight in the western part of town, resulting in the death of one of their officers.[‡] Near midnight, a patrol was ambushed, killing another GI.[**] The engagements were nearly all the same with soldiers hitting the streets to maintain presence, look for IEDs, or travel the roads on supply missions. The enemy would always get the first shots at a time

[*]KIA: Spc. Yoe M. Aneiros
[†]KIA: Spc. Clarence Adams III
[‡]KIA: 1st Lt. Timothy E. Price
[**]KIA: Spc. Chad H. Drake

and place of their choosing. The attack would always be a surprise. The enemy would melt away. The best the American soldiers could hope for was that their enemy would make a mistake in the initial strike and that they could get some "payback," as the soldiers would bring to bear their superior firepower. The soldiers had long come to see themselves as sitting ducks.

By now, it was clear that Baghdad was one of the most dangerous places on earth for Iraqis as well. Since the war began, the Sheik Omar Clinic, charged with keeping official records, had recorded 10,363 violent deaths in Baghdad and nearby towns. Iraqi dead included not only insurgents, police and soldiers, but also civilian men, women and children caught in crossfire, blown apart by explosives or shot by mistake, both by fellow Iraqis and by multinational forces. Moreover, they included the victims of crime that had surged in the instability that followed the collapse of Saddam Hussein's regime. The people of Baghdad had to contend with car bombs, clashes between Iraqis and coalition forces, mortar attacks, revenge killings, and robberies. "During Saddam's days killings were silent. Now the killing is done openly and loudly," said one resident[43] who lost his 31-year-old son the April before.

September 12 started with the shelling of the Green Zone. U.S. forces then sent out a patrol to pick up outposts it had set up on Haifa Street. As the Bradley fighting vehicle patrolled, soldiers on the ground set up security in order to pick up other soldiers. Staff Sergeant William Payne dismounted his squad along the side of the street. A car laden with explosives sped onto the street and detonated into the rear of the Bradley.

An instant later the blast's concussion hit his squad, knocking one soldier to the ground. The force of the blast disabled the 33-ton Bradley. Its rear ramp was engulfed in flames and the upper cargo hatch was blown off. Small arms fire began to rain onto the street. It was a prepared ambush. One fire-team leader shifted the squad into a new position so they could provide cover fire, while Payne and another soldier went to help the soldiers in the Bradley.

Payne ran 60 yards to the burning vehicle through the insurgents' gunfire. At the Bradley, Payne climbed up on top and helped two of the crewmen out of the turret. He then turned his attention to the infantrymen still inside the crew compartment. One by one he pulled them up through the damaged cargo hatch. Within seconds of retrieving the wounded soldiers the vehicle's load of ammunition exploded from the heat and fire.

Once back in a safe position Payne's squad teamed together again to cover the rescued soldiers as the medic treated them.

Up came another Bradley and with the additional firepower the ambushes slackened in their gunfire. The wounded were placed into the other Bradley and evacuated to the hospital in the Green Zone.*

Four U.S. soldiers were injured and the Bradley fighting vehicle was ablaze. Two OH-58 Kiowa helicopters flew in to cover the scene and found that a mob had descended upon the armored vehicle. On the vehicle one person was waving the black flag of al-Zarqawi's group. The helicopters made three passes, firing a total of seven rockets and thirty rounds from .50-caliber machine guns into the crowd gathered around the Bradley, killing thirteen persons and wounding sixty-one. Some of the killed or wounded were likely guerrillas, others were just curious from the neighborhood or were there celebrating the attack. In the street were a television cameraman and Mazen Tomeizi, a Palestinian producer for the al-Arabiya satellite network. He was among those hit by the helicopter fire. All told, between the mortar attacks, seven car bombs that day and U.S. response, twenty people were killed.

On September 17, the troops were back at Haifa Street with the newly trained Iraqi National Guard. It was clear, however, that working with green Iraqi troops was dangerous. Most of the Iraqi troops on that mission had received only two weeks of basic training. The Americans started taking fire from a mosque. After some confusion, the shooters turned out to be Iraqi National Guard in civilian clothes. The mission, lasting 10 hours, turned out to be a nightmare for the U.S. troops as the Iraqis opened fire on anything that might be the start of enemy contact. Once one Iraqi soldier would fire, the others, assuming they were in a firefight, would open up in the crowded downtown district. At times, the firing would get so out of hand that they would fire on the Americans who were in overwatch positions. Said one American officer, "They are so undisciplined; we are usually more scared of them than of the enemy. It's pretty easy to identify an American soldier, but they still shoot at us anyway."[44]

While disappointed in their performance, officers evaluating the operation did notice the fact that these soldiers were willing to fight. It was back for more training.

For the Iraqis working at the police and military academies, it was with the knowledge that they were a particularly favored target. At about 10:00 A.M. on September 18, six Katyusha rockets attacked the military academy in ar-Rustamiyah, Baghdad. That same day, Katyusha rockets hit the police academy and the Ministry of the Interior building next door. As usual, there were no casualties. Meanwhile, rockets hit the base of Camp Victory, again without effect. Again, at 9:00 P.M., three powerful explosions shook the airport. It was proving impossible to prevent

---

For his actions that day Staff Sgt. Payne was awarded the Silver Star medal.

such attacks unless the local population was willing to call police when they saw the rockets being set up. Locals would simply walk away, not wishing or daring to call the authorities. That same day on the road from Baghdad to the airport, an IED struck a Humvee, injuring three soldiers.

September 18 showed how dangerous it was to work for one of the many security guard companies in Iraq. The hotels that serviced the contractors were targets. An IED exploded in a small side street in the city center, killing one security guard and seriously wounding two in a passing car.

All that night, it seemed explosions echoed across the city. A little after 7 P.M., an American patrol was ambushed but managed to escape without loss. Two more ambushes happened that night, but again without effect.

The next day, 82mm mortar rounds fell in the Green Zone. Again there was no damage except to the reputation of the Coalition as the sounds thundered across the city. Another rocket struck the airport. But, for that September, it was a relatively quiet day. For the people in downtown Baghdad, the day after made up for it.

On September 20, a five-vehicle American convoy passed through a bridge at the end of crowded Haifa Street when an improvised explosive device detonated. No U.S. casualties resulted but return fire wounded at least fifteen Iraqis. It was difficult to impossible to determine how many were combatants and who were bystanders. The people in the way were caught between insurgents who often used a pray-and-spray method of engagement, and American soldiers who had no way to distinguish between insurgent and civilian, and with often less than a second to make the decision as to whether to fire or die.

The response to these daily attacks came on the morning of the twenty-first. After preparation and planning, the Coalition conducted raids throughout the day in nearly every neighborhood of the city's center. They arrested twenty-four. On the same day, there was a rare victory when Iraqi police discovered a car bomb before it could detonate. EOD specialists and the troops quickly cordoned off and secured the area. The vehicle exploded with no injuries.

EOD experts estimated the blast to be the work of more than 500 pounds of explosives. Windows shattered at a nearby mosque, and the northeastern wall of the structure was damaged by the car bomb. Nevertheless, even with the failure to kill an intended target, it still had an effect. For the people within a mile the sudden explosion and the pillar of smoke said as much as the headline in the paper about a successful attack would have said.

The next day, a Task Force Baghdad soldier died* and four others

*KIA: Sgt. Skipper Soram

were wounded when a car bomb detonated next to two Humvees acting as a traffic control point. The soldiers were guarding a city council meeting.

Again, the troops went after what was a battle for the control of central Baghdad. On the twenty-third, another two dozen suspected insurgents were captured along with a wide array of weapons and munitions during a 10-hour operation.

The operation kicked off at four A.M., involving elements of an Iraqi National Guard brigade and multi-national forces. Throughout the day, they conducted raids in nearly every neighborhood of the city's center.

Besides the twenty-four detainees taken was a large quantity of weapons and munitions. It was a rare day throughout Iraq. No U.S. military were killed.

But on September 24, the insurgents were on the move as well. A rocket struck in northern Baghdad, killing four Iraqis and wounding fourteen others. In southern Baghdad, one mortar round left a three-foot hole in the dome of the Kadamiya Mosque. Another round landed in the facility's courtyard, while a third landed in the street just outside the building. Some rocket-propelled grenades were also fired at the Italian Embassy, damaging its perimeter wall and injuring three Iraqis in adjacent buildings. Still, military officials felt that they were making progress. But just how little the insurgency needed to do to cause great harm in such a target-rich hunting ground came to light the next day.

On September 25, seven Iraqi Army recruits in a van were ambushed and killed. Insurgents threw two hand grenades at the van and then shot at it with their AKs. For the recruits trapped in the vehicle with their windows up, there was no chance to fight back.

On the morning of September 27, Iraqi National Guard troops and Task Force Baghdad soldiers raided again, detaining seventeen suspected insurgents. Not all the raids were so fruitful. Cordon and search operations were also conducted in southern Baghdad neighborhoods. Task Force Baghdad forces searched more than 150 homes and turned up only two known insurgents that morning. The troops uncovered only two machine guns, anti–Iraqi propaganda materials, and a lot of angry residents.

That same day, precision air strikes were called into Baghdad, using intelligence gathered to hit safe-houses.

Along Haifa Street, American troops and insurgents again battled on the twenty-eighth, with explosions echoing through the city. Dozens of suspected insurgents were arrested in raids, including a number of al-Zarqawi's group.

In each of the raids, one of the most important jobs was that of the exploitation team. Their job was to preserve captured equipment and documents seized during and after actions. This was a change from just a few months before, when military officers had scoffed at the idea of preparing cases for court. The press of adding additional prisoners to Abu Ghraib and bad publicity forced the issue on many commanders. Evidence preservation was now the difference between a terrorist going free and going to court.

On September 29, U.S. and Iraqi forces were back again, raiding suspected hideouts in the heart of the capital, sparking firefights. Iraqi security forces managed to arrest one leader operating on Haifa Street, cornering him in a closet as he tried to conceal his face with his wife's underwear. The capture of Kadhim al-Dafan, a key neighborhood leader in attacks in the area, was a major victory for the Coalition. Five other suspected insurgents were also taken into custody as forces fought on the street. The dozens of people rounded up behind a razor wire barrier with their hands tied gave locals a clear indication that the war was not a one-sided hunt for Americans as the insurgency portrayed in their propaganda. The troops also uncovered caches of weapons, ammunition and explosives secreted between graves of the nearby Sheikh Omar Cemetery.

September ended with regular raids by Coalition forces. They brought in lots of suspects but were unable to drain the swamp. Each day more recruits for the insurgency came in, often linked to the safehaven in Fallujah.

To the citizens of Baghdad and the Coalition workers in the Green Zone, the city seemed to be up for grabs in the month of September. Guarded by U.S. troops and the Iraqi National Guard, life was one of keeping at bay the insurgency with the area just outside of the Green Zone wall particularly dangerous. One of the more dangerous jobs was the clearing of the area just outside by the daily patrols. On September 21, Task Force Baghdad soldiers were lucky to come away with just wounded. At about 3:55 P.M., one such patrol stopped all civilian traffic to investigate an abandoned vehicle. The soldiers exited their Humvees and left the gunners on top to cover them. Another military convoy was passing when a different civilian car pulled in right behind them and detonated. Five soldiers were wounded. The gunner in the vehicle closest to the car bomb lost an eye and sustained burns over a third of his body.

Throughout this time, for the people living in the Green Zone, life was listening to the distant gunfire and explosions and the intermittent distant pop followed by a boom as insurgents shelled the Green Zone. There was, however, a sustained mortar attack against the Green Zone that was launched with impunity from the Baghdad neighborhood of Karrada on the other side of the Tigris River. Hardly ever was there any real damage or injury, but to the people working there it was a matter

One of the more dangerous jobs in Iraq was escorting civilian CPA administrators around Baghdad. Here a platoon readies to take civilian personnel to one of the ministries in Baghdad. Throughout its time in Iraq there was a shortage of military escorts, hindering the function of CPA in its role as the occupational government. Many just ignored the safety rules and braved the chance of being ambushed.

of time as far they were concerned. The attacks were having a marked impact on the confidence of the civilians. The idea of going into the Red Zone terrified many. Many civilians were restricted by security rules. This often made traveling outside impossible.

This sense of siege was particularly true for the State Department employees. Armored vehicles and escort were required to move about, and the military, short on escorts, could support only a fraction of the missions. Some Green Zone workers cheated, but most sought ways around the requirements by trying to get Iraqis to come to them. Often the bureaucracy's requirements for safety and the lack of escorts either delayed or simply left undone critical tasks.

Then there was the knowledge that Ramadan was approaching. After the violence that flared on last year's Ramadan, a month-long Muslim holiday, there was a sense of fear that the insurgents might kick off an offensive. The perimeter walls and tire wells of official vehicles parked in guarded lots were checked each day for explosives. Now, even some restaurants inside the supposedly secure sector were off limits to a growing number of diplomats and other officials. The variety of foods and overall comfort level of the main dining hall and other chow stations was declining as security problems interrupted the flow of convoys provisioning the Green Zone from outside Iraq.

CHAPTER 10

The Olympians

During the summer of 2003, the insurgency sputtered in the northern part of Iraq. There was a sense that events were going in the right direction. With the fall of Fallujah in May, there was nonetheless increasing alarm among American military commanders.

Intelligence was picking up a clear trend of insurgents and al-Zarqawi's operatives nesting in the Arab sections of Mosul, the biggest city in the north. With the Coalition standing back and giving up control to local authorities, Tal Afar, a city in the northwestern desert, was becoming another Fallujah.

In the north, the Stryker Brigade brought from Korea and the Iraqi National Guard spanned across the vast plains and deserts to control the insurgency, an area once held by the 101st Air Assault Division. This unit trekked about in their new wheeled armored vehicles, which were able to keep up with other unarmored vehicles on the road. The new Stryker Brigade was named "Task Force Olympia." This force, at less than a third its size of the unit it replaced, was to control what most people felt was the possible flash point of an ethnic struggle between Kurds and non–Kurds. Complicating the matter was the fact that the Coalition was depending upon the Kurds to provide a majority of the shortfall of American forces, to keep a lid on the violence in the north.

Here, there was a special aspect of Iraqi politics involved. By far, the largest ethnic group in the Iraqi National Guard were Kurds. Most were former Pershmerga who fought as militia allied with the Americans. It was no secret that most Kurds would have preferred an independent state. It was also clear that the Americans, the rest of Iraq, and the Turks to the north would not tolerate it. Thus, the Kurds made the best of the situation but always kept an eye on the possibility of independence should the Iraqi state fall apart.

The Kurds as well had an old score to settle. Saddam Hussein's Arabization program displaced many who were waiting in relatives' homes or villages in the north. Arabs had moved them from their homes. The

Most "non-combat" forces were issued soft-skinned vehicles, which made them vulnerable. This Civil Affairs Humvee ran into a rocket-propelled grenade in Baqubah, Iraq. It took more than two years before even a majority of the vehicles were armored.

Arabs and other minorities often feared that the Kurds might go the road of some former Yugoslav states, ethnically cleansing non–Kurds to make it more likely that a Kurdish state would be viable should Iraq descend into chaos. The people most frightened were the Turkmen. Many lived in Tal Afar, a northern city near the border with Syria that lay on smuggling routes for weapons and foreign fighters. In Tal Afar, there had been friction between the Turkmen and Kurds since the fall of Saddam Hussein. Some Turkmen sought an alliance with the Arabs involved in the insurgency.

The Turkmen accused the Kurdish militias of looting and destroying the offices of civil population registrations and the offices of property and deeds registrations after seizing all the archives and registers to carry out a Kurdification policy on Turkmen. They also accused the Kurds of bringing in tens of thousands of Kurds to the city of Kirkuk, from Suleymaniya, Duhuk and even from Iran and Turkey. These accusations were heard loudly amongst the Turkmen population in Tal Afar.

Nineveh provincial governor Duraid Kashmoula worked with sheikhs and local leaders to bring about peace and stability in the area. But then Kashmoula's son, Laith Duraid Kashmoula, was assassinated. Laith was driving to work when assailants pulled up next to his car and opened fire with their AKs. He was an employee in the Iraqi government's anti-corruption office in Mosul, the largest city in the northern Iraqi province. The governor's cousin and the previous governor of Nineveh province, Usama Kashmoula, were shot dead in an ambush two months prior. The Iraqi government gave permission for the Americans to step in and clean out Tal Afar.

September 4 started the month's action near Tal Afar with members of the Stryker brigade conducting a raid. When rescue efforts commenced for a downed helicopter, the rescuers were ambushed by RPGs, disabling one of the armored vehicles. As was so often the case when the insurgents tried to stand and fight, the ambush victims were able to turn the tables, killing five of the insurgents. The Americans believed they had a clear picture now of what they were facing: 250 to 300 insurgents.

It was on September 9 that the U.S. turned its might loose on Tal Afar. Fighting went on throughout the night on three streets. The U.S. military calculated that it had killed fifty-seven insurgents in the attack on Tal Afar. The provincial health director* said 27 civilians were killed and 70 were wounded.

The next day, Brig. Gen. Carter Ham believed that about 200 fighters remained in Tal Afar. Asked how long he thought it would take, Ham said: "I'd say a week."

It was not until September 14th that the some 3000 civilians that fled the city were allowed to return. Turkey warned the United States that it might halt cooperation in Iraq after the offensive at Tal Afar, which resulted in the deaths of scores of ethnic Turkmen. Turkmen community leaders were saying that at least sixty civilians were killed and another 50,000 people had to flee their homes amid the fighting. The Turkish media reported that Kurds were rushing into the city to take the place of residents who fled the fighting. The Turkmen political leaders made a point of saying that the area Iraqi National Guardsmen were predominantly Kurds and accused them of ethnic cleansing in order to establish a Kurdish state.

That did not deter the Americans. In Tal Afar on the seventeenth, the U.S. forces were back conducting cordon and search operations. The operation detained seven people.

By September 24, the military felt confident enough to declare it had chased the terrorists out of Tal Afar, after six months of violence. It had come at a cost for the residents.

*Dr. Rabie Yassin

The battle left houses riddled with bullet holes along Route Santa Fe, a main highway running through the outskirts of Tal Afar and used by the insurgents. Now the residents were returning to their city to begin the process of rebuilding the infrastructure, repairing houses, and reopening businesses.

For the last six months, civil affairs soldiers had been restricted from helping the residents because of violence. Now, the soldiers were moving in to assess damage and look for ways to aid the rebuilding. There were two focuses to support, the rebuilding of infrastructure damaged in the recent fighting and to improve upon the existing facilities in Tal Afar.

Civil affairs soldiers from the Stryker Brigade's 416th Civil Affairs Battalion and engineers from the 133rd Engineer Battalion toured sites in the city on September 18 and 19 to determine the extent of damage. They visited electrical and water facilities, police stations, and a grain silo to determine the most important projects in the city and to maximize new construction jobs.

During a visit to the electrical substation, they found that they could fix most of the city's electrical problems with minor repairs. Fighting and general lack of maintenance brought down some of the power lines in the city and a few transformers were damaged. The local electrical department was already working to fix these problems.

Many of the people who lived on higher ground were not getting water because there was not enough pressure in the lines to reach all the neighborhoods in Tal Afar, a problem that existed in the city before the war. To solve this problem, U.S. forces rented twenty water trucks to distribute water to the homes. To aid the city's policemen who responded to many of the recent attacks, the civil affairs soldiers provided them with two new vehicles and 140 sets of body armor. Troops also repaired the damage that was done to the police academy and one of the police stations during the fighting.

The military was also taking steps to improve the unemployment rate in the city. About 75 percent of the city's population were unemployed. Civil affairs troops selected local firms to contract the projects, employing people from the area.

"Without security, we cannot accomplish these projects," said an American officer, "We cannot find contractors who will work in an environment where they do not feel safe."[45]

As with the rest of Iraq, victories in Tal Afar were never complete, however. On the last day of September, insurgents ambushed Tal Afar's police chiefs, killing four Iraqi civilians and wounding seven others. Two of the injured were police officers.

Still, this was a clean victory when compared to the Marines' efforts

American troops found themselves carrying out tasks for which they had no training. Here soldiers from the 3rd Armored Cavalry supported by PSYOPs and Civil Affairs teams try to defuse a labor dispute in the Iraqi border town of al-Qiem.

in Fallujah. There was not the press and political outcry of April, and the collateral damage was at a minimum. Just as important, the rapid response in mitigating the damage after the fight was well received. For the leadership in General Casey's staff in Baghdad, there were a lot of lessons noted for future operations.

But General Ham could not rest easy. The insurgents' real target was Mosul. Somehow, with far fewer forces, the brigadier had to keep the lid on the city. If Mosul became another Baghdad, the entire operation in Iraq could unhinge. There were significant numbers of Kurds in the city and should Mosul prove ungovernable, it could be taken as proof that a unified Iraq was not possible and that the Kurds had best strike out on their own.

Even as the operation in the western desert was starting, the attention of Task Force Olympia was shifting back to Mosul. Insurgents fired a handful of mortars that landed near the provincial council office in Mosul, killing an Iraqi and wounding several others. The local hospital said they received eleven wounded, four of whom were seriously hurt. That same day, gunmen laid an ambush to shoot, and killed three Iraqi women as they were returning home from work at a U.S. base in Mosul. A fourth woman in the vehicle escaped.

At the same time as the big operation in Tal Afar on the ninth of

September, a unit took small-arms fire during a patrol in the central Mosul neighborhood of Al Uruba. No one was injured. Soldiers quickly maneuvered to the origin of fire and conducted a cordon and search of a residence, detaining nine people suspected of conducting the attack. Meanwhile, troops conducted a cordon and search operation in southern Mosul and detained five people suspected of conducting roadside bomb attacks. If they thought they had rooted out the insurgents, they were wrong. On the fourteenth, insurgents ambushed a Mosul patrol, wounding five and killing one U.S. soldier.* At Hawijah an IED struck a Humvee. The occupants got out of the disabled vehicle, but there was a sniper waiting. The sniper pulled the trigger, and one soldier died.†

With the Americans short-staffed, the Iraqis had taken an increased role regardless of their lack of training. The insurgents were taking advantage of the thin numbers. In Mosul's city center, explosions sent people rushing into the shops as insurgents attacked with four mortars. Amidst the screaming, one Iraqi police officer lay dead and another lay hurt along with seventeen townspeople. Firefighters rushed to the scene to carry the bloody and shocked victims to the local hospital.

The action in September for Mosul was not as intense as in Baghdad, but there was a tit-for-tat war. On September 16, Iraqi police thwarted a mortar attack when they stumbled upon four people placing a mortar in northern Mosul. Police shot at the mortar crew, who fled. Using a description from Iraqi police, U.S. forces later found the vehicle full of munitions. Mosul was one of the few places were the insurgents would use their light mortars for more than shoot-and-scoot raids. In one engagement, they fired twenty-six 60mm mortar rounds until the Apache gunships caught the gun team in their sights.

On September 18 in Mosul, insurgents armed with automatic weapons pulled up in two cars alongside the convoy carrying Mohammed Zeybari, manager of oil products. The gunmen opened fire on the convoy, killing five of his bodyguards and wounding four others.

On September 19, an Islamist militant Web site posted video showing the decapitation of three members of the Kurdish Democratic Party. In the video, a group calling itself Ansar al-Sunna, the same group that released the video the month before showing the killings of twelve Nepalese hostages, said that the members of the KDP and the Patriotic Union of Kurdistan were traitors serving "Zionists" and "Christian crusaders" fighting against Islam. The video statement said the three men, all truck drivers, were captured as they were hauling military vehicles

---

*KIA: Sgt. Jacob H. Demand
†KIA: Spc. Joseph C. Thibodeaux, III

near the town of Taji, about fifteen miles north of Baghdad. The group said it killed the men "to teach them a lesson they will never forget."

In Mosul, the Coalition forces launched a series of raids on the same day. They found a weapon stash and arrested sixteen.

On the twenty-first of September, soldiers raided a meeting of insurgents in a neighborhood of Mosul, confiscating weapons and intelligence documents. U.S. forces detained 20 people for "anti–Iraqi activities," including three leaders of a "known terrorist network."

Still, snipers were a present threat. One patrol came within the sights of one on September 22, losing a soldier.*

At the end of the month, Mosul was starting to taste the level of violence that regularly stalked the streets of Baghdad. A car bomb exploded next to a National Guard vehicle in eastern Mosul on September 27, killing three Iraqi National Guard and wounding seven other people, three Guard members and four civilians. On the same day near the village of Qayarrah, a patrol foiled a roadside bomb attack. They had collected a variety of weapons and munitions in northern Iraq when they noticed a 155mm artillery round in the median of the road. Soldiers from 1st Squadron, 14th Cavalry Regiment also discovered a large weapons cache in western Mosul.

Late the next day on September 28, a car bomb exploded as a U.S. military convoy was passing by, wounding six American soldiers. Five of the wounded soldiers suffered minor injuries and returned to duty.

On September 30, an Iraqi police official, Maj. Ghassan Mohammed, was killed along with his driver in a drive-by shooting.

In the backdrop of the violence and the inability of U.S. forces to do much more than conduct raids and respond to ambushes, the civic action teams were struggling to reach out. One such project was to farmers in providing seed. There had been a planting season the year before, but much of the crop was of such poor quality that the wheat was fit only for animal feed. New seed was brought in by the World Wide Wheat Company and they distributed more than 1,000 pounds of seed to Iraqi farmers located in the Ninevah Province. The problem was to get it to the farmers without its being stolen or simply destroyed by the insurgents. Finally, there was something the soldiers were capable of coordinating with an immediate and positive result.

The military leadership in the northern part of Iraq was now clearly feeling the strain. The success at Tal Afar buoyed their morale, but so long as there was a steady stream of insurgents coming up from the Sunni Triangle and in from Syria, they realized that they were just "sticking fingers in a dyke." Something would have to be done further south or

*KIA: Pfc. Adam J. Harris

the small force would eventually lose control of the level of violence. Once that happened, elections would fail and Iraq would fly apart, if only because the Kurds in the far north were so much better off than the rest of the country. They would not likely stay part of a failed state.

There were clear advances in the Kurdish areas to the north. Life was progressing well in the institutions of civil society. Judge Latif Mahmood, the chief justice of Kurdistan, the area of northern Iraq under Kurdish control, expressed it best. "The security situation is difficult in the middle [and south] of Iraq, especially for legal and judicial work. But we in Iraqi Kurdistan for many years have had a well functioning judicial system. The judicial system is in place, democracy is in place, there is a parliament in Iraqi Kurdistan, and a judge is free to make rulings in accord with his own convictions and without external pressure."

Mahmood said the security situation in Iraqi Kurdistan was stable enough that "I have no private guards or any gun at home."[46] Threats to judges were rare because police forces were strong enough to cope with criminal gangs, despite the violence elsewhere in Iraq. This was in sharp contrast to what Arab judges were saying to the south.

But Olympia did not have all the territory of interest to the Kurds. Kirkuk was a flash point as well and one of constant contention. Another U.S. soldier was killed* September 22, when insurgents attacked his patrol near Ash Sharqat, about sixty-five miles west of the northern city of Kirkuk. It was also were some of the more successful actions were taken against the insurgency. On the twenty-seventh, U.S. soldiers captured Husayn Salman Muhammad al-Jabburi, leader of a Kirkuk-Hawaijah based cell aligning itself with Ansar al-Sunna. Ansar al-Sunna was a faction of Ansar al Islam and had close ties with al-Zarqawi.

Still, working for the Americans was as dangerous anywhere in Iraq as was being an American soldier. Two Iraqis were killed the twenty-ninth, south of Kirkuk, when gunmen opened fire on a minibus full of people working at a U.S. base. Life as a soldier was not that quiet either. Four U.S. soldiers were wounded in an explosives attack on their convoy about twenty-five miles from Kirkuk. The Kirkuk airbase, a major U.S. installation, was the victim of attacks involving mortars and rockets.

But there were quiet victories as well. One of them was the start of oil exports from the oil fields in the Kirkuk area to Turkey.

*KIA: Spc. Joshua J. Henry

CHAPTER 11

Moqtada al-Sadr

The Shi'a of northeastern Baghdad had little use for the people of Fallujah. Some regarded the Baa'thist and Salafi elements as, in the words of one Moqtada al-Sadr aide, "no better than dogs and Jews."* But in September 2004, the Thrawa district of Baghdad was as much a no-go zone as Fallujah. With the forces of Moqtada al-Sadr firmly in control of the Thrawa slums, it seemed that any offensive in Fallujah might provide the opportunity the young radical cleric needed to spark a far wider revolt.

If Fallujah was a difficult nut to crack, the Thrawa district of Baghdad was impossible. In that district was a steaming slum, before known as Saddam City and now known locally as al-Sadr City. Nearly half of the people in Baghdad lived in what could be fairly termed as the black hole of Baghdad. The district was the poorest in the country. Homes were in disrepair, and there were places where the backed-up sewage system actually ran human feces through the streets. Electric lines were strung sometimes at chest level in parallel, on the off chance that electricity would come on. It was a good day if the electricity was on for three hours. In the summer, the place seemed unlivable. Even when friendly, movement through the area could be frightening, as one would quickly find himself in a packed crowd of people trying to sell something, begging for money, or simply gawking. The population consisted mostly of Shi'ite Moslems and unemployment was near 100 percent. During the Saddam days, there had been riots bordering on a public uprising. The police put them down brutally. It was the perfect place for a revolutionary.

Islam has two great branches of faith. The majority are Sunni, but a large minority, who happen to be the majority in Iraq and Iran, are Shi'a. The Shi'a draw their religious heritage from a split for leadership

---

*As offensive as that phrase is, it is hard to overstate the sense of resentment this author overheard from the Shia concerning the state of Israel.

116

when the Prophet died. After the Prophet's death, Muslims divided between those who believed their leader ought to come from among an election by his advisors and those who felt it should remain within Mohammad's bloodline. The Shi'a sought to keep the control of the religion within the family while Sunni sought to establish a Caliph (successor) through a wider selection.

The Shi'a challenged the authority of the Caliph. In the Battle of Karbala, which happened to have taken place in Iraq, the movement's leader, the Prophet's grandson, was killed. It set the pattern for a troubled relationship between the religious sect and the secular government. Ever since that time, the Shi'a were a problem for any government who ruled in Iraq.

Within the Shi'a, there were competing traditions and the tension between the two often resulted in a divide. The Shi'a had a long-standing stake in social justice. The corruption and greed of the secular government was often the target of Shi'a clerics. This was natural in that the Shi'a were often a minority and in the bottom strata of society. With Islam's general willingness to mix religion and politics (after all, the Prophet had been a ruler himself), some clerics, as they had in Iran, were willing to constitutionalize religion.

There was another school of thought that saw how the government sought to control Shi'ite clergy and thus corrupt it. This school saw mixing government and religion as dangerous and apt to lead to moral decrees designed to carry out the will of the ruler and not of God. Without a democratic tradition, the political differences were apt to manifest themselves through violence. But as a rule, within the Shi'a community there was a tradition of scholarly tolerance, so direct attacks against a Shi'ite leader by another was rare. Thus, even in Iran's oppressive governmental structure there was a lively debate between the two factions.

The al-Sadr family had a distinguished history within the Shi'a. Moqtada's great uncle founded the Dawa (Religious Call) movement, which was formed by Shi'ite theological students to combat Baa'thist and Communist influence in Baghdad's slums. The movement benefited from the regime's decimation of their communist rivals. Its leader, Mohammad Baqir al-Sadr, wrote books about Islamic politics and economics to prove that Islam provided solutions to all social questions. Mohammed Baqir al-Sadr was killed by the regime in 1980.

Saddam Hussein, thinking he had made the point about bucking the system, backed Mohammad Sadiq al-Sadr to head the religious post of al-Hawza (the main center for Shi'a instruction) in Najaf because he was an Arab Muslim. He wanted to rid the Shi'ite leadership of its Iranians. Mohammad Sadiq al-Sadr declared himself the wali or leader of the faithful. His work focused on the Mahdi or Shi'ite messiah who was expected to return on judgment day. He was less a canon lawyer or intellectual and more a mystic. His writings dwelled on the return of the Mahdi. Al-Sadr and his sons were assassinated by the regime in 1999 for opposing Saddam.

In comes younger son, 30-year-old Moqtada. The young leader promptly claimed the mantle of his father. In Thrawa, painted over the old murals of Saddam Hussein was the Santa Claus–like image of Moqtada's father. Moqtada al-Sadr referred to himself as in the line of "seyyed" (descendants of the prophet). Though barely a minor cleric, he made a ruthless power play soon after occupation, when his followers surrounded the home of Grand Ayatollah Allah Ali al-Sistani, an Iranian citizen, demanding that he leave the country. This followed the murder of the prominent Shi'a cleric, Abd al-Majid al-Khoei, who had returned to Iraq with U.S. forces after years in exile. Al-Sadr backed down when the Shi'a clergy en masse condemned the religious coup. Moqtada then turned to politics.

In June 2003, L. Paul Bremer, the head of CPA, considered Moqtada as a possible member of the U.S.-appointed Iraqi Governing Council, but other Shi'ite members rejected the idea. Moqtada and his followers fumed at the exclusion. He in turn refused to recognize the U.S.-appointed Iraqi Governing Council and declared a shadow cabinet.

Because they had to fight Saddam's army and secret police, all major Shi'ite political movements in Iraq developed paramilitaries. Moqtada al-Sadr's father formed his after the first Gulf War. From the summer of 2003, Moqtada al-Sadr reformed the militia as the Mahdi Army. With no jobs, schools, or other alternatives it quickly gained recruits. It was an immediate benefit by October 2003, for the Central Iraqi Criminal Court issued an arrest warrant for his role in the murder of Ayatollah Khoei in April 2003. But fearing the militia, Bremer ordered the warrant not be published.

In August of 2003, U.S. soldiers in a helicopter tried to remove a Mahdi flag from a communications tower, prompting an outburst by al-Sadr supporters. U.S. forces, taking fire from a crowd, shot back, and 13-year-old Wael Ayman was killed. The child became a symbol for the al-Sadr movement.

Ayatollah Kadhim al-Haeri, a student of Moqtada's father and his intellectual heir, lived in Iranian exile and started advocating for al-Sadr, sending advisors and aid. While Moqtada's politics were incoherent, lacking in Islamic theology and oriented solely toward gaining power, Haeri was a rigid follower of Islamic government with a clearly defined political program aimed at establishing a theocracy in Iraq. Between the

Soldiers repeatedly ran into situations their training could not have prepared them to imagine. Here a unit sent to evict a political party from a government building were confronted by a religious sect that proceeded to mutilate themselves with knives and ice picks and by eating glass to show their willingness to die for their beliefs.

ragtag militia and Iranian support, Moqtada was now a force with which to reckon.

The position of ayatollah was achieved by those clerics who studied and wrote on religion, including a manual for laypersons about the righteous practice of Shiism. Their authority was entirely moral and it was up to the candidate to attract a popular following. There were once hundreds of ayatollahs, but Saddam depleted their ranks. Now there were only four grand ayatollahs.

The most revered of the grand ayatollahs was the *marja* or source of religious authority. His fatwas or rulings on matters of religious law had enormous moral authority for the laity, and were often persuasive with other clerics. All Shi'ite laity had to choose a learned religious leader, whose rulings on religious and moral practice they would follow. Many followed al-Sistani.

Al-Sistani, at 74, was a skilled religious politician committed to a form of parliamentary democracy. Throughout the summer of 2003, al-Sistani had what could be called the only viable political organization in the country. Throughout southern Iraq, painted likenesses of the cleric gave the feel of a political campaign. People would hang posters of his face in the rear windows of their cars.

Shi'ite Muslims revered the city of Najaf as the site of the tomb of Ali, the son-in-law of the prophet Muhammad, considered by Shi'ites to be his vicar. Sunni Muslims honor Ali as well, and control of such a sacred shrine brought prestige and wealth through contributions of pilgrims.

Najaf also had Shi'ite seminaries, where clerics studied for years, graduating with a degree in religious jurisprudence. Those graduates who wrote and taught moved up to positions bestowed by the consensus of other clerics. The first step up from a simple student was *Hujjat al-Islam*, or proof of Islam. Al-Sadr's followers often use that title for him. Most, however, doubted he finished his formal studies.

Al-Sadr salted his speech with vulgarisms. An angry hothead with a ruthless streak, he gave some who saw him the impression that he lacked the intelligence to be a serious leader, leading to suspicions that he was a stooge for the people around him. But al-Sadr led a radical Shi'ite minority throughout the south that was loyal to his father. He appealed as much on economic grounds as to religious faith, and his lack of patience and his defiance gathered a following of the unemployed youth. A majority of Iraq's population was under twenty-five, and it was they who suffered most from the lack of jobs.

His movement was sectarian, nationalistic, and based on charisma, appealing mostly to the young and poor. His followers demanded an immediate withdrawal of U.S. troops and advocated an Iranian-style, clerically ruled state with himself as its spiritual leader. They viewed the caretaker government of Prime Minister Ayad Allawi as a puppet. Al-Sistani and the other Shi'ite ayatollahs could not take al-Sadr seriously, he being too young and not sufficiently advanced in his religious studies.

By tapping anti–American feelings, a feeling of dissolution by the younger Iraqis in the Shi'a elder clergy, nationalistic pride and the desperation of the urban poor, the radical cleric increased his following. Many of the members of the Mahdi army were sons of Shi'a in the south who left home because their farms could not support the large families, and because Saddam had not built the state-owned industries in the area to punish the Shi'ites for their lack of loyalty. Al-Sadr's methods angered wealthier, more established members of the Shi'a majority and other Shi'a parties with strong followings, but he had won support from younger men who saw him as a voice for change. They felt the clergy had let them down and saw no future for themselves. As members of the Mahdi army, they instantly received a degree of prestige and a sense of purpose no one else offered.

Al-Sistani, as the current source of religious authority for most Iraqi Shi'ites, depended for his leadership both on the support of other clerics and on popular recognition. He also had large followings outside of Iraq. But, because Shi'ite Iran itself had a number of grand ayatollahs, al-Sistani had little following there, although he himself was Iranian and spoke with such a thick Pharsi accent that Arabs had difficulty understanding him. Al-Sistani also had to watch his flanks with the other grand ayatollahs in Iraq.

The other three grand ayatollahs in Najaf were Bashir Najafi, a Pakistani; Ishaq Fayed, an Afghan; and Mohammed Saeed Hakim, an Iraqi. Hakim was a relative of Abdul Aziz Hakim, later to become the leader of the Supreme Council for Islamic Revolution in Iraq, the political arm of the Badr Corps. All three supported al-Sistani. The murder of Mohammed Saeed Hakim at the direction of al-Zarqawi in August 2003 only increased al-Sistani's hold on the Shi'ite faithful.

Al-Sadr complained about Iranian dominance of Iraqi Shiism; the religious leadership had long been multinational. His movement was strongly nationalistic even though he received aid from Iran. Al-Sistani was born in Iran and had lived in Najaf for fifty years. But few doubted his commitment to Iraq. The clerics in Iran, themselves divided but with a tradition of scholarly tolerance among the clerics, generally supported al-Sistani. Although many disagreed with al-Sistani, they nonetheless saw him as one of their own. An Iraq controlled by a Shi'ite-dominated parliament was acceptable to them. Al-Sistani was also a favorite with many of Iran's reformers. Realizing that there were still hard feelings over the Iran-Iraq war of the 1980s, he asked Iran to keep out of Iraqi domestic affairs. Thus, al-Sadr failed in March of 2003 to chase off al-Sistani.

The stage for much of the conflict that embroiled Moqtada was in the Grand Mosque of Najaf. Najaf lies about 120 miles south of Baghdad in Iraq's central plains on the western bank of the Euphrates River. It is home to 900,000 people. It is also the site of the tomb of Ali, the first imam of the Shi'a.

For 1,000 years it was a destination for Shi'a pilgrims, ranking in importance behind only Mecca and Medina in Saudi Arabia, holy destinations revered by all Muslims. Many Shi'a also made special pilgrimages in order to lay their dead there. It also had the Wadi-us-Salaam, or Valley of Peace, the world's largest Islamic cemetery and one of the largest cemeteries overall. Thousands of prominent Shi'a Muslim figures were buried there.

By the close of March 2004, it was clear that al-Sadr was going first to the use of force, rather than a political route. The militia was strong enough to keep the American army at bay in al-Sadr City and he was clearly inciting violence against the Coalition. Bremer closed down the *al-Hawzah* newspaper of Moqtada al-Sadr. Moqtada sent his people to the streets of al-Sadr City in protest.

With the Americans fighting in Fallujah on April 4, Moqtada ordered his forces to attack the Coalition, taking over the shrine in Najaf as well as Karbala and other cities in the south. Many al-Sadrists believed they were living in the last days, and that the advent of the Muslim messiah, or Mahdi, was around the corner. At the moment, the al-Sadrists were under the delusion that all that was needed to drive out the Americans was to challenge them and the people of Iraq would rise up en masse. Although al-Sadr's Mahdi Army entrenched in East Baghdad had little local support in the holy cities of Najaf and Karbala, it took over the cities. The people did not oppose him, but except for those who already were followers, neither did they provide aid. The Iraqi police simply ran away.

The Americans attempted to arrest or kill al-Sadr on the arrest warrant they received in October of 2003 but were holding onto until it was politically possible to execute the warrant. Al-Sadr militants flocked to Najaf. With intense fighting, the Americans quickly started handing the militia heavy casualties as a brigade from the 1st Armored Division rolled out of Baghdad and into the south. At the same time al-Sistani called on the Shi'a to remain calm and not attack the Americans. A major crisis loomed as the Americans were threatening to storm the Mosque of Najaf and Karbala. To the Coalition, now facing the prospect of losing Fallujah, Najaf, Karbala, al-Kut, and several other cities in the south, having already in effect lost al-Sadr City, as well as having their supply lines regularly ambushed, it was a matter of fight it out or leave Iraq altogether. L. Paul Bremer could not turn over to a transitional Iraqi authority a government that in effect controlled only half of Baghdad and only those patches of ground elsewhere that the multinational force physically sat upon.

Grand Ayatollah Ali al-Sistani sent in Sheikh Abdul Mahdi al-Karbalai, the Karbala representative, to conduct the negotiations with al-Sadr. The message was blunt. The old ayatollah was not going to bail out the cleric, and if he did not leave, his movement would die, for al-Karbalai was not going to condemn the Americans. To the Americans, the statement was equally stern. There would be no wholesale slaughter of the Mahdi Army. If he could convince al-Sadr to leave the shrine, the army would get a free pass home or the south would go up in flames.

Pressure by religious and tribal leaders, as well as residents of both Karbala and Najaf, forced al-Sadr's fighters to lay down their arms on May 21, paving the way for U.S. troops to withdraw from the thresholds of the holy sites. Most residents resented the fighters and called the

Mahdi army "outsiders" and "irresponsible" for disrupting their liveli-hood, which depended on the flow of pilgrims to the city.

The campaign against the Mahdi Army succeeded militarily, since the latter more resembled American street gangs than it did a military force. But it did not destroy al-Sadr and his followers. The American des-ecration of sacred Najaf and its cemetery angered many Shi'ites. One aspect that the Americans never grasped in the Arab culture was the power of revenge. All the Mahdi Army clansmen had relatives who would step forward to avenge them.

Moqtada al-Sadr was making it clear throughout the summer of 2004 that he was just biding his time to strike again. His rhetoric con-tinued to call for violence and intelligence showed that he was arming as fast as he could, although the quality of his troops left much to be desired. With it clear that a number of Sunni cities were rapidly failing and Fallujah already an open embarrassment, the threat of al al-Sadr's movement had to be dealt with.

The interim government in late July conducted a number of arrests of some officials in al-Sadr's offices in Al-Diwaniyah and Al-Nasiriyah, and arrested Mahdi Army members as they traveled to reorganize the force. In response, al-Sadr called for protests. A gun battle erupted August 2 in the holy Iraqi city of Najaf after U.S. and Iraqi troops approached the house of Moqtada al-Sadr. Six members of al-Sadr's militia and four Iraqi bystanders were wounded in the clashes. On the third, Moqtada al-Sadr's militia kidnapped eighteen police officers apparently to use as leverage to force authorities to release militants being detained. He also ordered his army to retake the great mosque yet again, while his follow-ers in the south started shooting at Coalition troops.

The Americans responded yet again with an offensive to secure the mosque, and this time they were determined to finish the job. A pitched battle was now underway in the city of Najaf, although the Mahdi Army was demonstrating a remarkable lack of combat skills. The only thing that was inhibiting the American troops was their desire to minimize the damage and not destroy the mosque. In the meantime, they were bring-ing up the best Iraqi troops they had to storm the holy site.

Looking for a peaceful way out of an oncoming crisis, leader Aziz al-Hakim and al-Sadr al-Din al-Qubanji, a Shi'a leader in al-Najaf, met with Moqtada al-Sadr at the office of Ayatollah Muhammad Mahdi Asifi. They discussed the management of the Imam Ali holy shrine and the for-mulation of a unified Shi'ite position with regard to the National Con-ference. This was an offer of inclusion to al-Sadr for a political rather than military route to power. Moqtada was not interested.

For the civilians of Najaf the fighting was particularly hard. The fear was looting. With the police gone, nearly all they owned was at risk of being carried off. For men of military age it was particularly hazardous because of the possibility of being mistaken by the Americans for a combatant. Insurgents opening fire and then throwing down their weapons had long victimized the Americans. Soldiers often had less than seconds to make the life or death decision as to whether to fire.

Negotiations between al-Sadr and the Iraqi government broke down on August 15. Al-Sadr said democracy could not prevail in Iraq while U.S. forces were besieging Najaf.

Najaf's police chief, Ghaleb al-Jazaeri, ordered journalists to leave the city.

The Americans moved in a battalion of 500 ING to storm the mosque. By the end of August 24th, Iraqi and U.S. forces moved to within 500 yards of the Imam Ali Mosque and shrine. The government warned fighters inside that they would be killed if they did not surrender. The Iraqi Defense Minister Hazim al Shalaan was bellicose: "If they do not, we will wipe them out."

"God willing, we'll be moving in tonight," an Iraqi commander of one unit said. U.S. M1 Abrams tanks reinforced positions along the southern flank of the mosque. Black smoke rose from the area and automatic gunfire crackled after an overnight bombardment from warplanes and artillery.

On the twenty-fifth of August, al-Sistani announced his intention to return from Britain after a 20-day medical visit to London, and then rushed back to Iraq. Despite his 73 years and "cardiac weakness," it seemed that only he could save the city from disaster.

Al-Sistani's return to Basra was more like a coronation than just a cleric coming home. Thousands of faithful traveled from all regions of Iraq to accompany him to Najaf, despite the risks.

August 26th turned out to be bloody in a battle the Americans could not understand, but watched in fascination. Al-Sadr's militia ambushed the unarmed supporters of Grand Ayatollah Ali al-Sistani in Kufa, and twenty people were killed.

Moqtada al-Sadr also called upon his masses to converge and passed by a military base. The crowd of several thousand started chanting their solidarity with al-Sadr and denouncing Iraqi interim Prime Minister Ayad Allawi. Some in the crowd had weapons. The Iraqi National Guard opened fire as the mob passed the military base. Two were killed and twenty-three wounded.

That same day, word came that Shi'ite cleric Moqtada al-Sadr reached an agreement with the Grand Ayatollah Ali al-Sistani. As part of the deal, Iraq's government would drop the murder charges against al-Sadr. Multinational forces were to leave both Najaf and Kufa, leaving security to local forces.

Najaf and Kufa were to be weapons-free cities.

Just that morning a mortar attack killed twenty-five people and wounded scores of others in nearby Kufa. Snipers also opened fire on thousands of demonstrators, killing another twenty-three people. More than 100 people were wounded in the attack.

The ayatollah called on demonstrators converging on Najaf to stay in their homes or stay where they were until further notice. Al-Sistani earlier had called on those same Iraqis to march to Najaf to help put an end to the violence. In a statement released the same day, Allawi reminded "outlaw militias" that the amnesty law was still standing and open to all the elements that opted for peace and would merge into the civil society.

The next day the Iraqi police appeared, securing Najaf's Old City and the Imam Ali Mosque as al-Sadr and al-Sistani representatives worked to transfer control of the mosque compound from al-Sadr's militia to the Marjiya, the Shi'ite religious authority. Al-Sadr called on his troops to hand over their weapons before leaving.

"Do this so they won't condemn you and they won't condemn me," the speaker read from al-Sadr's letter over the mosque's sound system. Residents returned to their homes, a cleanup operation started at the Imam Ali Mosque, and Moqtada's partisans, who just hours before were shooting at both the Americans and unarmed al-Sistani demonstrators, · disappeared.

Thus in September, Moqtada, having twice taken to the field, twice been beaten, but twice survived, went back to al-Sadr City to find another way to gain control of Iraq. With Moqtada having a firm control of al-Sadr City, the Americans and al-Sadr faced off with one another. Al-Sadr City was subdivided into six sections and it was in the easternmost section that Moqtada was strongest.

While al-Sadr may have buoyed his image among the young unemployed in al-Sadr City by September, he made few friends in Najaf. He had twice brought the Americans and the destruction they caused to fight with what could at best be regarded as an undisciplined gang. Most of his army could best be described as closer to criminals than a military unit and they had a reputation of treating the locals roughly and being liberal in their appropriations of property.

He also destroyed the main industry of the city, pilgrimages, by timing his takeover attempts with traditional pilgrimage times. The local merchants were not pleased. On the fifth and sixth of September, there were demonstrations in Najaf by the locals against Moqtada al-Sadr and his Mahdi Army. Demonstrators shouted, "Take your hands off the city! The people of Najaf do not want you!" They also called the Mahdi Army members "thieves."

Behind the scenes, Moqtada was under intense pressure by the Shi'ite clergy, the loose collection of Shi'ite tribal forces called the Badr Corps, and the Shi'a political establishment. The threat of al-Sadr was useful in forcing elections upon the Americans, which if fair would result in Shi'a control of Iraq, but only if Moqtada could be brought under control.

Quietly, in the southern part of Iraq, clerics were contacting the heads of households, asking them to get under control the grandsons, nephews, and sons that had joined the al-Sadr movement. This was the bulk of al-Sadr's militia. Why die for al-Sadr at the hands of the Americans when they could get what they wanted without bloodshed? Worse, the violence was threatening the election. At the same time, the Shi'a were undergoing a campaign making it clear to the Americans that no delay in the election would be tolerated.

While the U.S. military had avoided another public relations nightmare in Najaf they were still frustrated that Moqtada remained a military threat. The American military leadership did not have much faith in the Shi'a intervention without the application of force. So long as he could strike from al-Sadr City with even an undisciplined force, he was a danger. As well, there was the matter of his being the only Shi'a force that would not consent to the idea of a democracy. Strategists understood that sooner or later, the Shi'a would gain control of Iraq if only because of their numbers. There were other Shi'a militias but they could be bargained with to keep their members from attacking the Americans by the promise of winning at the ballot box. If Moqtada could be converted to that line of thinking or be eliminated, the resistance would in effect cease to be a resistance. The Iraqis against the Coalition would then be merely the Sunni holdouts. It might be a civil war but it would be a civil war the Coalition could manage. After all, in practical effect Iraq had been in an intermittent state of civil war for the last fifteen years. But Moqtada would just not co-operate.

As early as May, the commander of forces in the al-Sadr City area, Colonel Abe Abrams of the 1st Cavalry Division's 1st Brigade Combat Team, was begging CPA for more help in construction projects to undermine al-Sadr's popularity. CPA's Baghdad Central tried to accommodate with sewer projects, but found it impossible to get the contractors in without first dealing with al-Sadr, and was inhibited by the red tape. Al-Sadr was willing to take the money and expertise but required that only his people be hired and that the projects not be tainted with an American presence. Efforts to bring in American contractors to oversee a project threatened violence, and the American contracting companies started to drag their feet for fear of casualties and liability.

If the carrot wasn't working, the stick looked even less appealing. Al-Sadr City with its closely packed population was a problem fully ten times the size of Fallujah. To go house to house was out of the question. In May, Abrams had taken to doing thunder runs to at least keep a presence, but the results were often bloody and not fruitful in dislodging the militia. A typical thunder run would center on a platoon of Bradleys roaring down the street in the dead of night with the soldiers not daring to leave the tracks. The results were ghastly.

On a typical night, gang-like groups would challenge the armored force. Completely unskilled, the militia would be cut down wholesale by the armored personnel carriers' machine guns and 25mm chain-guns. The 1st BCT would easily chop down fifteen or so a night with little or no loss, but the next night would find the same numbers. What made it so tragic and worthless as a military victory was that nearly all of the militia were teens, some hardly so. As it later came out, many were intoxicated with drugs. Al-Sadr's people took control of the al-Sadr City health facilities and appropriated the prescription drugs for their military use. In the more respectable neighborhoods around al-Sadr City, the Mahdi Army was called the "pill army" because often its members were clearly whacked-out on a combination of religious fervor and drugs.

With the deal brokered in Najaf there was some hope that Moqtada could be converted into seeking power through less violent means. On September 12, in the background of the bombs, patrolling, and ambushes, intense negotiations were underway with Coalition leaders concerning al-Sadr City and Moqtada's control of the slum. At issue was his militia and arms. The deal over Najaf did not cover al-Sadr City and a careful dance was underway between the central government and the al-Sadr political movement. Neither side was willing to move on its position, but was willing to put into place a face-saving way for the other to back down. From the Iraqi government's point of view, the present situation was untenable. The Coalition was able to make things uncomfortable for al-Sadr, but he in fact was as much in control of the sprawling slum as were the Sunnis in control of Fallujah.

Under Shi'a pressure, al-Sadr called his followers across Iraq to end fighting against U.S. and Iraqi forces. This peaceful accommodation with al-Sadr started on shaky ground in early September, as talks broke down when the Iraqi government refused demands for American troops to keep out of al-Sadr City. Just days before, while combat still continued in Najaf, fighting in the slum killed ten people and wounded one hundred and twenty-six. Since then, however, the impoverished district had been calm. A representative for al-Sadr said an agreement was initially reached with government negotiators on a six-point proposal that would have barred American troops from entering al-Sadr City without Iraqi government permission. But the government negotiators backpedaled the next day, expressing concern that such a deal would incite residents of other Baghdad neighborhoods or Iraqi cities to also call for restrictions on the movement of U.S. troops.

With news starting to filter in of the pressure from family elders to abandon the violence, al-Sadr used his newfound freedom from prosecution. Al-Sadr sponsored a rally in his hometown of al-Kufa. In a defiant speech read out to 2,000 supporters during the first Friday prayers al-Sadr announced, "Many, but not all, think that the American army is invincible. But now it's appeared only truth is invincible," Sheik Jaber al-Khafaji said in a statement read on al-Sadr's behalf. "America claims to control the world through globalization, but it couldn't do the same with the Mahdi Army." Al-Sadr portrayed the American withdrawal from Najaf's devastated Old City as a sign of U.S. military weakness. "We should keep in mind the lessons of what happened in Najaf."

Al-Sadr started applying those lessons around the slum of al-Sadr City. On the 7th of September, al-Sadr's people fired two RPGs at two patrols, which escaped unharmed. Three IEDs exploded near three other patrols without effect. Five IEDs daisy-chained together attacked another convoy near al-Sadr City but again there were no casualties. Another patrol was not so lucky, but the soldier survived his wounds. There also was a mortar attack, which missed its target. Two other RPG attacks wounded U.S. soldiers, and there were additional attacks that killed two soldiers[51] that day near al-Sadr City. To the soldiers patrolling around al-Sadr City this was a continuation of the whole summer. One company of about 150 soldiers had twenty Purple Hearts over the last two months. The Mahdi Army would choose the time and place to attack as the Americans tried to control the area through patrols.

While the 1st Cavalry was patrolling and trying to conduct pinpoint raids in the packed slum, it was also trying to conduct civil affairs missions. The local commander, Colonel Abe Abrams, was determined to make progress across the "no smile line" that divided al-Sadr's controlled area from the rest of Baghdad.

"It's tough," said one soldier. "A guy will shoot a weapon at you, hand it to someone, and then run into his cousin's house to wave at passing U.S. troops. They have a great ability to melt into the neighborhood."[47]

These could be as dangerous as the "combat" missions. One such mission sent in to deliver a truckload of food and cooking supplies to a women's hospital in al-Sadr City was just leaving the hospital when an explosion rocked the last vehicle. An RPG hit an armored Humvee, wounding one of the soldiers. Fifty-caliber machine guns pelted the area where the ambush occurred and the stricken Humvee drove up to the rest of the column.

The column stopped and gave first aid for arm and shoulder wounds of a stricken soldier. An Iraqi interpreter and another man came running up, carrying a wounded Iraqi man on a stretcher from where the attack came from. The wounded Iraqi was carried to the hospital.

Again the column started to leave and another RPG round came at them, missing this time. A machine gunner took out the RPG gunner, and the U.S. soldiers left for their base.

As a general rule, the U.S. forces gave back more deadly than they received. Iraqi officials claimed that fifteen Iraqis were killed in the exchanges and scores were wounded on the seventh. The next day, insurgents detonated a roadside bomb near al-Sadr City that killed one U.S. soldier* and wounded two others who were part of a bomb disposal team. Another patrol had an injured soldier from an IED. Two more patrols were attacked by RPGs and four other IEDs exploded with no casualties. Again, there was an ineffective mortar attack. On the other side of the ledger, the U.S. military claimed at least thirty-five Iraqi combatants killed and more than two hundred others injured in the fighting.

The difference between al-Sadr City and the attacks elsewhere was that the Coalition could see a pattern and relate it to specific stages of negotiations. With Sunni attacks, there were no patterns, no one to talk to. The Coalition felt that once al-Sadr realized he was losing his hold on al-Sadr City the violence there could end.

By now, there was disturbing intelligence. There were indications that al-Sadr was ready and able to move quickly to retake Najaf yet a third time. On September 20, at 2 A.M., U.S. forces and Iraqi police raided the office of al-Sadr next door to the Imam Ali Mosque in Najaf. They arrested al-Sadr aides Sheikh Ahmed al-Shaybani and Sayyid Hussam al-Hassani as well as some of the cleric's bodyguards, confiscating thousands of weapons. Al-Sistani condemned the raid. But in doing so he was making a wider point. There was no clerical outrage in the deaths of the Shi'ites in al-Sadr City. The criticism of the Coalition only underscored the sense that the Shi'ite leadership blamed Moqtada as much as the Americans for the violence.

For months, the Coalition had been trying to negotiate with the sheiks in al-Sadr City in an attempt to bypass Moqtada al-Sadr. The Coalition had scheduled 160 million dollars' worth of public works projects but was unable to do so without al-Sadr's permission. As had happened so often before on September 20, an agreement with the often self-proclaimed leaders was concluded, but for now it was an agreement that was dependent on others not present.

If the agreement was thought to bear any real fruit, the next day made clear who was really in charge in al-Sadr City as Coalition forces

*KIA: Sgt. James D. Faulkner

sought to clean out pockets of militarists. On September 21, al-Sadr's people responded to the American operations by shooting thirty-two mortar rounds and five more rockets. The marksmanship was terrible, damaging solely civilian dwellings. The usual attacks came on schedule against Coalition forces elsewhere in the slum when an American vehicle was hit by a blast. One soldier was taken to a nearby military hospital while three others suffered minor wounds and returned to duty. Several civilian vehicles were damaged in the blast and subsequent fire.

Meanwhile, the Americans announced that charges had been preferred against two Task Force Baghdad soldiers, alleging they were involved in wrongfully killing three Iraqis. The announcement was widely played in the Arab press.

On September 22 in al-Sadr City, American troops and Iraqi forces were at it again, "targeting pockets of insurgents and terrorists." Now Colonel Abrams was taking on a new strategy. The goal was to carve out the hardest part of al-Sadr City and then start a sewer project to give a clear choice to the people between al-Sadr's controlled area and that of the interim government. Hospital officials said ten people were killed and ninety-two wounded. Insurgents launched fifty-two mortar rounds and two rockets, often landing on people's dwellings. That same day, U.S. officials announced a project for a new sewer system in the southern area of al-Thrawa employing 1,000 local Iraqis.

Late September 23, U.S. helicopter gunships fired down on mortar positions inside al-Sadr City. The clashes that day between Shi'ite militants and U.S. troops killed at least thirteen Iraqis and left more than fifty wounded. But an IED attack injured three soldiers and one armored vehicle was burnt.

That day something else happened more lethal than both the Americans and al-Sadr's militia combined. A virulent form of hepatitis broke out both in al-Sadr City and the predominantly Sunni town of Mahmudiya. It was particularly dangerous to pregnant women. Health officials blamed it on the collapse of the sewage and water system. With the willingness of the Americans to fix the problem, the violence was now threatening tens of thousands of the most vulnerable. The pressure on Moqtada al-Sadr was intensifying.

A roadside bomb exploded in al-Sadr City September 24, setting a U.S. military vehicle ablaze and wounding three soldiers. Troops seized a few more blocks of al-Sadr City's labyrinth of winding alleyways and gray cinder-block tenements. The Americans continued the plan of trying to make parts of the slum a model of law and order. Once the shooting stopped on this newly-won turf, the military worked with contractors to start construction on sewage, water, and electricity to weaken the support for al-Sadr's fighters. There was a sense within Colonel Abrams' command center that they were starting to make headway against Moqtada.

On September 27, insurgents fired three mortar rounds from al-Sadr City at a nearby U.S. Army base, but the shells fell short and exploded in a civilian neighborhood. The Americans were not idle; they continued with operation "Iron Fury 2."

U.S. jets pounded suspected Shi'ite insurgent positions in the slum. Explosions lit up the night sky for hours before dawn. Mangled vehicles, debris, and shards of glass littered the streets. Dr. Qassem Saddam of the Imam Ali hospital in al-Sadr City, admittedly sympathetic to al-Sadr, said five people were killed and forty were wounded, including fifteen women and nine children. At least two children wrapped in bloodstained bandages were displayed to the press lying in hospital beds along with a man suffering burns from head to toe.

Al-Sadr tried to generate publicity to portray his fallen as martyrs. In al-Sadr City mourners carried the coffin of a fallen insurgent, marching in an organized procession through the slum. But it was clear that there was no general outpouring from the residents.

In a statement, the U.S. military said it conducted what it called "precision strikes" and denied reports of heavy civilian casualties.

An al-Sadr City resident speaking to Reuters disagreed with that assessment: "As usual the warplanes dropped bombs without any reason, there was no resistance," he said. "They used to say the Mahdi Army attacked them, but there was nothing yesterday. What is the guilt of the children and the women and the houses that were destroyed?"[48]

The U.S. developed a new tactic in the Baghdad slum, with eight tanks and seventeen Humvees to draw out the militia, tempting them to lay roadside explosives and otherwise expose themselves. Waiting above would be an AC-130 gunship. On September 28, U.S. aircraft struck. The local hospital reported that one Iraqi was killed and three injured.

Again, September 29 brought another air strike at a patrolling al-Sadr militia vehicle in al-Sadr City. The strike targeted an insurgent rocket team. The insurgent vehicle blew up, igniting four to five secondary explosions from munitions inside. The pilot reported that the vehicle was fired on and destroyed in an open area away from buildings and other people. Maithem Mahmoud of al-Sadr General Hospital said one man was killed and a woman injured in the strike. The 1st Cavalry had turned the tables on the IED problem. If the insurgents knew where the Americans would be, an IED would be waiting. But in the confined area of al-Sadr City, if the Americans could give the Mahdi Army a predictable route to attack, the Americans had the technology to set their own trap.

That same day the U.S. cavalry troopers came under fire as twenty-one mortar rounds landed in or around "War Eagle," a base of the 1st

Cavalry Division on the edge of al-Sadr City. But U.S. forces scored a victory against the mortar men who often harassed their post. A single round fired from an artillery piece struck a vehicle the insurgents had used as a platform for their mortar. Following a trail of blood from the vehicle, soldiers found three bodies of the attackers with other body parts strewn around the area. Battle Damage Assessment claimed six insurgents killed.

In the backdrop of the fighting intense negotiations continued with Moqtada al-Sadr. Quietly the Muslim clergy in the south were pressing the revolutionary to step back. Implied was the threat that they would keep him out of the political victory once the Shi'a won the election, which if fairly run they surely would. Al-Sistani was an old man, they told him. He would have to wait but perhaps not that long. There was the sense that they were on the brink of making a deal.

By October, the spokesmen for the ayatollahs were pressing Moqtada al-Sadr to the point that the leader of the Mahdi Army was seriously discussing the possibility that some of his aides would run for parliamentary seats while he stayed behind the scenes. Adil Abdul Mahdi, the finance minister, official within SCIRI, and contender to lead a future Iraqi government, also was pushing al-Sadr to come to heel. The revolutionary was still hedging his bets and was unwilling to let go of the military option. People within the al-Sadr organization were offered compensation and an inside track on contracts from the government in exchange for abandoning al-Sadr.

There was talk within the inner circle of the al-Sadr movement that by accepting participation in the elections the increasing pressure to give up the militia might ease, allowing for the survival of the Mahdi Army.

Fighting in al-Sadr City killed nine Mahdi Army militiamen October 1. As of October 4, Abrams was still keeping up the military pressure, killing another five in al-Sadr City. Meanwhile, Moqtada al-Sadr was negotiating with the U.S. for an end to military operations.

On October 5, there was heavy fighting in the Shi'ite slums. Colonel Abrams continued his military operations in the ghetto as that night AC-130 howitzers struck repeatedly and tanks rolled in.

As late as the first week of October, Moqtada al-Sadr was playing his dwindling hand of cards, indicating once again that he would boycott the elections. But, in light of al-Sistani's support of the elections, he was rapidly losing popular support among the more mature Shi'a population.

By the close of the first week of October, negotiations were intense between the Allawi government and Moqtada al-Sadr. The U.S. military had been using air strikes and tank fire to attack Mahdi Army positions in the city, wreaking havoc in the densely populated slum, but unlike before there was not the outcry against the Americans. The deal being offered was that the Mahdi Army would turn over its heavy weapons in a five-day period, and that al-Sadr would get the credit for the 500 million dollars in projects already allotted for the Thrawa slum. Unlike with Fallujah, there would not be the equivalent of a separate Fallujah Brigade made up of his followers, but the patrolling within the city would be done by one of the newly created, U.S.-trained and multi-ethnic Iraqi National Guard battalions. Otherwise, Colonel Abrams would continue his operations of taking control of parts of the slum, inserting the projects, and al-Sadr would watch a continued decline in his territory and popular support.

Moqtada pressed to have only local police to patrol, but by now al-Sadr City had only 500 policemen. In past fights with the Mahdi Army, the police tended to defect to the Mahdi Army or simply melt away.

Prime Minister Ayad Allawi was assured that Moqtada was cornered and no concessions were needed. He offered an amnesty to fighters of the Mahdi Army if they surrendered their weapons, accepted the presence of Iraqi police forces, and abided by the law.

On the seventh, a senior aide to Iraqi Shi'a leader Moqtada al-Sadr, Muayad al-Khazraji, a religious judge, was released from Abu Ghraib. He had been held for nearly a year. That day, Moqtada agreed to stand down his militia. In a broadcast on al-Arabiya television, aide Ali Smaism said the militia would disarm if al-Sadr's aides were freed from U.S. detention, if U.S. forces stopped "persecuting" al-Jaish al-Mahdi, and reparations were paid. Al-Sadr, via his aides, also demanded financial assistance in the rebuilding of al-Sadr City.

On October 11, members of the al-Sadr Movement began turning over heavy weapons to the U.S. in exchange for a cessation of hostilities. Unlike the situation in Fallujah, the weapons turn-in started off promising. On the first day at one station in the district, there was a surrender of about a dozen machine guns, 12 mortar rounds, 38 mortar launchers and a sniper rifle. On the next day, it was clear that the weapons collection program in al-Sadr City was markedly more successful, with the pace of weapons turn-ins picking up substantially.

October 12, Grand Ayatollah Ali al-Sistani issued a formal legal ruling requiring believers to register to vote in the voter registration drive set to begin on November 1. The ruling stated, "It is incumbent upon all citizens eligible to vote, both men and women, to register their names correctly in the voter registration lists." He said that voters were responsible for making sure their names were correctly recorded. He called on his aides to form popular committees in their regions to help citizens to accomplish this task, so that all might be enabled to participate in the elections, "which we hope will be held at the scheduled time, and which we hope will be free and fair." This act closed the door on Moqtada's abandoning the political route.

On October 17 there was one close call in the relationship when Allawi visited one of the turn-in stations to publicize the progress. Insurgents caught wind of the event and fired a mortar round at an office where weapons had been collected from the Mahdi Army militiamen. While Prime Minister Ayad Allawi had been scheduled to visit the site, the timing was off and he had not yet arrived. He did ultimately meet with al-Sadrist leaders.

In the meantime, the U.S. military noticed a drop-off in the numbers of weapons turned in and were certain Moqtada was holding out. They were telling the Iraqi interim government that the program was not a real success. The Iraqis simply shrugged. "What did you expect?" asked the local commander of the Iraq police, sarcastically. "Why would they give them to you when they could sell them to Fallujah?"

There was another problem: all the IEDs the Mahdi Army laid as a defense of the slum. They were in such large numbers that the Iraqi National Guard could not safely patrol the area. The U.S. military was demanding they clear them if the cease-fire was to hold. The concern should have been not clearing them, but policing them up. The residents were feverishly getting them off the streets as valuable explosives for sale.

CHAPTER 12

The South

A number of strategists believed that Fallujah was just a sideshow. In the final analysis, the Sunni Iraqis in general and Fallujah in particular could make things bloody, but it was the Shi'a Iraqis in the south who were decisive. It was the southern cities that the Americans needed to keep quiet. Should military and other security officials lose a grip on Shi'a willingness to seek a pluralist Iraq, all would truly be lost.

August 2004 saw an attempt by Moqtada al-Sadr to seize control of the Shi'a south by taking over the holy city of Najaf. That proved a miscalculation in that the U.S. military and the Iraqi central government proved quite willing to risk offending the Shi'a population and storm the Shi'ite holy shrine in that city. Moreover, the Shi'a population did not rise in mass indignation to the defense of al-Sadr's gambit to establish himself as the Shi'ite warlord. Faced with the likelihood of a major military defeat and being proclaimed a usurper by the Shi'a clergy, he agreed to end his occupation of the Grand Mosque of Najaf. But it left him a powerful force in Iraq with the stature of being the only single leader willing to face off the United States military. He also got the interim government to dismiss the warrant for his arrest on the charge of murder. This left the Coalition with an imperfect victory and a complex if less violent southern Iraq.

In the far south, a religious movement seeking to establish *vilayat-e-faqih* (rule by the religious clergy according to the Shi'ite faith) was developing. Early on, the Lebanese Shi'ite militia, Hezbollah, had infiltrated Basra and surrounding areas, so much so that with the help of other Shi'ite militias it had become a force in and of itself.

Most of Iraq's males had received military training under the Baa'th rule of Saddam Hussein. New militias sprang up, often as a means to protect themselves as makeshift police, sometimes in an arms race with competing militias. The Coalition was powerless to stop the trend.

Iranian intelligence bankrolled these new forces through "welfare funds" ostensibly given to mosques and shrines. Shi'ite militias had no trouble gaining arms and ammunition. Iranian Shi'ites came across the porous border, including Iranian revolutionary guards, who established pockets, especially in Ammarah and Basra. On occasion, they were willing to fight for al-Sadr, then switch sides. The British, Polish, and Spanish forces, not willing to risk casualties, often simply ignored the problem. In March, when intelligence reports pointed out that checkpoints coming in and out of Karbala had closed traffic, the Polish commanding general charged with the area simply replied to his intelligence officer that there were no militias.

In Corneesh, near the Sheraton Hotel in the former residence of the governor of Basra, a political party, the Sayyed al-Shohada, operated as a cover for Iranian intelligence. The Coalition watched this nearly open operation closely but did nothing to stop it.

This party, like many Shi'ite militias, called itself a branch of the al-Majlis al-Alla (Supreme Council of Islamic Revolution in Iraq, SCIRI) led by cleric Abdul Aziz al-Hakim. However, the officers of this organization were not local Iraqis. It was difficult to distinguish between Iranians and native Iraqis in southern Iraq, as many Shi'ites spent many years in exile in Iran during Saddam's rule. Coalition intelligence tracked a number of leaders in the Dawa Party, the SCIRI, and members of Moqtada's Mahdi Army with connections to Iran and assumed most took orders from its intelligence services. The militias in the south flourished, taking advantage of the troubles of the U.S.-led occupation forces elsewhere.

There were other indications of Iranian designs. After the fall of Saddam's regime, Iranian money helped Hezbollah send volunteers into southern Iraq from Lebanon. Hezbollah leaders helped Iraqi Shi'ites establish the Iraqi Hezbollah to fight against the British, with the ultimate goal of establishing *vilayat-e-faqih* (Islamic Republic), in line with Iran. Hezbollah had long been supported by Iran.

The Iraqi police moved their offices to a new building in front of the Shatul Arab waterway. With the old building unoccupied, as with other places in Iraq, political parties moved in. The Iraqi Hezbollah now had its headquarters right in the middle of Basra, in the old police headquarters. The Iraqi Hezbollah established as well a branch in the city of Ammarah, just north of Basra. This combination of Shi'ite militias and Iranian intelligence in Basra and Ammarah was taking place under the watchful eyes of the British, who were responsible for security in the south. They were reluctant to risk a major clash.

These Iranian-supported militias were just one Shi'ite political force. There were other forces, notably Moqtada, who had a powerful grand ayatollah, Kazim al-Haeri from Iran, as a backer. But, after vowing to fight to the "last drop of my blood" in Najaf, Moqtada called on his militia to put down their arms and leave the Imam Ali Shrine in Najaf. He was now facing a challenge in the south by other Shi'a forces. He was watching many of his loosely organized forces convert to competing militias.

Espousing a more moderate secular-leaning Iraq to Moqtada's vision of a country more in line with *vilayat-e-faqih*, al-Sistani was walking a tightrope. Al-Sistani's power was completely moral, having no real fighting forces. But this gave him additional power in that it did not threaten other militias and political groups and made him acceptable as a force for moderation to the Coalition.

But in the end, it was guns that worried the U.S. military, and al-Sadr had the guns. The interim Iraqi government and Moqtada's representatives continued talks on the future of his militia, thus making him a very public player. The focus of a peace plan was not in the Shi'a south but in the Baghdad neighborhood of al-Sadr City, and most living there had relatives in the south. At the same time, Moqtada was developing an alternative "political program."

Still sidelined in the south were many Arab nationalists (former Baa'th Party members), tribal chiefs, former Iraqi army top brass, and last but not least many of the clergy and prayer leaders at mosques, both Shi'ite and Sunni. The Coalition banned from government the people who formed the foundation of power under Saddam, the Baa'th Party, and the army. Many of these supported the insurgents.

For the central government, the principal tool it had to make inroads revolved around money. The job of clearing the rubble, repairing the damage, and rebuilding all that was destroyed the month before in Najaf was estimated to cost $500 million. Despite the price tag, U.S. commanders saw the battle of Najaf as a success story, a blueprint for winning control of other "no-go" zones in Iraq. Hit them with a big stick and then throw on a bushel of carrots.

But Najaf and Karbala were uniquely tolerant of the U.S. presence compared with other Iraqi cities. Oppressed by former dictator Saddam Hussein and long open to outsiders because of the pilgrim trade, Najaf welcomed the U.S. invasion without a fight. Many residents despised al-Sadr and his followers as Baghdad-based thugs and thieves without respect for Najaf's senior Shi'ite clerics.

Even during combat operations in Najaf, work continued on several projects that had been underway before al-Sadr's attempt to take the city. Civil affairs soldiers and Marines worked on the construction of the Sadeer Canal in Najaf and a new bridge in Qadisiyah. Already planned reconstruction on the An Najaf Teaching Hospital was ongoing. A recent flooding problem was stabilized and pipes and pumps were brought in from Baghdad to fix the problem.

These were all part of military operation, which was possible there only because the public support kept the lightly armed soldiers and their contractors safe. The plans were that civil affairs forces would help in the reconstruction of government buildings damaged in the fighting. New construction included plans for a building for the Provincial Council, which was currently collocated with the Governor's office. Schools and mosques in both Najaf and Kufa would be refurbished, repaired, and where necessary, rebuilt. A women's center for internet and newspaper access was also under construction in Qadisiyah.

In al-Hilla, U.S. army civil affairs under Polish command targeted construction funds at two elementary schools as well as contracting improvements for the Babylon University's Law School. No one was fooled into thinking that these projects were a massive overhaul of the Iraqi infrastructure, least of all the Iraqis, but the projects were carefully targeted to what were genuinely needed public improvements designed to win public support more than actually cause a widespread improvement in lives. That was beyond the scope and budget of the units involved. Still, they were very different from the "shock and awe" style of military prowess the world had come to identify with the United States.

All told throughout the country, 650 projects were underway although it was difficult to say, outside of the south and the Kurdish north, how many were actually being built. The Coalition started over a third of the projects since the beginning of September. Supposedly, these projects employed over 100,000. If the security situation allowed, 18,000 projects were planned, obligating seven billion dollars. These were not unusual projects for the American military but were possible only where the local populace allowed it.

For the most part, casualties for America's allies were far less, as Washington realized that they had signed on expecting operations more like Kosovo's peacekeeping than real war. Thus, they were placed in less threatening areas, and when violence kicked up as it did in April, the U.S. heavy formations would move in. That did not leave them immune to attacks, however. On September 13, a Polish explosive ordnance disposal (EOD) team along with its security escort came under attack from insurgents using rocket-propelled grenades (RPG) and small arms. That same day near al-Hilla, Iraqi National Guardsmen ran into a roadside bomb, killing three of their number and wounding three more. The night before, insurgents attacked Camp Zulu with mortars in the Wasit province and the next day a roadside bomb struck but to no effect.

There were Coalition victories in the south as well. Near Nahr Wand, in the Karbala province, Polish, Bulgarian, and Iraqi National Guard soldiers launched a search, finding a large store of weapons on September 16th. The same day, Marines uncovered a large cache of weapons and ammunition after stopping to investigate an improvised explosive device near Iskandariyah. On September 18, several insurgents were killed when an explosive device they were preparing backfired near the Wasit Province town of Suqayra. On September 23, in the town of al Mashru, Iraqi security forces and multinational forces found and seized a large weapons cache and detained twenty suspects. The next day more than 320 large-caliber artillery shells were found during a joint forces search in Babil province.

The British, with their experience in Northern Ireland, interacted better than the Americans with the locals using their "Smile, Shoot, Smile" tactics. They also better handled the breakdown of tasks, realizing that the true purpose of an urban patrol was not to get into a fight but to gather information. In their patrols, a carman, spotter, recorder, and cameraman would be detailed. The carman would have studied the intelligence reports and looked for cars on the watch list and concentrated on identifying possible car bombs coming their direction. The spotter would study the intelligence reports for people on the black and gray list as well as watch people closely to prevent a dropped grenade. The cameraman would take digital pictures of suspicious vehicles, people, and places for the patrol report. The recorder would keep careful notes, which would be the basis for the debriefing after the patrol was over.

The British would need that skill in September. During the al-Sadr offensive in August in Najaf, they had limited their patrols to immediately around their bases. With the al-Sadr offensive over, it was time to get back on the streets where the Iraqi police and National Guard were outgunned. They also well understood the stakes in keeping the pressure on Moqtada al-Sadr at this juncture.

But no amount of skill could keep a patrol safe where a deliberate ambush was waiting. Two British soldiers were killed on the twenty-eighth of September when their convoy was ambushed in Basra. British troops killed three Shi'ite militiamen in clashes before Coalition forces withdrew from the office of Moqtada al-Sadr in Basra. Mahdi Army elements opened fire on British soldiers after they took the office. This was not the first raid of the office. Earlier in the week, police raided al-Sadr's offices and seized weapons.

British troops then conducted several raids of weapons caches, which sparked more fighting. Al-Sadr's military leader started making threats of a wider campaign. "The al-Mahdi Army is ready to carry out these military operations against British forces, oil fields, and oil pipelines in Basra," Sheik Asaad al-Basri said. The military offered to repair the office following its raid and left it under the control of the Iraqi police. It would be up to them to decide if al-Sadr's people could go back in. Al-Sadr's leadership made their usual bluster: "Basra governor Hassen Rashed must return all weapons. Otherwise, I will send a battalion of the Mahdi Army to arrest him," Sheikh Assad Basri said in a sermon at the Muslim weekly prayers.

Local hospital officials claimed that eight civilians were wounded in overnight clashes amid continued fighting. Within hours, the anti–Coalition press in Baghdad reported that more than one hundred Iraqi civilians were killed and over two hundred and fifteen others wounded, with troops destroying forty houses and damaging fifty cars. Unlike before, the Arab press was not picking up on the story. The claims were starting to lose their effect as they became more outrageous and not supported with real visual images.

In the south, the Iraqi National Guard was taking on more of a role in the day-to-day military activity. That made them more of a target. On September 29, in Iskandariyah, thirty miles south of Baghdad, insurgents attacked an Iraqi National Guard patrol, killing two soldiers and wounding three. However, compared to the north these were rare occurrences. For most Iraqis in the south, life was far more normal.

While this was all going on, there was another quiet unreported war within the Shi'a population. A coalition of the Badr Corps was opposing al-Sadr's militia. These were the armed wing of the Supreme Council of the Islamic Revolution in Iraq (SCIRI), and the Da'wah Party. These were the militia that also supported al-Sistani although he had no direct links with the group. They saw elections as the way to power and al-Sadr's tactics as an impediment.

CHAPTER 13

The Sunni Triangle

"Sunni Triangle" has slipped into the American lexicon as a depiction of life under constant danger and frustration. To the soldier working there in scores of unknown villages and cities, life was a constant seesaw of fighting off boredom and moments of danger with little sense of progress. It was the Sunni people there with whom the insurgents of Fallujah had the most in common. It was also in the tribal areas that the Baa'thist insurgents felt they had the best chance of defeating the Americans.

The Sunni Triangle is an imaginary patch of ground in Iraq where a majority of the population is Sunni Arab. It runs from the city of ar-Ramadi through Fallujah to just north of Baghdad through Baqubah to Balad Rus at its base and then north up through Samarra, Tikrit, and Baiji. Some included the cities of Mosul and Kirkuk in the Triangle but those cities had as many Kurds, Assyrians, and Turkmen as Arabs. The Sunni Arabs have always been a minority in Iraq, but since the occupation by the British during the First World War had been its political master. Saddam Hussein, himself a Sunni Arab, favored this group with public works projects and wealth funneled down through the Baa'th Party.

Sunni Arabs made up most of the Republican Guard, as was the case of most of the officer corps above the rank of major. The Baa'th Party subsidized most tribal sheiks of the Sunni tribes. The way Iraqi society worked under Saddam, a worker—whether a common laborer, a doctor, or college professor—received officially much the same pay. But Baa'th officials would get bonuses on Baa'th holidays, and loyal tribes were granted gifts, of which, in turn, a percentage filtered down. There was no way to live in anything but poverty under the salaries paid, but each profession had its way of cheating the system. A teacher combined his class with other teachers and went to work only half or less of his time, working on the side. A college professor would hold a seminar on his class and charge each student $200. If you didn't take the seminar, you didn't pass the course. Death certificates and marriage licenses required an extra five to fifteen dollars for the authorizing signature. The system tolerated this corruption so long as you had a Baa'th protector. If you did not, you had to play by the rules and starve. Most the Sunni had protectors, and many of the others did not.

The sudden end of this culture of corruption placed the Coalition in a difficult position from the beginning. The Baa'th benefactors were gone. There was no way in a democracy that Sunnis would be better off either politically or economically than they were under Saddam Hussein. Worse was the blow to their pride and the fear of revenge from the people, whom they had so brutally ruled over the last generation under the regime of Saddam. Saddam's old cronies also had money to spend. There was a $2,500 bounty on any American soldier killed. As was predictable, it was in the Sunni Triangle and the Sunni neighborhoods of Baghdad that serious attacks started mounting as early as May 2003.

Where possible, U.S. commanders reached out with the public works funds called "CERP" to help area communities. The 1st Infantry Division alone had ninety-five million dollars to spend on such projects. It was common to hear commanders say that their greatest problem was unemployment, and they were often asking for more help with social programs. Thus, the person most sought after was the officer handling the unit funds. Said one brigade commander, the person who controls the money, controls the battle.

Each local area was highly individualistic and the varied approaches by local commanders brought differing results. In Baiji, for example, the 1st Infantry Division dispatched its troops to help build a health care clinic and make improvements to the electrical power plant. The electrical plant in Baiji was considered a critical asset, as was the oil refinery there. From the beginning when the 1st Battalion of the 7th Field Artillery took over the town, they found that they had two different groups causing problems, the insurgency and the local crime mob. In the case of Baiji, a local traffic police officer operated the criminal activity. He had full control over the oil refinery and anyone who wanted a job had to go through him. Though the mob was not the insurgency, they still could be dangerous and unpredictable, as one Civil Affairs team of the 415th Civil Affairs Battalion discovered. In September, while the team was approaching the plant, the guards there took the team under fire.

The security of Baiji's oil refinery and electrical plant was a major concern; the civil affairs team was in the process of contracting to build a wall around the facility. The pipelines were occasionally attacked but easily repaired. Hiring the local sheiks to protect the pipelines, just as Saddam had done, generally worked well. For the crime gangs, for the most part, the military simply came to a tacit arrangement. The military stayed out of the businesses of the facilities, the wall was built, and the oil flowed.

For the troops, one of the most aggravating aspects of duty was General Order Number One, which forbade the use of alcohol by U.S. troops. CPA would regularly throw parties at the pool in the rear of the CPA headquarters where non–American forces, senior officers assigned to the civilian authority, and civilians would imbibe in the presence of the U.S. enlisted. This picture is a typical morning after at CPA.

Security concerns often curtailed such projects. The insurgents targeted contractors or forced them to give their profits to local guerilla leaders. The violence forced the lightly armed civil affairs teams managing the projects to travel with heavy escorts, making any such effort a drain on the unit's combat power and less attractive to unit commanders. Thus, the insurgents had effectively separated the U.S. military from the Sunni population, which was in fact the prize to be won or lost.

What was remarkable was that they accomplished so much over the summer of 2004, as was seen by September. All through 2003, the Triangle mounted a serious death toll as Brigade Combat Team commanders struggled, each with his allotted area trying to get the local leaders to curtail the insurgent attacks. A patchwork of approaches developed as the U.S. commanders opted to keep the control on the tactical unit that "owned the ground" instead of a unified command of civil affairs and reconstructive efforts. This brought varied results.

On Highway 1, Reading north from Baghdad, you passed a large military area on the right. Destroyed Iraqi armor blocked its gates. To the left ran a railroad track that ambushers had on many occasions used for cover. Along the way was the town of Taji. The people there rarely gave a friendly wave to the Americans. According to one soldier stationed there, "...if you like a simple life with just an occasional rocket or mortar round to liven things up then this is the place for you." Many of the residents had family that served with the Republican Guard and still held a grudge. Casualties were sharply reduced by keeping down the contact with the locals but Taji remained in September a dangerous place. On September 13, a patrol was ambushed at Taji using small-arms fire and an improvised explosive device. The short skirmish killed two U.S. soldiers.*

Two weeks later, a fourteen-vehicle supply convoy was moving two miles south of Taji. A bomb rose into the air and spun around an armored Humvee gun truck, the last vehicle in the trail of supply trucks. The explosion blew in a door and shrapnel flew at the three people inside. Still, between the armor on the door and their armored vests, only the driver inside was slightly injured. The occupants checked on the top gunner. All knew he was not so well protected and would be the one most likely to be hurt. The soldier was slumped in the turret, his arms braced against the sides. The other vehicles swung back to the bombing site. Soldiers secured the area and medics worked on the gunner. Cars were piling up behind the site. Dozens of people gathered outside shops along the road watching the frantic action around the smoking Humvee. The soldiers were unable to determine who set off the IED. No one came forward to point out who planted or exploded the roadside bomb. The soldier sustained a head wound and could not be revived.†

Head wounds and IEDs sparked a debate within the military. The troops now deployed had new lighter helmets. The new helmets were as strong as the old ones but provided less protection in the back and sides. This lighter helmet made a lot of sense to infantry units facing fire from the front, but IEDs usually struck from the side or back. Doctors noticed an increase in deaths from the soldiers using the new helmets when they ran into roadside bombs.

Saddam's hometown was Tikrit. From the beginning, the Americans paid particular attention to the city, placing a division headquarters in Saddam's Water Palace. For the most part, there was always an uneasy truce between the Americans and the local Sunni leaders. However, IEDs and mortars were a problem. Small-arms ambushes were less of a problem. That is not to say September did not see them at all.

Near Tikrit, close to the village of Ash Sharqat another convoy was

*KIA: Staff Sgt. David J. Weisenburg, Spc. Benjamin W. Isenberg
†KIA: Spc. David W. Johnson

attacked on September 20, killing one U.S. soldier.* The soldier died when he stepped out of his vehicle to investigate a roadside bomb and it exploded. Two days later near Tikrit, a roadside bomb detonated near a dismounted patrol, killing another U.S. soldier† on the twenty-second of September. The U.S. forces responded with aggressive patrolling, engaging insurgents near Baqubah on September twenty-seventh. These were dangerous for everyone nearby. In the course of the fighting, a farmer was killed in the crossfire.

But there was one bit of political good news. The Georgian defense minister had assured that his country would be deploying 300 troops to Iraq who would join the 159-strong contingent already there.

There were hundreds of small nameless towns in the Sunni Triangle. All of them were dangerous, and more of the Iraqi National Guard was taking them over. Seven Iraqi civilians and three National Guardsmen were wounded in clashes overnight on September 24, in the town of Dhuluiyah forty miles north of Baghdad. The fighting wounded ten more, including a woman and a child. The fighting started the day before when a U.S. military patrol came under attack from rocket-propelled grenades near an abandoned police station. The insurgents launched an assault aimed at taking control of the main police station. The town, home to a number of the Wahabi sect of Islam, was harboring foreign fighters operating out of Samarra. An Iraqi National Guard soldier was killed early the twenty-seventh of September in a roadside bomb blast near Muqdadiya north of Baghdad. Just the night before, another roadside bomb killed four Iraqi civilians and wounded a fifth in nearby Kan Beni Saad.

Balad Rus was a small Arab village on the eastern corner of the Sunni Triangle. It had always been a flash point between the Kurds further to the east and the Arabs. With its mixture of Sunni and Shi'a population it was a hotbed of the insurgency. On September 18, an American column narrowly escaped an ambush there without loss. Nevertheless, that isolated village incident became an important victory in the information war for the insurgents. Iraq, with its newly found press freedoms, fostered a number of pro-insurgency newspapers that spread the word of thirty-eight American troops killed. Throughout the Iraqi campaign, these small papers generated an intensive war in the minds of many in the street. Information warfare became a major tactic of the insurgency, on one hand claiming fictitious victories while intimidating the mainstream press with threats against the reporters, publishers, and their families.

*KIA: Spc. Joshua J. Henry
†KIA: Staff Sgt. Lance J. Koenig

Of the entire Sunni triangle, the military considered the village of Balad the most important to military officials because of an air base nearby. At the beginning of the operation, CJTF-7 turned a nearby air base into the logistical hub called "LSA Anaconda." The massive base was perfect to house the COSCOM of the American CORPS and provided the central supply and support base of the American forces in Iraq. It was also in a reedy, swampy section of Iraq, which provided perfect cover for insurgents. Early on, ambushes and IEDs were common around the base. It was here that the mortar attacks first became a problem. It was an area that American troops could never secure despite the large amount of firepower expended there. In large measure, the nearby village of Adwar was a big problem. Many of the people who lived there were officers in the old Air Force, without any jobs and leaning towards a return of the old regime anyway. The civil affairs team at LSA Anaconda asked for funds six months before to hire the former air force officers as police officers, but CPA ignored the request. As it was, they were paying them their former military stipend for doing nothing. Adwar was a source of many who shelled the base. The massive base was sometimes shelled three times in a single day.

One of the most dangerous jobs in the U.S. military belonged to a combat support unit that traveled long stretches of highway under constant threat of attack. These trucks, moving slowly on empty desert roads, were easy targets. The job became increasingly dangerous as the convoy approached its destination. Near LSA Anaconda was a favorite place to attack supply convoys.

A large percentage of the soldiers working out of the massive base were reservists, often assigned to transportation units. These trucks rarely had armor. On the morning of September 9, the family of one such reservist received a knock on the door with the news of their son's death. "I felt my heart sink from my whole body," the soldier's mother said. "I asked them if they were sure ... and then I asked God to hold on to me and give me the strength to support my family." September 8 claimed the soldier's life and seriously wounded another when their supply truck ran into a roadside bomb.*

Two days later, on September 10, one U.S. soldier was killed as his patrol was responding to IED and mortar attacks on the base.†

QRF (quick reaction force) duty in the early stages hardly lived up to its name. A base commander would assign a platoon the job and everyone knew that on short notice they would simply roll. But the summer of 2003 found that often the troops would not get out in time to catch

---

*KIA: Spc. Lauro G. DeLeon Jr.
†KIA: Spc. Edgar P. Daclan Jr.

the enemy, and when they did roll, often an ambush waited. For the insurgency, predicting when and where the Americans would be was all they needed to kill a soldier and then run. Those working with a QRF were the most predictable group to pick on.

By September 2004, the assignment to a QRF was hard and dangerous work. First, there were tactical drills. Unlike raids, these could not be planned on every detail of the operation. Each call would come with the QRF not having much if any intelligence; each situation would be different. That meant training, and training, and training battle drills in the hot summer sun.

Even then, the QRF would always be at a disadvantage. The insurgents would attack at the place and time of their choosing, knowing what they would be facing ahead of time. On September 27, a 1st Infantry Division soldier was killed* at about 10 A.M., when a patrol returning from the scene of a fatal traffic accident involving an American soldier was attacked with small-arms fire. The patrol returned fire but could not fix and destroy the ambushers. Three days later, the Americans there lost their last soldier for September when, on the thirtieth, another IED hit a convoy.†

Most soldiers who worked in the Sunni Triangle in 2003 rated the city of Baqubah as one of the worst. The city quickly developed as one of the hotbeds of insurgents. It was where the 4th Infantry Division had conducted many of its first cordon and search operations. It was where the Americans first started taking multiple casualties.

The death toll in the city, known for its IEDs, quickly mounted as soldiers desperately sought to round up insurgents and at the same time establish good will with civic action projects. It was one of the places where the brigade combat team turned loose the civil affairs teams to work directly with the people, often at great risk and casualties to the reserve soldiers that made up those units. It was also one of the few places in the Sunni Triangle that managed to keep the general population on the Coalition side. With the population not supporting the insurgency, it turned its wrath on the local police, killing scores.

In Baqubah, the 1st Infantry's 3rd BCT commander, Colonel Dana Petard, developed a reputation for reaching out to the community. He established a neighborhood watch and an Iraqi version of a 911. He met regularly with three groups of local leaders, the government officials, the Sheik's Council, and an advisory council made up of local community leaders. He also turned to his civil affairs team, the MPs and JAG officers and told them to get out there and find out what was going on. The

*KIA: Sgt. 1st Class Joselito O. Villanueva
†KIA: Spc. Allen Nolan

Following the collapse of the Iraqi police during the fighting in Fallujah and with Moqtada al-Sadr in April 2004, millions were redireced to rebuilding and training the police. The Police College in downtown Baghdad became the focal point of the effort, and in turn was sometimes shelled several times a day.

insurgents became so alarmed at his success that they placed a $60,000 bounty on his head.

There were attacks in September, but they were usually from professionals and not the large units of local cadre found in other places. Attacks came in spurts, as insurgent bands formed outside the area passed through. Two U.S. 1st Infantry Division soldiers were injured when insurgents attacked their patrol September 2 at nearby Dhuluiyah. Shrapnel from the rocket-propelled grenade injured the soldiers. Insurgents attacked an Iraqi army patrol at nearby Buhritz the same day. The ambush wounded eight Iraqi soldiers and a twelve-year-old girl. Buhritz was one of the most dangerous areas in the province in that it was entirely Sunni and hardened in its support of Saddam Hussein. It quickly became a foothold for Wahabists. It was a principal base of operations for attacks in Baqubah.

It was nearly two weeks after the attack in Buhritz, late on September 14, that militants opened fire on a van carrying policemen, killing eleven Iraqi police officers and their civilian driver. A message on an

Islamist Web site claimed responsibility. The attack on the police was particularly bloody, but the people in and around Baqubah continued to join the police and the rest stayed on the job. Again in Baqubah on the sixteenth, guerrillas detonated a roadside bomb, killing four policemen and one civilian. To the insurgents the police were now the real threat, the Americans having gained a surprising level of support for having started badly in the pro–Saddam city.

Four days later, on September 18, a mortar round landed near the Baqubah Technical College, injuring eleven students. Two additional mortar rounds landed but did not explode. The apparent targets were Iraqi National Guard and Iraqi police personnel as they responded to ·investigate a report of an improvised explosive device. That same day insurgents attacked the U.S. base in Baqubah with 120mm mortars. These were all in stark contrast to Fallujah, were the attacks seemed to come from a popular uprising on a regular basis rather than professional insurgents.

But, even with the progress made, Baqubah was still a dangerous place for any American soldier. On September 24, an RPG ambushed a convoy. A soldier later died of the wounds suffered in the attack.*

The people most at risk, however, were the public officials. The Iraqi government had created a private guard service called the FPS (Facilities Protection Service), but there were never enough, thus many local government officials lived in fear. They had good reason. Two translators working for the Americans were murdered that summer, and the U.S. bases were under constant observation. The military tried to provide two truckloads of medical books to the medical school in the city. The day before, insurgents came to the president of the college and told him they would attack the school if they accepted the textbooks. They turned the texts away and asked soldiers not to come back. It did not help the president, however; shortly afterward, the insurgents launched an assassination attempt, injuring the college president and killing his driver.

Combat in the Sunni Triangle outside of al-Anbar had gone well as far as the 1st Infantry Division was concerned. September cost the division a total of eleven men killed.† It was a high price to pay but other months had been worse. As far as the "Big Red One"‡ was concerned, they were making grudging headway.

---

*KIA: Sgt. Tyler D. Prewitt
†KIA: Spc. Joseph C. Thibodeaux, Spc. Brandon M. Read, Spc. Michael Martinez, Spc. Edgar P. Daclan Jr., Spc. Marva I. Gomez, Spc. Joshua J. Henry, Staff Sgt. Lance J. Koenig, Spc. Gregory A. Cox, Sgt. 1st Class Joselito Villanueva, Sgt. Tyler D. Prewitt, Staff Sgt. Mike A. Deenie
‡The Big Red One is the nickname of the 1st Infantry Division.

CHAPTER 14

Facing Reality

The military officials of MNFI, Multi-National Force Iraq, felt that the Fallujah solution had been forced down their throats. Complaints by the military to the politicians brought back reminders of the political nightmare of the April offensive. Further, there were claims that a political rather than a military solution would reduce the violence.

The violence increased as cities in the Sunni Triangle sought their own Fallujah arrangement, and Fallujah itself was acting as a safe-haven for continued insurgent operations. Adding to the problem, al-Zarqawi's organization, although a small percentage of the insurgency in numbers, was creating a disproportionately large number of deaths and political damage through his beheadings and suicide car bombs.

Many in the military leadership were becoming more vocal to put an end to the embarrassment of the defacto independent city-state of Fallujah.

For now in Fallujah, America's only available weapon was its technology. On the first of September, a U.S. air strike targeted two safe-houses used by followers of Abu Musab al-Zarqawi in southwest Fallujah. A Predator drone observed al-Zarqawi associates removing a man from the trunk of a car, executing him, and then burying the body. The Americans said that the attack on the reported Fallujan safe-houses was based on "multiple sources of Iraqi and coalition intelligence." The Iraqi Ministry of Health said the air strikes killed twelve people and wounded eight others.

On September 7 and 8, Fallujah again came under American bombs. There was little doubt in this case that the strikes hit home. Drone aircraft saw bands of fighters, many wearing loose black pants and T-shirts, lounging outside abandoned buildings facing the U.S. lines, seeking to escape the intense sunlight of the day as the temperatures topped 115 degrees. Most hid their faces with Arab headscarves, weapons at their sides. Some quenched their thirst from coolers beside them. Most appeared to be in their late teens or early 20s and 30s, but a few looked middle-aged. Said one staff officer, "They're hanging out there like they are at some ... health spa." Military officials claimed one hundred enemy casualties although they admitted that they could not confirm the actual body count. Hospital officials said the attack killed two people.

Any celebration by the Coalition was short-lived as gunmen kidnapped the deputy governor of Anbar province, which included Fallujah. The U.S. hit again the next day, hitting a two-story house with two adjacent homes substantially damaged. On September 8, a patrol ran into an ambush near Fallujah.* The war around Fallujah was now a cat and mouse game for both sides, but from the city, car bombs and kidnapping squads were fanning out.

If it wasn't clear before, it was beyond denial now: Fallujah was a threat to the entirety of Iraq. However, according to General Richard Myers, the chairman of the U.S. Joint Chiefs of Staff, Washington's strategy for retaking rebel-controlled areas of Iraq depended upon the training of Iraqi forces to take a major part in such operations. The implication was that the Iraqis were just not ready yet to carry their share of the load. Completely unspoken was what, if any, effect such an offensive might have on the election back home. No one would touch that issue, but there was an understanding that no matter how carefully managed, a repeat of last April's scenes on television would have an unpredictable impact on the American electorate. Even if necessary, it was a matter of conjecture as to whether politicians in Washington would agree.

At the same time General Myers was speaking on why Fallujah could not be retaken, the politicians were speaking on the fact that the U.S. death toll had reached one thousand in Iraq. Said the Democratic challenger for President in Cincinnati, Americans owe it to their memory and to all U.S. troops to do what is right in Iraq. The Democratic candidate said that the President Bush had made the wrong choices. This was clearly not a time to take gambles. After the stinging experience in April, reinvading Fallujah was clearly a gamble.

On September 12, two more Marines were killed.† The day after, Marines called another air strike on Fallujah. The estimated enemy casualties were fifteen. Nevertheless, the violence throughout the al-Anbar was increasing. Three Marines died at enemy hands that day.‡ The next day another Marine died** under rocket fire. Outside of Fallujah, more direct action came. On September 14, there were clashes between U.S.

*KIA: Pfc. Jason L. Sparks. The soldier had been in Iraq only a week.
†KIA: Pfc. Jason Poindexter, 1st Lt. Alex Weatherbee on his 2nd tour in Iraq. Pfc. Poindexter had been in Iraq for less than a week.
‡KIA: Lance Cpl. Mathew D. Puckett, Cpl. Adrian V. Soltau, Cpl. Jaygee Meluat
**KIA: Maj. Kevin M. Shea. At the time of his death he was being considered for an award for valor for earlier action.

forces and insurgents in the western Iraqi city of Ramadi, killing ten people and wounding more than a dozen others. An ambush during the action killed one American soldier.*

On September 16, the Marines and insurgents from Fallujah traded blows. A Marine Humvee came under attack. The blast killed the driver, who was also the squad leader, and wounded two other Marines.† Another tank officer died that day as well from a separate incident.‡ At the same time, air strikes came down on a Fallujan home that insurgents used as a munitions depot. MNFI launched another strike that night at Qaryat ar Rufush where intelligence predicted that ninety insurgents were staging. Battle damage assessment estimated that the strike killed sixty of the insurgents.

Recognizing what was a reality, the Marines disbanded the controversial Fallujah Brigade after it became clear that brigade members were actively assisting insurgents in the city. The Fallujan soldiers refused to dress in the new Iraqi military uniforms, the same as the ING (Iraqi National Guard) that were working with the Americans, preferring instead to wear Hussein-era army fatigues. Those soldiers from the brigade not aiding the insurgents simply did nothing to rein in the militants. There were also reports that soldiers from the brigade actually joined up with militants to fight U.S. Marines in al-Fallujah. Some 800 AK47 assault rifles, 27 pickup trucks, and 50 radios that the Marines gave to the brigade ended up in the hands of the insurgency. In one incident, the leaders of two Iraqi National Guard battalions that had worked with the Fallujah Brigade were kidnapped and one was beheaded.

Trying to put the best face on the original decision, General Conway stated, "The early success of the Fallujah Brigade was ultimately its downfall. You had to have a force that came from Fallujah in order for it to be accepted by the people. They're very xenophobic ... but in the end those were the same things I think that dictated the demise of the Fallujah Brigade. Because they were from the local area, they were emasculated as far as their ability to do something very aggressive."

On September 16 and then 18, the U.S. Marines announced "Operation Hurricane," described as "clearing operations" in Ramadi aimed at the Dahman network, which was linked to al-Zarqawi.

On September 17, U.S. forces carried out a night air strike, targeting a building in central Fallujah where they thought followers of al-Zarqawi had gathered. Hospital officials said two people were killed and ten others wounded. The Americans claimed sixty insurgents killed. That

---

*KIA: 1st Lt. Tyler H. Brown
†KIA: Cpl. Steven Rintamaki
‡KIA: 1st Lt. Andrew K. Stern

hundreds of men were seen digging mass graves to bury the dead seemed to bolster the military's numbers. That same day another Marine was killed.*

The Americans struck again the next day, hitting an armed checkpoint. U.S. F-16 aircraft pounded the al-Juraythi neighborhood of the city, killing seven and wounding five others. The aircraft returned that night to the industrial zone of the city, striking in the eastern and western districts of al-Fallujah. However, there was another defeat for the Iraqi government that day when residents found the body of al-Anbar province's deputy governor, who was kidnapped several days before. It was no longer possible with any credibility to call the Fallujah experiment anything other than a failure.

Within the military, there was a debate as to whether to take the risk of fighting an early battle in Fallujah. Within the C3 staff of Multi-National Force Iraq, the successor headquarters to CJTF-7 once Lt. General Sanchez left, tacticians wrestled with why they were not bringing an end to the insurgency.

"Metrics" had been the byword for the American force since they arrived in Iraq. In the American army, measurements of success were always stated in numbers. But, by their reckoning, the insurgency should not have gotten this far in the first place. In 2003, they had the land and had destroyed the force. Unable to articulate why things had gone wrong, they could not quantify how to make things go right. Debates within Camp Victory developed into a freeform debate that was unfamiliar territory for many of the officers.

A senior commander said Fallujah and the city of Samarra, an enclave sixty-five miles north of Baghdad where U.S. forces had avoided a decisive battle with insurgents, did not have to be pacified before national elections in January. More important to quell, he said, were insurgencies in provincial capitals, such as Baqubah, about thirty-five miles northeast of the capital, and ar-Ramadi, sixty miles to the west of Baghdad.

"Fallujah and Samarra don't necessarily make the list," the commander said. "They're not provincial capitals. They're not major cultural centers."[49]

While the U.S. military intended to intensify a joint campaign with Iraqi forces to attack insurgents by the end of the year, the effort would likely initially focus on small cities, the commander said. "Do you go right to Fallujah?" he said. "It's a big chunk to bite off. Can you isolate it and let it fester for a while?"

KIA: Cpl. Christopher Ebert, who had seen some of the hardest fighting in Fallujah in April.

Some Marine officers in Fallujah contended that waiting for Iraqi forces to be trained gave the insurgents time to recruit new members, harden their defenses, and plot new attacks.

"We need to take out that rat's nest," said one senior Marine officer in Fallujah, who spoke off the record because his views contradicted those of his commanders. "The longer we wait, the stronger they get."

Some of Fallujah's residents, eager to end the hostilities and open the city to reconstruction projects, shared that view. "If they invade Fallujah now, it will be better," said a senior tribal leader. "Every day that passes, the resistance increases. Their numbers increase. Their power increases."[50]

Although Marines blocked off the main road from Fallujah to Baghdad, other routes into the city were open, allowing insurgents free passage to other parts of western Iraq and Baghdad. On most days, there were no checkpoints to search cars leaving Fallujah, where U.S. intelligence established that insurgents assembled many car bombs and launched other insurgent operations.

Some U.S. military officers turned that argument around, saying that attacking the city could lead Zarqawi's followers and other foreign fighters to flee to other parts of Iraq, making it harder to track their movements. These officers said that in the current situation, the insurgents remained in the city, and the military could rely on informants, reconnaissance drones, and spy satellites to target them with air strikes.

"Zarqawi has massed his folks there, and he is presenting targets for us on a regular basis," a military official in Baghdad said. "It's a heck of a lot easier to target the Zarqawi network when we see groups of fifteen or twenty having a meeting in Fallujah than it is when we see three- to four-man cells spread out all over Iraq."[51]

U.S. commanders believed the targeting of foreign fighters was starting to create a rift among insurgents in Fallujah. Initially, the Mujahadeen Shura Council welcomed the outsiders. This group of clerics, tribal sheiks, and former Baa'th Party members effectively ran the city and elements of the insurgency. There were complaints by clerics of the beheadings, which some thought were against the tenets of Islam, and the numbers of Muslim civilians killed in the car-bombings. Zarqawi's agenda extended beyond the goals of residents, who wanted to keep U.S. forces out of the city. He and his supporters had turned the city into a base for wider attacks against Iraqi officials and security forces. Then, there was Zarqawi's hostility towards the Shi'ites, whom those seeking to broaden the "resistance" realized they needed. Zarqawi's Salafi views regarded the Shi'a as only nominally Islamic.

Many Fallujah residents were growing weary of Zarqawi's followers for other reasons as well. His loyalists, most of whom adhered to the strict Salafi school of Islam, were seeking to reestablish a pure Islamic Empire. Some also attempted to instill hard-line social restrictions, demanding that women cover their hair and harassing men for not growing beards. Although Fallujah was a deeply religious city, many residents followed mystical Sufi beliefs, such as praying by the graves of relatives, which the Salafis regarded as blasphemous.

American intelligence reported combat between residents and foreign fighters. The fighting had broken out after residents, fearful of air strikes, sought to evict foreigners from their neighborhoods.

A delegation from the Fallujah Shura Council announced its willingness to negotiate with Iraqi government officials, aimed at a settlement that would allow Iraqi security forces to enter the city.

The council was willing to reestablish Iraqi control of the city with locally based security forces but non–Iraqi fighters loyal to the council would be allowed to stay in Fallujah, and U.S. forces had to remain outside the city. Iraqi government officials expressed an unwillingness to permit foreign fighters or create exclusion zones for U.S. forces.

The head of the Shura Council, Abdullah Janabi, who had invited foreigners to the city in April, issued a statement calling Zarqawi a "criminal."

"We don't need Zarqawi to defend our city," he said. He made a distinction between what he called "Iraqi resistance fighters" and foreign fighters engaged in a campaign against Iraq's infrastructure, foreign civilians, and Iraqi security forces. "The Iraqi resistance is something, and the terrorism is something else. We don't kidnap journalists, and we don't sabotage the oil pipelines and the electric power stations. We don't kill innocent Iraqis. We resist the occupation." Zarqawi's actions, Janabi said, had "harmed the resistance and made it lose the support of people."[52]

There was also a realization that the activities of al-Zarqawi's organization had become so odious that he was threatening the existence of the city-state. "There is no Zarqawi in Fallujah, nor the so-called followers of Zarqawi. The people of Fallujah do not need Zarqawi to defend them. If there is someone called Zarqawi, I am not grateful for his attack on our policemen," said al-Janabi.[53]

To both the Iraqi interim government and the Americans, this sounded like a rehash of the old Fallujah Brigade and an indication that all the Council wanted was help to chase out the "biggest worm in a barrel of rotten apples." They had no doubts that the Council planned to fill the local security forces with people that would continue the insurgency or at least intimidate them to turn a blind eye.

Faced with the obvious, the U.S. military announced that it intended to take back Fallujah and other rebel areas by year's end. The commander did not set a date for an offensive but said that much would depend on the availability of Iraqi military and police units. They would have to occupy the city once the Americans took it. General Casey suggested that operations in Fallujah could begin as early as November or December, the deadline for restoring Iraqi government control across the country.

"We need to make a decision on when the cancer of Fallujah is going to be cut out," the American commander said. "We would like to end December at local control across the country."

"Fallujah will be tough," he said.

At the same time, the Americans and the Iraqi interim government were willing to give negotiations to disarm the rebels a final chance. Members of the Mujahadeen Shura said they were planning to come to Baghdad to meet with Iraqi officials to talk about disarming the rebels and opening the city to Iraqi government control.

"Although the Americans have lied many times, we are ready to start negotiations with the Iraqi government," said Hajji Qasim Muhammad Abdul Sattar, a member of the Shura.

Dr. Ahmed Hardan, a Fallujan doctor who would take part in the negotiations, said that at least some members on the council might be willing to strike a deal with the Americans. Under the proposal to be discussed, Dr. Hardan said, the guerrillas would turn over their heavy weapons and were willing to allow a military force gathered from not just Fallujah but from around the Anbar Province to enter the city. That unit would replace the Fallujah Brigade.

The Iraqi government again demanded that the insurgents turn over their heavy weapons and that "foreign fighters" leave the city. Because not all of the Shura council was willing to participate, there too was the belief that the people at the table could not deliver on their promises. The Marines scoffed at the idea of a purely Iraqi force controlling the city now.

The new Marine commander, Lt. Gen. John F. Sattler of the 1st Marine Expeditionary Force, had taken over, and he made no secret of his plans. "We need Iraqi security forces with us. We need to be side by side when we move in, so that when it is said and done, when you open your door the next day and look out, there's an Iraqi policeman, an Iraqi National Guardsman, an Iraqi soldier on your street."

That was a difference from his predecessor. "The Marines we have there now could crush the city and be done with business in four days. But that's not what we're going to do," Conway had said before. "Since the handover of sovereignty to an interim Iraqi government in late June," he added, "Fallujah is an Iraqi problem. If there is an attack on the anti–Iraqi forces that inhabit the city, it will be done almost exclusively by Iraqis."

Meanwhile, on the nineteenth, in Fallujah a U.S. tank opened fire on a metal-storage depot as workers loaded up a van. A doctor at the main Fallujah hospital said three bodies and two people with shrapnel injuries were brought from the area.

September 20 brought U.S. air strikes on a bulldozer and a dump truck full of sand at a "municipality project" in western Fallujah. The strikes killed three people and wounded five others. U.S. military officials said the American-led multinational forces fired on construction equipment used by insurgents to build "fortified fighting positions." This was a clear indication that the Americans intended to assault the city. In the meantime, the steady losses continued as two more Marines died in combat.*

While all of this discussion was ongoing, from their bunkers just outside the city, the Marines could see no more than the first few rows of brick-and-concrete homes along Fallujah's urban fringe in the sweltering heat and occasional shelling. From every post was the sight of a half-dozen houses flattened. One hundred and twenty millimeter tank rounds had punched holes into others. Insurgents had used them to fire at the bunkers, which were fortified with dirt-filled Hesco barriers. The Marines could do nothing but wait, and watch, and get shot at.

After a rare day without a Marine death, the 22nd brought back the continuing pattern of a Marine a day killed.† Then, as if to make up for the light casualties of the last few days, September 24 was particularly tragic. Four Marines died.‡ The Marines were, however, able to hit back, conducting precision air strikes on a group of insurgents seen training in an open field south of Fallujah. Military officials reported the individuals were part of a mortar and rocket-propelled grenade training team. Coalition forces observed ten to twelve individuals as part of the team and fired artillery. The team ran into a cave that supplied their efforts with weapons cache storage. Coalition forces then directed an air strike on the cave with precision-guided munitions. They were getting ready for what all knew would be a battle.

On September 25, the U.S. hit again from the air. Following the air strike, local hospital officials said Americans killed seven people and injured ten. Intelligence sources indicated that approximately ten terrorists were meeting at this location. On September 25, a small-arms attack killed one U.S. soldier.** Insurgents challenged Marine positions in a

*KIA: Lance Cpl. Steven C.T. Cates, Sgt. Foster L. Harrington
†KIA: Sgt. Benjamin K. Smith
‡KIA: Lance Cpl. Aaron Boyles, Sgt. Timothy Folmar, Lance Cpl. Ramon Mateo, 2nd Lt. Ryan Leduc. Boyles had earlier been awarded a Purple Heart.
**KIA: Spc. Robert Oliver Unruh. In a tragic finish to this soldier's death his mother collapsed and died days after learning her son had been killed, and just hours after seeing his body. Some who knew her said she died of a broken heart.

small skirmish that same day outside of Fallujah but the defenders took no losses. As almost everywhere in Iraq, harassing mortar fire could be lethal. In Ramadi, a round found and killed one soldier on the twenty-sixth.*

In Iraq, the United States was losing the public relations war as the harassment—rather, the defeat—of the insurgents of Fallujah continued. People were ready to believe that the U.S. was conducting senseless killing, whether or not the reports were justified. On one night, U.S. war-planes were spotted over the city, and residents told reporters they saw a plane firing rockets into the city. Dr. Walid Thamer of the Fallujah General Hospital, which the insurgents controlled, said at least three people were killed and nine wounded in that attack. U.S. Marine officers said they only fired flares. On September 27, in the Tamim district of Ramadi, fighting between U.S. Marines and Sunni Arab nationalists left four Iraqis dead and ten wounded.

If the warnings from the local commanders were not clear that the Americans were coming, Secretary of State Colin Powell made it loud and clear. "The U.S. military will move into insurgent-heavy 'no-go zones' in Iraq to clear the way for legitimate elections in January," Secretary Powell said on the twenty-seventh. That same day, as though to punctuate the need to end the stalemate, there was a suicide car-bomb attack, killing four Iraqi Guardsmen at a checkpoint jointly manned by both U.S. forces and the Iraqi National Guard near Fallujah. The U.S. struck back that night, bombing what it called a "terrorist site." Iraqi officials in Fallujah said at least two people were dead, including a child, and at least six injured. And again they hit at about 4 A.M. the next day.

One final voice was needed before an offensive could start: the Iraqi government. That came on September 28. "I think we waited more than enough for Fallujah," the prime minister said in an interview aired on the Arab television network, al-Arabiya. He indicated they would use Iraqi security forces in any operation against the city. The same day the U.S. again sent in air strikes on safe-houses. The squeeze was on to frighten the civilians out of Fallujah to get them out of the way for the oncoming battle.

The next day, Iraqi Defense Minister Hasim al-Shalaan repeated the warning that U.S. and Iraqi forces would start a military offensive during October to retake rebel-held cities in Iraq. But that did not help the soldiers on the field at the present. In Ramadi, one Iraqi civilian was killed in a firefight that ensued after insurgents attacked a U.S. patrol September 29. The gunfight also injured a number of U.S. soldiers. Mean-

---

*KIA: Capt. Eric L. Allton

while, another soldier fell victim to an IED that exploded next to his vehicle.*

The thirtieth saw what had been the pattern for the entire month of September. U.S. forces struck a suspected safe-house of al-Zarqawi. According to the Fallujah hospital, three people died and eight others were wounded in the air strike. Four children were said to be among the hurt. Coalition forces reported "significant" secondary explosions after the blast.

In the meantime, medicines and food were reaching the Iraqi city of Fallujah, regardless of the danger. It was, however, little comfort for local residents in Fallujah, as those who chose to stay were under intense pressure. "We are paying for something we didn't ask to happen. Peace will only be a dream in our lifetime. We are just toys in the middle of all of them, with our lives at great risk," said a shop owner.

Perhaps the greatest cost of the situation in Fallujah was the cost in credibility with Iraqis outside of the city. People were leaving the city with new stories that were repeated by the press to an Arab population eager to find fault with America. "When the Americans first came to Iraq, they came to Fallujah without a problem," said one man in Baghdad helping families who fled Fallujah. But, he said, the U.S. offensive against Fallujah in April, and more recent air strikes, had changed even the view of those who before did not care. "There was a resistance in April, but now it is innocent people, normal people who are dying in these attacks from the sky."

*KIA: Pfc. Joshua K. Titcomb

CHAPTER 15

A Race to Establish the Norm

When the Coalition first rolled into Baghdad in April 2003, the leaders within the newly established occupation government and CJTF-7 told the planners to expect an occupation of only three months before Iraq took over as a democratic government. With violence rising, the disintegration of the Iraqi army, the lack of political consensus, and the military unable to reduce its force, it was obvious that the Iraqis could not just take over with the American army as their Praetorian Guard. By December 2003, the White House laid down the law. An interim government would have to take charge by July 2004 with elections to follow as soon as possible. With considerable elbowing and cries of unfair treatment by the different ethnic groups, over 1000 "leaders" gathered to elect a 100-person council over the summer. The insurgency, many of which were Baa'thist and thus not invited to participate in government, just kept on fighting and gathering new recruits, now using its newly won safe-haven in Fallujah.

In the backdrop of all the violence and kidnapping dramas of September, Iraq was living and dying with the consequences of a rapidly building insurgency racing with an interim government to establish itself as the norm. Both sides instinctively struck at the other if only symbolically, as if to say they we're in control. To the leaders of the insurgency, anything that discredited the Coalition or interim government was fair game. The objective was to make the people feel they had no choice but to fight. The Coalition's principal weapon was any effort to establish normalcy. Thus, the insurgency targeted the police and public works projects.

The insurgency started with a major advantage. Sympathizers within the Iraqi government and Iraqi forces, as well as the Iraqis working for the Coalition, media, and NGOs, often provided excellent human intelligence without violently taking part in the insurgency. Saboteurs operated within the government and every aspect of the Iraqi economy. The Coalition was only now developing a genuinely effective counterintelligence

When the Americans first arrived they took over the Presidential Palace for the new occupational government. The palace had four huge statues of Saddam on it. One of the first contracts let out was for their removal.

arm in Iraq. With the failure by the military to win over the Iraqi population, local commanders usually worked without any true support from concerned citizens.

One of the more curious dramas was the arrest warrant for a major politician whom the Americans had favored. Ahmad Chalabi had helped convince the Americans to attack Iraq in the first place and wrangled himself into a position of power with American backing. As was the case in most of the leadership of Iraq, he came into a position of power and wealth with less than clean hands. In 1992, a Jordanian court convicted Chalabi in absentia for embezzlement, fraud, and breach of trust after a bank he ran collapsed with about $300 million in missing deposits. Some $100 million, 14 percent of the bank's loans, went to family members and close friends, and most of those were not paid back. When the Jordanian government insisted in 1989 that banks keep 30 percent of funds on hand, the institution was overextended and unable to comply. The bank folded. A court sentenced Chalabi to twenty-two years in prison. From the beginning, Americans suspected that he, along with other members of the Interim Council providing political advice and cover for CPA, were using their positions to operate schemes to enrich themselves, if not taking outright bribes. This came to a head when there was evidence that counterfeit money was being funneled through his office in the official currency exchange from the Saddam dinar to the new Iraqi dinar. The Americans got a warrant and raided his compound. True enough, they found large sums of counterfeit cash. The Iraqi Central Criminal Court issued an arrest warrant. Chalabi denied the charges and said political opponents were trying to smear him.

Nevertheless, after extensive court hearings,* they could not tie the cash directly to him, only to a relative. The court dismissed "for lack of evidence" the charges against Ahmad Chalabi, the one-time Pentagon favorite. The whole affair looked terrible from the outside if only because Chalabi's nephew, Salem Chalabi, headed the special tribunal in charge of trying ousted Iraqi leader Saddam Hussein. September in Baghdad started with an ominous note both for the city and the new Iraqi government. Iraq's new National Council began its work at Baghdad's Convention Center in the secured "Green Zone." The new government pinned its hopes on this group to gather their support that would lead to nationwide elections and a new constitution. The one hundred members of the new legislative assembly were chosen by over one thousand participants at a national conference the month before. Of the one-hundred National Council members, forty-five were Shi'a Muslims, forty-four were Sunni Muslims, and two were Assyrian Christians. According to U.S. officials, fifty-five were secularists, twenty-two were Shi'a Islamists, and seven were Sunni Islamists. This was the start of a new government in earnest, choosing a legislative president, two vice presidents, approving a ninety-eight point administrative law, and forming standing committees, although their role was more advisory than lawmaking. The parliament only had rights to question the prime minister and the ministers that held the real power, and make political trouble if its views were ignored. They were likely to raise such questions. A poll commissioned in September to gauge the mood of the populace found that only forty-three percent of the population believed that the interim government was effective at all. That was down from sixty-three percent in July.

One who showed up was Ahmad Chalabi, now cleared legally if with a soiled reputation, and still leader of the Iraqi National Congress.† Chalabi was lucky to get there at all in that his entourage was ambushed near Latifiyah, about a forty-five minute drive south of Baghdad. Two of his bodyguards were wounded but Chalabi escaped.

---

*Zuhair al-Maliky, Iraq's chief investigative judge.
†A political party made mostly of exiles.

As the first session was underway, five mortar rounds landed less than 250 yards away. The blasts shook the building, sending people rushing away from the windows. One Iraqi was injured. Two other large explosions came just outside of the "Green Zone" a few minutes later.

The security threat went past those in the council and to those running the government. The ministers providing mundane services required a large armed force to keep them alive. The Transmigration and Displacement Minister, one of the few women in positions of authority, for example, had to rely on as many as thirty guards. Like most members of Iraq's interim administration, the minister lived in a fortified compound in central Baghdad. Blast walls fifteen feet high encircled the enclave, and visitors had to undergo a series of searches at checkpoints complete with armed guards and razor wire. Her deputy minister escaped an assassination attempt himself.

Prime Minister Ayad Allawi had escaped four assassination attempts in the prior three months alone. Dozens of government officials were killed while a number of others escaped assassination attempts.

There was a sense of fear throughout those working in the government. There was considerable worry over their children and families.

Said the husband of the Iraqi minister, "I don't feel rest until I receive a call from my wife. I am always worried about her and especially for the kids. Kidnapping is my biggest fear."

The other high officials had a long list of assassination attempts, and September just added more. On the first day of the month, insurgents came out of a car with two RPGs near the home of the Minister of Justice, Malik Duhan al-Hasan. The minister was a man in his 80s and a well-respected lawyer with connections going back into the 1950s. The insurgents fired their rockets at the encircled house, protected by a high wall and massive concrete barriers. No one was hurt, but the attackers easily made their escape. It was the second attempt on the Minister's life since he took office in May.

Not all the Iraqi political leadership was involved in the council held in Baghdad in the beginning of September. Some disenchanted political groups, tribal leaders, and individuals who failed in getting assembly seats in August for the Iraqi National Conference, gathered in Beirut two days before to kick off what they termed a preparatory conference for a competing Iraqi National Founding Council. The chairman of the council, Abd al-Amir al-Rikabi, came out as the spokesman of the sixty-member preparatory committee elected at the conference. The attendees were tribal chiefs, Kurds, Turkmen, and Assyrians, civil-society representatives, nationalist leaders, Nasirite and democratic parties, Islamic leaders, including Muslim Scholars Association members, and representatives

Life for most people in the Green Zone was work much like what they did at home. The difference was the regular explosions at night and the car bombs that happened several times a week at one of the checkpoints.

of Shi'a cleric Moqtada al-Sadr, with only one thing in common. They wanted the Americans to leave Iraq.

The preparatory committee called for the council to move its activities inside Iraq through the establishment of offices in Baghdad, Karbala, and al-Basra. The council intended to act as an "executive government" in Iraq in competition with the interim government. Conference attendees complained that Iraqis were subjected to a formula set by the occupation that did not coincide with their vision for Iraq. One thing no one ever agreed with at any conference sponsored by the Americans was what groups made up the population of Iraq. One interim council member remarked, after listening to the Turkmen saying they made up 10 percent of the population, the Kurds 25 percent, the Shi'ites 65 percent, the Assyrians 10 percent and the Sunni Arabs 45 percent, that the government in Baghdad made up only 150 percent of Iraq.

Al-Rikabi voiced opposition to the former Iraqi Governing Council and interim government, saying that the Iraqi state did not reflect Iraq's pluralistic nature. Conference attendees also advocated resistance against the occupation, saying it was a legitimate national and religious right. The conference was also attended by Socialist Progressive Party leader Walid Junblat, and representatives from the Lebanese Communist Party and the Popular Front for the Liberation of Palestine (PFLP).

The jihadists had their voice as well, and they expressed it through audio tapes which they passed around, giving general instructions that were simple and to the point. Attack any time, any place.

On one such tape, a man named Sheik Abu Anas al-Shami, one of al-Zarqawi's key commanders and a member of the organization's religious committee, preached that any nation built on secular principles was "in the light of Islamic law a tyrannical infidel and blasphemous state." Anyone associated with it, he continued, especially soldiers and police, whether or not they are good Muslims, could be killed, as "they do not represent themselves; they are means in the hands of the tyrants." Even Muslims "who pray" could be killed to punish the Iraqi government or U.S. forces. "If the infidels have good people among them, and our fighting against them necessitates annihilating these good people, we are permitted to kill them because we are ordered to do so," he said.

These were not idle threats. A typical story circulating read, "My brother's friend had been killed in al-Anbar governorate last week, 'al-Tawheed wa al-Jihad' which belongs to al-Zarqawi is responsible for that, and they killed his wife too, because they were 'cooperating with the occupier.' In fact, they were doctors and supplying Iraqi National Guards with some necessary medical things. They've been beheaded also." Whether true or not, these street stories buzzed through Baghdad.

Another such tape, recorded in the voice of al-Zarqawi, described Americans as "oppressors" and "doglike aliens" and criticized the Western media for denigrating the will and character of Muslims. But al-Zarqawi targeted his harshest criticism at his former ally, Harith al-Dhari, an Iraqi Sunni Muslim leader and chairman of the Association of Muslim Scholars, and the closest person the Sunnis had to the Shi'ite religious leader al-Sistani. U.S. intelligence had reports that al-Dhari was funding and organizing groups within the insurgency. Faced with repeated complaints, al-Dhari criticized al-Zarqawi's practice of decapitating hostages. On the tape, al-Zarqawi called al-Dhari a coward "who accepted humiliation" and accused him of "extending (his) hands to the enemy."

To the jihadists, questions of democracy and representation were missing the point altogether. To many within the groups the very idea of government by the people went counter to their aim of government by God. There was no room for compromise in their view and most felt that any means that advanced a Salafi agenda was sanctioned by God and thus beyond question.

Some inside the insurgency complained that al-Zarqawi's willingness to sanction terrorist attacks against all civilians had created splits among the various rebel groups. A number of nationalist insurgents, some who were old Baa'thists with no desire for an Islamic state, objected to killing innocent Iraqis. They said the armed insurgency was being taken over by the well-funded and motivated international jihadists answering al-Qaeda's call for a holy war. Nationalist insurgent groups were attempting to create their own leadership and to forge ties with moderate Islamists based in Fallujah. Their goal was to create a political party that could contest and win elections held after U.S. withdrawal.

This view was shared at the time by the fugitive former President Saddam Hussein, who cautioned his people to keep a distance from the Salafi groups. This view was not shared, however, by many of his lieutenants who were willing to accept aid from any source and were particularly impressed both by the Salafis' ability to draw attention and spread fear. Jihadists often found at least toleration if not support from nationalist insurgents who in turn felt that sooner or later the rest of Iraq would have to turn to them to restore order to Iraq.

"Thinking has started to move toward asking what happens after the Americans leave. So far we have only shown that we know how to act militarily, but the military wing cannot lead the country into the future,"[54] said an insurgent leader calling himself Abu Khahil who spoke to several news sources.

Meetings aimed at establishing a political face for the insurgency were underway for months. An earlier conference collapsed. The very problems of who represents what in Iraq were as vexing to the Iraqi insurgency as they were to the Americans. Everyone said they represented more than they obviously had, and about the only thing they agreed upon was they wanted the Americans out. Nevertheless, a number of people were trying to spark a debate among the insurgents on what kind of country they wanted to create.

The push for political legitimacy now flowed from their success at fending off U.S. forces in Fallujah and Samarra. "Things have moved so fast, the events are ahead of our thinking," said Abu Khalil. "A year ago, the Americans' departure was a dream, but now it's realizable. We control entire cities, and we're looking to expand."

At the same time, the leadership of the Sunni clerics was supporting the insurgency. Sheik Abd al-Jabbar Abd al-Sattar, a member of the Muslim Scholars Association, told al-Jazeera television in a September 21 interview that he did not understand why the world paid so much attention to the killing of two American hostages when Iraqis were dying every day.

When asked whether the killing of the hostages was justified given the suffering of the Iraqi people under the occupation, Abd al-Sattar claimed: "I am not justifying. I want the world to pay attention to our issue and our justice. I want to hear the world denounce what the occupiers are doing in our country. What makes those people carry out such actions is the crimes they see in the Iraqi arena," he contended.

Regarding the kidnappers' demands that all female prisoners be released from Iraqi prisons, and the U.S. contention that only two women, former regime members, were in custody, Abd al-Sattar picked up on what was being written by anti–American internet bloggers: "The U.S. government considers the Iraqi women prisoners to be nonprisoners. It gives them the same status of the prisoners in Guantanamo.... This is why, according to [U.S.] understanding, it is telling the truth and there are no Iraqi women prisoners. However, there are dozens and perhaps hundreds of Iraqi women prisoners in the occupation prisons."

Asked what the difference was between the case of American and British hostages versus the case of the French journalists and Italian aid workers, on whose behalf the association claimed to be working for a release, the cleric said: "The French are innocent and the two Italian women are innocent. As for the Americans, they have admitted that they are rebuilding military bases for the U.S. army." He also cited a fatwa, or religious edict, that claimed, "...the one who helps the occupiers ... is considered like the occupier himself and should be fought and confronted."

There were moderate Muslim clerics both inside and out of Iraq, but the violence was polarizing, particularly in the Sunni community. One prominent Islamic cleric who once condemned the September 11 Twin Towers attack in New York was now telling his followers to resist the U.S. military in Iraq, and to provide weapons and funds to the insurgents. Egyptian cleric Sheik Yusuf al-Qaradawi demonstrated just how difficult the U.S. struggle in Iraq had become. "We believe that all Iraqis should stand together in one rank to resist the occupation," Qaradawi said.

The cleric called resistance to the United States "a religious duty." He also sanctioned attacks on Iraqi civilians who commit "the crime" of assisting "the enemy," and urged Muslims around the world to refuse to work for any companies that served "the occupier."

"If a Muslim land is occupied, then its people should fight the occupier," Qaradawi continued. "Others should also help them with funds and weapons, in spirit through prayers and in any way possible."[ii] Qaradawi's comments were noteworthy because he was influential throughout the Muslim world and had been a voice for moderation.

After bin Laden's attacks in New York and Washington, Qaradawi denounced the murders of innocent civilians and encouraged Muslims to donate blood to the victims. "Our hearts bleed" for those who died in the attacks, Qaradawi at the time said.

Despite the differences between the members of the insurgency, they still had a ready-made issue that sold well to the Iraqi public. Throughout the religious and ideological struggles was the suspicion that oil was the only motive and aim of the foreign forces in Iraq.

As violence in Iraq continued, government ministers and security forces were not the only ones under threat. University professors and others in the academic community also came under attack by insurgent groups. Eight of Baghdad University's professors had been murdered since the fall of the Saddam Hussein regime. Some reports put the figure across Iraq as high as 40 professors and academics killed, with at least five assassination attempts made on such people every month.

The apparent targeting of academics led to fears of "brain drain," as those with the financial means to leave Iraq did so. According to the Iraq University Teachers' Union, one thousand of Iraq's estimated fourteen thousand university professors had left. Nabeal Younis, a professor of international relations at Baghdad University, said the militant Islamists want to eliminate what they see as strong competition from intellectuals with a more modern outlook.

"Their aim is to get the country empty of any kind of thinking, or think-tanks, or any kind of mind [intellectual] people. We are not rich. We are not businessmen. We just have our opinion. We tell the truth in an academic way. This is the only thing we have. So when they try to assassinate, kill, or threatened most of us, there must be a reason, and the reason is the mind."[56]

The academic community blamed the lack of security brought about by the U.S.–led invasion of Iraq. Despite repeated pleas for assistance by the academic community to the Ministry of Higher Education and U.S. forces, Mr. Younis said the group remained at risk.

"We've told the Ministry and they did nothing. We told the Americans and they did nothing. We don't have enough money to get our own bodyguards. So we have to depend on ourselves."[57]

The Iraq Center for Research and Strategic Studies was an independent research group based in Baghdad. The group had to move its office after gunmen opened fire on its original office. Insurgents attacked the office at night and no one was hurt.

The group's director, Sadoun al-Doulame, referred to the targeting of Iraq's intellectuals and government ministers as revealing the weaknesses in the security apparatus and the number of groups competing for power in the new Iraq.

"We have a golden opportunity to build a new society, a new state. And, as I said, every group [is] trying to build that state, that country, according to its interests. And, the terrorists have special interests. And, they want to build, to modify Iraq, according to their ideology. That's why. Therefore, they regard all the intellectual people as a first enemy. And, they condemn them as a spy for the Americans and so on."[58]

This was life not just for the upper parts of society but for the common citizen. On an average day, the morgue's daily intake had grown from 7 to up to 25 bodies. The biggest part of the violence was simple vengeance. In the first eight months of 2004 nearly 3,000 people in municipal Baghdad, which had about five million residents, had died from gunshot wounds. A surge of killings in September had only increased the pressure. The murder rate rose over the summer, in spite of more than a year of promises from the Americans about the increasing effectiveness of the Iraqi police and security forces. By the close of 2004, the Baghdad Central Morgue would have counted 8,035 deaths from unnatural causes in Baghdad alone, an increase from 6,012 in 2003 and a figure up from 1,800 in 2002.

For the people living in the troubled parts of Baghdad it was even worse. Haifa Street, a major artery in downtown Baghdad that was crowded with shops, homes, and government offices, was known locally as "Death Street" because of the constant attacks there. Said one resident, "Every morning when I go out, I say goodbye to my wife and daughters because we know we may not be coming home," he says. The view was reflected in the public attitudes. Nearly two out of three Iraqis disagreed with the government's handling of security in both Baghdad and Fallujah in a government-commissioned poll.

In the backdrop of the war within most Arab areas, the civil violence of simple crimes was overcoming the civil structure. The Iraqi court system, never a strong institution, was simply overwhelmed. Iraqi judges said they found themselves hard-pressed to cope with the rising criminality. They also complained about the radical restructuring of the courts, just as CPA had done to the country's other institutions.

The judges were critical of the initial disbanding of the Iraqi security forces, creating a law and order problem that emboldened criminals to directly challenge authorities. Judges were routinely threatened by criminal gangs before trials, and in some cases assassinated in campaigns of intimidation.

The judges complained that the Iraqi judicial system had been weakened by Coalition forces engaging in security sweeps. When Coalition forces detained people in Coalition-run prisons like Abu Ghraib, family members were often unable to find out where they were kept. Almost comically, the soldiers taking the detainees into custody could not keep track of the inmates because they could not spell their names. The Arabic alphabet was so foreign that the Americans would often write even common names with multiple different English spellings. The families turned to the Iraqi judiciary, but they had no more information than the relatives did. This made the judges even more vulnerable to threats, and lacking adequate protection a number of them were killed.

Judge Noman Fathy Hassan, deputy chief of the Court of Cassation (top appeals court) in Baghdad, said, "The security situation here is very difficult, and there is a confusion and overlapping of responsibilities between the international forces and the judiciary in Iraq."

In the days running up to the transition of authority from a legal occupation, one of the aims of the Coalition was to criminalize the insurgency. By September, the Central Criminal Court of Iraq had now been in existence for nearly a year and had to show for it 76 trials involving 120 defendants. Ninety were convicted with thirty found not guilty. Some sentences were stiff, leading to 30 years, but the usual prison term for planting a roadside bomb was only three years. By this time, U.S. forces had detained well over 10,000. The Coalition simply released most suspects after interrogation and weeks to months of detention. The relatives of these detainees swamped civil affairs units and Iraqi courts with complaints about loved ones caught up in these detentions. It was a no-win situation. Many who were part of the insurgency developed a contempt for the Coalition from the short stay in detention, while the innocent, outraged at confinement for up to several months, seethed at the felt injustice.

Some military commanders, realizing the harm done by arresting and holding people only to let them go, started paying those who were held and not charged. Some American commanders, not skilled at gathering evidence but believing the detainees to be insurgents, were outraged at this. Still, it did pay off locally, although the Americans rarely received publicity by the gesture. On one occasion, an al-Jazeera reporter was accompanying the Iraqi provincial governor through the Baqubah jail as a follow-up on the Abu Ghraib story. When they came across the commander of American forces in the area, Colonel Dana Petard, paying each of the detainees released $25 along with an apology for being wrongfully arrested, the reporter refused to film or report on the scene, saying that the story did not "appeal" to his viewers.

There were days in Iraq when the government seemed to make undeniable progress. Perhaps the greatest successes of the month came on September 11 and had little to do with weapons at all. The Coalition scored a significant victory when the annual Shi'a pilgrimage to the Kadimiyah Shrine in northern Baghdad occurred without incident. The interim Iraqi government touted the absence of American involvement during this Islamic holy day as proof of the progress made.

The most improvement was in southern Iraq. In September, tens of thousands of Iraqi Shi'ites marched to Karbala to mark the birth of Imam Mahdi (AS), whom the Shi'ites believed to be the messiah.

One of the most difficult jobs given to the CPA was the reestablishment of the Iraqi court system and the Ministry of Justice. During the rule of CPA, three people served as senior advisors for the herculean task. One was a retired colonel brought back to active duty, Daniel Rabini, shown here. At one point he became so frustrated with the lack of personnel that he wrote to Ambassador Bremer, saying they were asking him to "make a duck with a pile of feathers."

Karbala was the scene of fighting when al-Sadr launched a revolt against the U.S.–led occupation in April, taking advantage of the combat in Fallujah. Now strings of lights and bunting hung in the plaza between the holy shrines of Imam Hussein and Imam Abbas. Brightly colored flags were everywhere. Local shops displayed street trays of sweet covered cakes and stuffed biscuits. Merchants profited in a rare good payday.

Families gathered around a wooden sword with a double-pronged point, thought to be like the one used by the great Imam in his last battle. He was the first of the twelve Shi'ite imams (holy men), Prophet Mohammed's son-in-law, and was their symbol of a new Iraq.

Others went to the opposite side of the plaza to touch a wooden crib lined with green cloth, elevated on a marble pedestal, and supposed to represent the birth of Imam Mahdi more than a thousand years ago. This was a festive occasion with more of the air of an Easter parade than a solemn religious celebration.

Imam Mahdi was the last of the Shi'ite imams. According to tradition, he disappeared mysteriously in the ninth century. Shi'ites believed he would return to deliver humanity, much the same as Jesus promised to lead the world into its golden age.

Many were enjoying the freedom to celebrate after decades of oppression under Saddam Hussein. Under Saddam, open displays of Shi'a faith could lead to prison. They complained as well about the violence plaguing Iraq after Saddam's fall and the bloodshed in Shi'ite areas like Baghdad's slum of al-Sadr City.

Security was very tight in and around Karbala. It was provided by local guards, not the police or military. No cars were allowed within a radius of almost six miles and guards from Iraq's Shi'ite religious authority and mainstream political parties searched all those entering the city. The aim of this measure was at preventing a repeat of the devastating suicide bombings in Karbala and Baghdad that killed close to 180 in March during the commemoration of the holiday known to Shi'ites as Ashura. Organizers also were determined to keep al-Sadr's zealous supporters in check. Still, a few hundred young loyalists of the radical cleric came to the plaza brandishing posters and chanting anti–U.S. slogans. But there was no violence at the pilgrimage site.

The religious celebration, however, had an ominous precursor. Two days before, two Iraqi pilgrims were killed and four others wounded when someone threw a hand grenade at a tent erected on the side of the road just south of Baghdad. No one would own up to the attack, but there was no need. The Shi'a knew that Sunni extremists were sending a message.

If there was any chance to establish a peaceful norm, oil had to flow to pay for it. Riding the boon of so much oil money, the people of Iraq were addicted. The oil revenues subsidized the price of gasoline and food. It paid for free electricity and medical care, and took the place of taxes. It paid for the state-owned industries that did not make a profit, the salaries of a large government payroll, and the new security forces.

The first day of September also saw continued attacks on Iraq's principal source of revenue. Saboteurs attacked a key oil pipeline linking the Iraqi town of Baiji and Turkey. A bomb planted under the pipeline set off a fire. Some thirty local families had been forced to flee the area, and the road between Kirkuk and the Baiji refinery was cut by the choking black smoke and fire. On September 24, gunmen killed a senior official of Iraq's North Oil Co. in the northeastern city of Mosul, less than two weeks after his boss escaped an assassination attempt. Also, saboteurs attacked an oil well near Baghdad and a pipeline in the south. For the most part, oil production and export was one of the most striking victories of September. The month brought the highest flow of revenue since the fall of the Hussein regime with 1.83 billion dollars into Iraqi coffers.

Iraq managed to keep the oil flowing in large part by using the same methods Saddam had used. They paid the local tribal leaders to guard the pipelines.

On the reconstruction front, delivery of electrical power to the people had been a priority of first the military and now the new interim government. It was not going well. Throughout the country, private generators were the only reliable sources of electricity. Saddam had provided electricity on a political basis. Areas such as the Sunni Triangle and government areas in Baghdad got electricity 18 to 22 hours a day while other areas would get none at all. The new government distributed it equally, giving only 8 to 12 hours a day. For the people in the Sunni Triangle, this was only proof that they were now worse off than under Saddam. In places like Baqubah, the rolling blackouts used six-hour rotations, two hours on and four off. In smaller towns such as nearby troubled Burhitz it was one hour on and five off. The sewage systems, and thus public health, had actually deteriorated throughout the country.

On the eleventh, a significant victory for the government came with two additional electrical generators coming on line. The lack of power and rolling blackouts were in large measure the way the populace judged the effectiveness of the central government. The military tracked carefully the slow advance in expanding the electrical grid. Anything that added a few extra minutes or hours of electricity was seen as being as much a victory as the capture or defeat of an insurgent band.

The insurgents also had an acute appreciation of the importance of the power grid. Two weeks later, on September 14, an attack on a pipeline in northern Iraq melted cables leading to a power station, causing blackouts in parts of the country. Two days later the electrical grid itself came under attack, but maintenance workers quickly restored the power.

Electrical power was not the only basic service under attack. One of the results of the new freedom was that everyone could now have a car. Iraqis driving cars imported, often stolen, from Europe and Russia now choked streets that were once drivable. With gasoline officially priced at about three gallons a U.S. dollar, if one were willing to wait in long lines, and about twice that on the street corner sold from plastic jugs, a living was possible as a taxi driver. Shortages of gas quickly developed, particularly where gas could be smuggled across the border at a market price of a dollar a gallon. One sure way to get the populace riled at the government was to cut off the gasoline. On September 27, insurgents at Latifiyah just south of Baghdad launched an attack on a group of gasoline tankers, in which they killed ten persons and wounded twenty-six. They sprayed machine gun fire at the tanker trucks, setting all five ablaze, after which they engaged in a running gun battle with members of the

National Guard who were accompanying the convoy. Tankers without a convoy escort were often stopped, but only to take out a percentage of the gas for the insurgents.

There was other plodding movement towards a nation state. On September 18, Iraq's national carrier, Iraqi Airways, resumed international flights after being grounded by war and sanctions for fourteen years.

Security was key to any reconstruction effort. However, accelerating employment opportunities for Iraqis was also an important part of the country's economic and political environment leading up to the January elections.

There were real advances in the underpinnings of Iraq's economy that did not get much attention. There were more than 1.5 million telephone subscribers in Iraq, including some 738,000 cell phone subscribers. That was 85 percent more than existed before the war. Crude oil production was up in September, although the energy sector remained a favorite insurgent target. The Americans rehabbed some 2,400 schools nationwide. In northern Iraq, the Kurdistan regional government opened an Internet cafe and training center that allowed 2,000 people access. Perhaps one of the greatest successes not covered by the press was the start of school for six million Iraqis without attacks on the schools themselves although there was fear that such might happen. Every city in Iraq was under orders to open at least one center to teach reading and math to 10- to 14-year-olds who dropped out of school. This program alone would bring as many as half a million children back to school. The increased teacher's pay from a little over $60 a month prior to the war to $165 allowed teachers to actually report to work and teach.

There were other unsung successes. In Tikrit, the Americans rebuilt a 5.4 million dollar bridge. The U.S. had undertaken thousands of projects ranging from water and sewage facilities and road repairs to new computers for ministries and crop-dusting. The military civil affairs units operated in hundreds of small neighborhood projects, often in cleanup efforts. Usually they were small garbage collection projects paying workers from three to six dollars a day to clean the streets. Sometimes more was handed over, such as on September 26, when ten garbage trucks were given to a Baghdad neighborhood. These projects involved the presenting of large-dollar grants. Nevertheless, one of the most remarkable successes went completely without notice by the popular press. On September 9, General Motors signed a contract with the Ministry of Industry to produce 230,000 cars in Iraq.

There were big plans as well. The American government had already allocated $393 million to refurbish 200 of Iraq's 240 hospitals and $150 million for a new children's hospital in Basra with "top level care for pediatric oncology, plastic surgery, burn treatment, specialized surgeries, and high risk pregnancies with the latest technologies in radiology, ultrasound, physical therapy and other procedures." But to many Iraqi ears on the street, if they heard it at all, it sounded like empty promises in the background of the street rumors and al-Jazeera.

Under Saddam, schools were militarized and secular. To revitalize the education system, the U.S. had spent $225 million to renovate 2,400 of Iraq's 18,000 schools, print nine million new textbooks and retrain one in ten teachers. There was a great deal of academic freedom now but how that freedom was used was sometimes dismaying.

Many Iraqis were opting out of the public school system. Under Saddam, school was only allowed to teach the strict, state-approved curriculum. But now, private schools were free to teach whatever they liked. In a sign of the changing times, the focus was now on Islamic education. Instead of teaching the alphabet, some schools taught students to memorize basic verses from the Koran and taught how to wash before prayers.

At universities too, religious hard-liners took hold. At Baghdad's Mustansiriya University, self-appointed morality police guarded the campus gate. They sent at least one grad student away because she was wearing pants.

The director of Iraq's education ministry opposed the fundamentalist trend. Radicals were trying to use their new freedom to deny the freedom of others. However, he admitted the chaos made it difficult to control. And the government no longer controlled the hundreds of Shi'ite religious seminaries known as the Howza, teaching Islamic theory and law.

What was a clear threat to a normal society were the attacks on academic professionals. Nevertheless, the predicted attacks on coeducational universities by extremists never occurred.

In the meantime, Coalition forces were desperately trying to prevent another nightmare, open sectarian civil war, despite what was clearly an attempt to ignite civil war along those lines. On September 18, Sheik Hazim al-Zaidi, the Sunni imam of Baghdad's al-Sajjad mosque, was kidnapped while leaving the temple in the capital's al-Sadr City. His body was later delivered back to the mosque. A second cleric, Sheik Mohammed Jado'ou, was gunned down on the twentieth, in southwest Baghdad's al-Baya'a district. Jado'ou was leaving prayers at his al-Kwather mosque when gunmen in a vehicle drove next to him and opened fire. The two clerics were members of the influential Sunni Committee of Muslim Scholars, a group that weighed in on key issues, provided religious interpretations and had helped with negotiating the release of hostages.

The Sunni clerics were not the only targets. On September 30, guerrillas attempted but failed to assassinate a local leader of the Shi'ite Supreme Council for Islamic Revolution in Iraq.

September gave rough treatment politically to the Iraqi venture and many thought that the battle would not be won or lost in Iraq at all, but in Washington. What worried officials most was the mood back in the states. "We are at a very critical time," a senior staff officer declared. "The only way we can lose this battle is if the American people decide we don't want to fight anymore."

From the beginning, both civilian and the military leadership feared that the American electorate would lose faith and abandon the effort. The majority of the public affairs effort in Iraq was always aimed not at the local or regional Arab audience, but at the American media. Commanders were constantly asked to bring forth "good news stories" that could be covered by the American media.

Quick success was now out of the question. For those who saw Iraq as simply transplanting democracy to the Arab world, this was all becoming increasingly frustrating and unlikely. It was becoming evident to even the upper reaches of the bureaucracy of the State and Defense Departments that, as put by the CATO institute, "...the American government may need to compromise its democratic ideals with a healthy dose of pragmatism. Democracy is an evolutionary development rather than an overnight phenomenon."

Because the security situation had not improved enough to spend the reconstruction funds allocated, the Pentagon had to publicly address the failure. On September 14, the State Department asked Congress to allow shifting $3.4 billion in Iraq reconstruction funds to help beef up security.

U.S. Ambassador to Iraq, John D. Negroponte; Army Gen. George W. Casey, commander of Multi-National Force Iraq, and Army Lt. Gen. David Petraeus, commander of Security Transition Command Iraq, developed the plan. Faced with hard choices, they decided that without a significant reallocation of resources to the security and law enforcement sector, the short-term stability of Iraq would be compromised and the longer-term prospects for a free and democratic Iraq undermined.

Members of Congress were pointed in their criticism on the lack of progress in reconstruction projects. In the hearing asking Congress for permission to transfer some money from electricity, water, and sewer projects to police, border patrols and other security measures, as well as private sector development and short-term job creation projects, the bipartisan criticism was sharp. Republican chairman of the Foreign Relations Committee, Senator Richard Lugar of Indiana, warned that diverting reconstruction money could actually hurt security in the long run, arguing that the rebuilding effort was important for winning the support of Iraqis. "It is exasperating for anybody looking at this from any vantage point. Now having finally gotten to this monumental decision of [wanting to transfer] three-point-four [billion dollars], it sort of begs the question, what happened to the other 14 billion?"

The top Democrat on the Foreign Relations Committee, Senator Joe Biden of Delaware, agreed, recalling that the administration appealed for "urgent" congressional action on what it called the "urgently needed" reconstruction package last year.

"How much money have we spent of this urgent supplemental? It is incompetence from my perspective. The emphasis on these [security and job-growth] priorities will mean that we will have less to spend on large-scale infrastructure projects, such as sewage treatment plants and power plants. Projects in those sectors that were scheduled to begin in 2005 will be delayed, which unfortunately means we cannot guarantee that as many Iraqis will have these essential services by 2007, as we had originally intended."

More political damage came to the mission in Iraq when drafts of a report from the top U.S. inspector in Iraq concluded there were no weapons stockpiles, but said there were signs the fallen Iraqi President Saddam Hussein had dormant programs he hoped to revive at a later time. A principal logic for the invasion of Iraq had been to prevent his using weapons of mass destruction against his neighbors or America. In a 1,500-page report, the head of the Iraq Survey Group, Charles Duelfer, was finding Saddam had imported banned materials, worked on unmanned aerial vehicles in violation of UN agreements and maintained a dual-use industrial sector that could produce weapons. Duelfer also said Iraq only had small research and development programs for chemical and biological weapons.

Duelfer concluded that Saddam intended to restart the weapons programs at some point, after suspicion and inspections from the international community waned. After a year and a half in Iraq, however, the United States had found no weapons of mass destruction. From those managing the combat forces in Iraq, there was fear that continued erosion of the logic for the invasion would reduce the support for continued operations.

The report was similar to findings reported by Duelfer's predecessor, David Kay, who presented an interim report to Congress that October. Kay left the post in January, saying "We were almost all wrong" about Saddam's weapons programs.

More bad news was circulating in the States. An intelligence report leaked to the *New York Times* warned that the prospects for stability in Iraq were not good and that current trends pointed toward a continued deterioration of the security situation there. By the end of 2005, the possibility of full-scale civil war involving Iraq's Shi'ites, Sunnis and Kurds could not be ruled out. The National Intelligence Estimate (NIE) predicted three scenarios, ranging from a tenuous stability to political fragmentation to the possibility of civil war.

That same day in an interview, Kofi Annan, the UN Secretary General, was repeatedly asked whether the war was "illegal."

"Yes," he finally said, "I have indicated it is not in conformity with the UN Charter, from our point of view, and from the Charter point of view it was illegal."

Caught up in a tough political campaign, President Bush countered, saying, "The Iraqis are defying the dire predictions of a lot of people by moving toward democracy.... It's hard to get to democracy from tyranny. It's hard work. And yet, it's necessary work. But it's necessary work because a democratic Iraq will make the world a freer place and a more peaceful place.... I'm pleased with the progress...."

Meanwhile, the other members of the Coalition, while not able to point a way out, were providing the grist for questioning the Iraqi venture in the first place. Iraqi interim Prime Minister Ayad Allawi warned that terrorists were flooding into his country from across the Muslim world. But former British Foreign Secretary Robin Cook told London newspaper *The Times*, "There were no international terrorists in Iraq until we went in. It was we who gave the perfect conditions in which al-Qaeda could thrive."

Facing an assembly of world leaders, UN Secretary General Kofi Annan criticized the violation of basic laws around the globe from cold-blooded massacres and prisoner abuses in Iraq to the seizing of children in Russia and widespread rape in Sudan. He condemned the massacre of civilians in Iraq "in cold blood, while relief workers, journalists, and other non-combatants are taken hostage and put to death in the most barbarous fashion." However, Annan also said Iraqi prisoners were "disgracefully abused," an implicit criticism of the U.S. treatment of detainees at Abu Ghraib Prison.

In the wake of Kofi Annan's statement that the war in Iraq was illegal, President Bush faced the UN General Assembly. President Bush delivered an unapologetic defense of his decision to invade Iraq, saying that his decision helped to deliver the Iraqi people from an outlaw dictator.

On September 23, Prime Minister Allawi appeared beside the president in an apparent bid to stem the tide of bad news to the American public to say that the upcoming election could be held tomorrow in 13 of the 15 provinces. John Kerry's campaign manager referred to Allawi as a puppet of the president. Insurgents were quick to repeat that statement in their propaganda.

September 29 saw the first presidential debate. Kerry hammered the president on the war in Iraq. "I think that's wrong, and I think we can do better ... we are 90 percent of the casualties and 90 percent of the cost, $200 billion, $200 billion that could have been used for health care, for schools, for construction, for prescription drugs for seniors, and it's in Iraq. And Iraq is not even the center of the focus of the war on terror. Iraq was not even close to the center of the war on terror before the president invaded it."

But with all the criticisms he did not call for a retreat. "We have to succeed. We can't leave a failed Iraq."

It was elections that the interim government and the Americans counted upon to establish legitimacy and a normal society. Planners emphasized that security would be an absolute necessity if elections set for January were going to be seen as successful in areas of Iraq now largely dominated by Sunni insurgents.

In the present city-state of Fallujah and those places seeking to copy it, such as Samarra and al-Sadr City, elections seemed out of the question. The U.S. military was growing concerned itself that American and Iraqi forces could not secure those areas without a full military assault.

Part of the problem in retaking areas held by Sunni militants was delays in getting Iraqi security forces properly trained, equipped, and ready to take charge. The military had to get the Iraqis trained and up to speed where they could take on and secure the area by themselves. The "Iraqi solution" of sending in Iraqi forces to secure insurgent areas was looking to be so far in the future as to make it impossible before the elections.

Political parties were as important as military forces to the Coalition effort. Without people willing to participate in the election there was no chance to advance past the violence. A growing number of Iraqi political groups were taking steps to organize ahead of the January elections despite numerous comments the week before by government and UN officials who said that elections might be postponed due to increasing violence.

Interim Iraqi Prime Minister Ayad Allawi worked to counter the talk of a delay in the election when he vowed on the 20th of September that the country will "definitely ... stick to the timetable of the elections in January next year" during a meeting in London with British Prime Minister Tony Blair.

Iraq's two largest Shi'a groups entered into discussions in early September about forging an alliance in preparation for the January elections. Leaders from the Supreme Council for the Islamic Revolution in Iraq (SCIRI), led by al-Hakim, met with representatives of the Islamic al-Da'wah Party on the fifth of September to discuss the possibility of merging the two parties into an alliance. SCIRI was also courting smaller Shi'a groups, such as the al-Fadilah Party, and an al-Sadr splinter group led by Muhammad al-Ya'qubi. A SCIRI-Da'wah alliance would form the largest political grouping in Iraq and place the alliance in a strong position for the elections. There was afoot a gathering of the Shi'ite political groups papering over the question of whether there should be an Islamic republic or a secular democracy. They would argue that out among themselves after they got power. Perhaps more significant, Moqtada al-Sadr was being left behind. Al-Sistani's patience was forcing Moqtada to either play political ball or be marginalized.

Starting in early September, Moqtada al-Sadr was feeling the pain as the Shi'ite establishment was peeling away his support, offering deals to splinter groups within his organization. Al-Sadr's *Ishraqat al-Sadr* weekly published an article on the eighth of September calling on SCIRI and the al-Da'wah to include the "al-Sadr trend" in its alliance. "We demand that the leaders of SCIRI and al-Da'wah Party hold negotiations with the leadership of the al-Sadr trend in order to work out a form that unifies the Shi'ite people and to ensure the victory of their unified list because we are heading toward an important stage the building of the new Iraqi state," the article said. The article was hailed as a landmark event in that al-Sadr himself said that he had no interest in participating in the political process.

However, he had made similar statements in the past, only to recant. Al-Sadr said that his movement was in the process of writing a "political program" that contained twenty-five articles addressing the political, economic, and social issues that he raised during his Friday prayer sermons over the summer of 2004. Still, there was hope among the Americans for al-Sadr's participation in the political process, which they saw as a critical piece to turn the corner. All that was needed was a little pressure in his home base to take away the military option. Colonel Abe Abrams was providing that.

Three Sunni groups, the National Front for Iraq's Tribes, the National Democratic Party, and the Iraqi National Movement, organized a rally in Baghdad on September 11, calling on the Iraqi people to unify ahead of the January elections. It was unclear whether these groups would forge a political alliance ahead of that vote.

One of the concerns about elections was the appearance of U.S. troops charged with security around the polls. There was increasing pressure to turn over local security to Iraqi control before votes were cast. Hard analysis was pointing to that being unlikely across the board and threatening to sap Iraqi troop strength away from Fallujah after its fall to assaulting forces.

On September 20, Lieutenant General Walter Sharp, the director of strategic plans and policy for the Joint Chiefs of Staff, predicted that more than 50 percent of Iraq, in terms of land area as well as population, would be under "local control" by 1 January. He defined "local control" as a locality assuming management over its own security and government, with limited or no oversight from U.S. forces. This was a concern for planners because if Fallujah were taken, there might not be enough Iraqi forces to take over the security there.

On the twenty-fourth of September U.S. Defense Secretary Donald Rumsfeld said Iraq's scheduled January elections might not take place in areas of that country where violence remained rampant.

In response the Shi'a were emphatic in their demands. "Mr. al-Sistani insisted on the following: First, elections should be held in its due time as scheduled. Second, he affirms and insists that the UN should play a crucial and a key role in monitoring elections so those elections can be credible and transparent and people of Iraq can be truly and really represented in legislative and constitutional councils," one of his spokesmen said.

Grand Ayatollah Ali al-Sistani was growing increasingly concerned that nationwide elections could be delayed and even threatened to withdraw his support for the elections unless changes were made to increase the representation of Shi'ites. His aides expressed al-Sistani's concern that voting might be delayed through Lakhdar Brahimi, the former Algerian foreign minister. The ayatollah often maddened officials with his indirect methods.

Ayatollah al-Sistani was also concerned that the democratic process in Iraq was falling under the control of a handful of the largest political parties, which co-operated with the U.S. occupation and were composed largely of exiles. Ayatollah al-Sistani was worried about discussions underway among those parties to form a single ticket for the January elections. He believed that would limit the choices of voters and smother smaller political parties. To the Shi'a, the more parties, the better. In a legislature full of small groups, the Shi'a bloc of the Islamic south would always be the biggest dog in the pack. The ayatollah, who earlier sent tens of thousands of Iraqis into the streets to demand early elections, was worried that a so-called consensus list of candidates being discussed among the larger political parties would artificially limit the power of the Shi'ites, who were in the majority.

"If he sees that what this is leading to is unfair and unfree elections, then he will not take part in it," an Iraqi close to Ayatollah al-Sistani said. "He will declare the elections to be illegitimate."

All of this political wrangling was starting to unnerve the generals, who still were sore from last April. They feared that politicians back home might bolt. There was a full court press to shore up support in America. "We are in fact moving in the direction that will allow Iraq to emerge as a democratic and representational state. I think that our military activities there have moved it ahead in a positive manner," General

Abizaid told host Tim Russert on *Meet the Press*. "It's a tough fight, it's a hard fight. But we shouldn't lose heart because there are difficult times. We know that there will be fighting through the elections."

"If everybody in Iraq was in the resistance, Prime Minister Allawi would not be trying to lead his nation forward to a better future. If everybody in Iraq happened to be part of the resistance, they wouldn't be volunteering for the armed forces," Abizaid said. "There's more people that are coming forward to fight for the future of Iraq than are fighting against it."

The ideological battle lines were now starting to clear up, with the Americans seeking to turn the conflict into one that would turn the country over to the Shi'a majority intact with the means to hold it together, while the Sunni were desperately trying to make the Americans the issue.

"Yes, there is a resistance. Yes, it is hard," a general noted. "But the truth of the matter is that Iraqis and Americans and other members of the Coalition will face that resistance together [and] will, through a series of political, economic and military means, figure out a way to defeat it and will move on to allow the elections to take place and a constitutional government to emerge."[59]

The four-star CENTCOM commander said that Americans needed to brace themselves for a long war in the Middle East and Central Asia, though not necessarily one that required huge numbers of American troops. However, the war would be long because the battle was between extremists and moderates.

"It'll be a long process. It'll be a difficult process. But it'll be one that can be successfully fought not only at home, but in the international community and with the peoples of the region to set the standards for good government and the standards for a moderate lifestyle," he said.

There were realists among the American leadership, particularly within the State Department. On September 27, U.S. Secretary of State Colin Powell said that the insurgency in Iraq was getting worse, and that U.S. forces would increase efforts to defeat militants who were determined to disrupt the democratic process in Iraq. The unspoken message was that the U.S. had no choice other than to go forward with the elections or risking fighting the Shi'a as well as the Sunni while trying to stave off the foreign radicals seeking to take control of the resistance. The question was only whether the interim government and the Coalition could keep the thing together long enough to hand the power over to the people most likely to win the election regardless whether everyone could participate.

Meanwhile, events on the ground made the point most eloquently. On September 15, the decapitated bodies of three men, their heads strapped to their backs, were found dumped in nylon bags by a roadside of Baiji. September 15 also saw the fourth assassination attempt against Interim Prime Minister Allawi. His guards became suspicious of a car outside Baghdad's Green Zone compound housing the government and the U.S. and other embassies. The car then blew up and a battle between gunmen and his guards ensued. Two non–Iraqi Arabs were arrested.

By the close of September, the daily and weekly updates from the U.S. State Department did not encourage policy makers. A year and a half since the fall of Saddam Hussein only 33,000 of the 85,000 Iraqi police had completed their training. Their total numbers were considered 50,000 short of the needs. Only a little over 40,000 of their number had even the outdated body armor discarded by the U.S. military. The U.S. catalogued 172 insurgent attacks over the last two months. Issues of sovereignty were becoming more pronounced. Iraqi judges were starting to complain about Coalition forces clashing with Iraqi law.

There was one bright spot, however. In the wake of constant press reports about the lack of Iraqi support for the government, there was no shortage of people willing to volunteer to serve in the police. The problem was how to get Iraqi's security forces ready fast enough.

By September, there were only six Iraqi army battalions in service, each with about 700 soldiers, the Coalition deployed three in Najaf. By February, U.S. officials planned to have twenty-seven trained and deployed Iraqi battalions. The Americans were supposed to train twelve battalions by the end of October that might allow the retaking of Fallujah. U.S. military commanders in Baghdad realized that there were not enough Iraqi troops available until the end of October. There was a sense of vulnerability because they didn't have the capacity to take on an offensive.

From the beginning, there was no plan to include those who had served in the old Iraqi Army. This slowed the start of the new force to a crawl. From May of 2003 to April of 2004, CPA officials met in a working group swapping ideas with little or no Iraqi input.

There were those who stated that the military did not appreciate just how bad it was in Iraq, and that they were overly optimistic. Statistics collected by private security firms, which included attacks on Iraqi civilians and private security contractors, were more comprehensive than those collected by the military that focused on attacks against its troops. In fact, many military commanders had long stopped relying on the intelligence "significant events" report as being wildly inaccurate. Over thirty days, more than 2,300 attacks by insurgents had been directed against civilians and military targets in Iraq, in a pattern that spread out over nearly every major population center outside the Kurdish north.

The period covered by Special Operations Consulting's data represented a typical month, with its average of 79 attacks a day falling between the valleys during quiet periods and the peaks during the outbreak of insurgency in April or the battle with Moqtada al-Sadr's militia in August for control of Najaf.

During the month of September, those attacks totaled 283 in Nineveh, 325 in Salahuddin in the northwest and 332 in the desert badlands of Anbar Province in the west. The Sunni Triangle comprised mostly the Salahuddin and Anbar provinces. In the center of Iraq, attacks numbered 123 in Diyala Province, 76 in Babylon and 13 in Wasit. These lower figures were coming from Shi'a areas although there was not a single province without an attack in the thirty-day period.

The number of attacks had risen and fallen over the months. The highest numbers were in April, when there was major fighting in Fallujah, with attacks averaging 120 a day. The average was now about 80 a day.

The type of attacks included car bombs, time bombs, IEDs, rocket-propelled grenades, kidnappings, hand grenades, small-arms fire, mortar attacks, and land mines. These incidents combined to kill 503 Iraqi civilians for the month of September alone. These numbers were far different from the intelligence reports given to military leaders.

But numbers did not tell the whole story. Both President Bush and interim Prime Minister Ayad Allawi were counting on the police to ensure elections took place on schedule in January. "In Iraq, we confront both an insurgency and the global war on terror, with their destructive forces sometimes overlapping," Allawi said in Washington. "I can tell you today they will not succeed." A strong, credible homegrown security force was an essential building block.

However, with a long-held reputation for incompetence and corruption, the Iraqi police force faced an uphill battle. Under Saddam Hussein's regime, they were the enforcers and often profited from his brutal rule. They subsidized their small salaries by whatever they could steal from those they were supposed to protect. Despite U.S. military-run police training, the attitude of both the cops and the public had not changed. In Iraq it was not just the Americans who needed to "win hearts and minds," to create stability, but the Iraqi police force as well.

There was also a plan for a growing paramilitary force to cover the situations in between the military and police functions, but these forces were also still in the infancy. In fact this "Civil Intervention Force" of a projected 4,800 members had not yet been established. But, on a local level they were being established. The SWAT teams still did not have a common uniform. Some dressed in fatigues, some in jeans, with knit shirts, ski masks or green bandanas tied around their heads. The tactics were simple. They piled out of their pickups and swept in groups of 30 or 40. They busted into one house, then another, in suspect towns. They detained a few men on lists or reported to be of interest. Contractors for

Dynacorp, acting as an adviser and liaison to the Iraqi police, would come along. At times, they noted that the police behavior was unacceptable. Claims of stealing and brutality were common.

By now, it was clear that the Iraqi security apparatus was struggling despite what was often a genuine display of courage by the Iraqis themselves. More than 700 Iraqi police officers had been killed since the Americans had reestablished the force.

By the close of September, there was still a differing of opinion between the Defense Department and the State Department as to the situation on the ground. Again, on September 29, Secretary of State Colin L. Powell acknowledged that the insurgency was strengthening and that anti–Americanism in the Middle East was increasing. "Yes, it's getting worse," he said of the insurgency on ABC's *This Week*. At the same time, the U.S. commander for the Middle East, Gen. John P. Abizaid, told NBC's *Meet the Press* that "we will fight our way through the elections." Abizaid said he believed Iraq was still winnable once a new political order and the Iraqi security force was in place. The sales job to go forward with elections no matter what, was on.

There were, however, military victories. On September 12, there was a coordinated attack on the Abu Ghraib Prison just east of Fallujah. For the insurgents it was a disaster. The attack began as several mortars exploded just outside the Abu Ghraib prison complex at about 6 A.M. The attack resulted in no injuries and only alerted the security forces. About twenty minutes later, troops spotted three civilian pickup trucks with machine guns on a road near the complex. As the Marines opened fire on one of the vehicles, another pickup truck approached at high speed. As it drove through a chain-link gate marking the outer perimeter, the Marines immediately started shooting from the wall towers of the secured compound. While under the withering fire, the vehicle exploded, sending out a fireball and shock wave that knocked many off their feet. None were injured as the truck had not reached the main security wall of the complex. The explosion scattered a number of 155-millimeter artillery rounds along with the debris of the vehicle. The troops later found the other pickup trucks used in the attack, and captured seven individuals. The insurgents were clearly unable to challenge in direct combat.

The press hardly noticed any of this because of what happened that day in Baghdad. Fighting in the city center resulted in the death of a reporter on camera that in turn was the story for the next several days.

No statistics on numbers of attacks could measure what was perhaps the most important political equation facing Prime Minister Ayad Allawi and the American military: how much of Iraq was under the firm control of the interim government. That would determine the likelihood, and quality, of elections in January. This was in large measure because the military, in the wake of a political campaign in America, avoided areas that would cause high casualties.

The number of attacks was not an accurate measure of control in Fallujah. Attacks had actually dropped in the town itself, but the town was controlled by insurgents and was a "no-go" zone for the American military and Iraqi security forces. It was a place where elections could not be held without dramatic military intervention. The same was true about Samarra, a city in the Sunni Triangle north of Baghdad. Commanders simply had their hands tied both by the need to keep losses down and the realization that they had little they could do to actually reach out to the people in the area. Delivery of aid, using up combat assets to escort and protect that delivery, just did not seem to be a useful exercise in the minds of combat commanders.

Nor was the presence of a high level of violence a decisive matter as far as elections were concerned. The statistics showed that there had been just fewer than 1,000 attacks in Baghdad during August. Since April, insurgents had fired nearly 3,000 mortar rounds in Baghdad alone. Those figures did not preclude having elections in the Iraqi capital; it only showed where the insurgents were pressing to extend their control.

Officers pointed to a separate list of statistics including the number of schools and clinics opened. They also cited statistics indicating that a growing number of Iraqi security forces were trained and fully equipped, and they noted that applicants continued to line up at recruiting stations despite bombings of them.

Most of all, military officers argued that despite the rise in bloody attacks during the past thirty days, the insurgents had yet to win a single battle.

The commanders without exception pointed out that there had not been a single military defeat of an American force in the field. The military believed that Fallujah was a political, not a military defeat. It also overlooked what the insurgents counted as a victory. In the insurgents' minds, they won victories every day with each successful car-bombing and every time a soldier fell to a roadside bomb. Earlier in the year, one exasperated CPA official, after reading the day's headlines, bemoaned that it didn't matter how many the U.S. military killed because the loss of a hundred to the insurgents meant little and the loss of one to us meant everything.

What no one in General Casey's staff could measure, however, was what was under the surface in Iraq. There was no telling how many people were having insurgents coming up to them and saying they would be murdered if they voted next January. There was no way to determine how many people, especially Sunnis, would stay home simply because the

Sunni leadership that was willing to run for office did not excite or inspire. There was simply no Sunni that appeared to represent their interests and could gather support from the majority Shi'a. Therefore, with no objective means to measure success in Iraq, the whole affair was devolving into one big political spin operation.

In a joint appearance in the White House Rose Garden, Mr. Bush and Dr. Allawi painted an optimistic portrait of the security situation in Iraq.

Dr. Allawi said that of Iraq's 18 provinces, "14 to 15 are completely safe." He added that the other provinces suffered "pockets of terrorists" that inflicted damage in them and plotted attacks carried out elsewhere in the country. In other appearances, Dr. Allawi asserted that elections could be held in 15 of the 18 provinces.

Both Mr. Bush and Dr. Allawi insisted that Iraq would hold free elections as scheduled in January. There was a sense of embarrassment at the "completely safe" part of Prime Minister Allawi's statement in Baghdad. American government officials explained that optimistic assessments about Iraq from President Bush and Prime Minister Allawi had to be interpreted as a declaration of a strategic goal. Despite the attacks, there would be elections. The comments were meant as a balance to the insurgents' strategy of roadside bombings and mortar attacks and beheadings, all meant to declare to Iraq and the world that the country was in chaos, and that mayhem would prevent the country from ever reaching democratic elections.

"The question is not whether there are attacks," said one Pentagon official. "Of course there are. But, what are the proper measurements for progress."

Some Iraqis shared their prime minister's optimism on the likelihood of elections, and a closely related census. "We are ready to start," said Hamid Abd Muhsen, an Iraqi education official who was supervising parts of the census in Baghdad. "I swear to God." As for the Sunnis, they were making it clear that they did not want elections. "We think the elections will be fake," said Abdul Salam al-Qubesi,[60] a leading Sunni cleric and a member of the association.

At this point, if it were not clear before, the American administration was making it clear now that the Shi'a were in the driver's seat and the ayatollahs had a firm hand on the wheel. September was a turning point in that if there was an election as planned in January the likely result would be continuing Sunni violence, perhaps even a civil war, but with the Shi'a in charge. There would not be a resistance to the American-supported Iraqi government because it would be the majority actually running the government. The Americans were buoyed also by an Iraqi public opinion poll that showed less than eight percent of the Iraqi public believed a civil war likely. But, without that election, the Shi'a would likely support the Sunni insurgents and America was not in a position to fight a protracted war against the majority of Iraqi people.

There were risks. The Shi'a might well simply tell the Americans to go home. But with the Sunni unwilling to submit to a Shi'a agenda; with Iran, although Shi'a themselves, not Arabic and not fully trusted; with the Shi'a not unified; with a Kurdish population willing to fight for their rights and possessing the only militarily viable force native to Iraq; with Iraqi security forces still fragile; and with America's ability to offer financial aid, being asked to simply go away was not likely. Elections in January were no longer optional and it seemed whatever was normal anywhere else would not likely happen in Iraq. However imperfect, it seemed that an Arab example of rule by the majority standing against radical Islam was possible due in large measure to the sacrifice of a handful of American soldiers and Marines.

There was one thing for sure: if there were to be elections, places like Fallujah had to be taken under control lest they not only discredit the results but also provided a springboard to attack the polling stations en masse. Tal Afar provided some important lessons but there needed to be a rehearsal on a grander scale.

To many Americans the race to establish the norm had been lost with the continued violence. The safe havens for the insurgents patterned on Fallujah made for an easy explanation for the failure. If so, it was only a technical matter of how to retake control of the rebellious cities.

CHAPTER 16

Deadly Samarra

Samarra had been under insurgent control and a virtual "no-go" area for U.S. troops throughout the summer. With the transfer of authority from formal occupation in late June of 2004, the Iraqi officials were to take over the day-to-day security with the U.S. military venturing out of their base camps only when the Iraqi police or National Guard needed their additional firepower. What the Coalition did not take into account was the likelihood that the insurgency would simply co-opt these very security forces. In Fallujah, this came about almost instantly. In Samarra, it was less dramatic but nearly as complete. Local military commanders were able to reduce their casualties by reducing their exposure. Left unattended, local police simply switched sides.

Samarra had always been a troubled area. In the 1990s, Saddam Hussein had to send in a battalion of Republican Guard to control the city. Samarra suffered from a complex tribal make-up. In places such as Tikrit, there was a single tribe and thus a strong man with which to deal, but Samarra had five tribes and the insurgency was better able to play them off on one another.

The military was more than aware at this point that police and National Guardsmen could switch sides. They had watched police and Iraqi National Guardsmen do so first-hand at Najaf, Samarra, Karbala, and Fallujah in April. Pushed by political considerations to give Iraqis another chance, they saluted smartly and let go any expectation of quality control through oversight. The existence of military uniforms at police stations required increased exposure and thus casualties. Besides, a number of commanders thought it was just not their job to baby-sit the police. After all, if the situation got out of hand, they could move in and "kick ass," which was what they were good at. They did not consider the political damage that such a highlighted setback could cause.

As early as July, the 1st Infantry Division Headquarters in Tikrit was talking about the problem in Samarra, and how they would have to take back the city. The battalion commander charged with Samarra had in effect stopped operations in the city, and once the division command realized the mistake, it relieved the officer charged with "owning" the ground.

Talking the military officials into retaking the city was easy. The officials in Baghdad were another matter. For now, the army had to toe the line. Early in September, the 1st Infantry Division commander wrote to a correspondent, "Samarra is a city where Iraqis are taking charge to throw out anti–Iraqi forces. No one has ceded the city to insurgents and there is no cordon. What we have in Samarra is the good people of Iraq, led by far-sighted provincial and city leadership, senior sheiks, and clerics, standing up to the enemy."

It was a curious thing to write because, at the same time, the PSY-OPS teams were handing out leaflets saying that the U.S. forces were coming to take back control of the city. The lessons of Fallujah in April were noted and the squeeze was on to get the civilians out of the line of fire. It was working and many were leaving for a safer place. Some went to Fallujah.

The city council had stopped functioning. In August, Tawhid and Jihad gangs ransacked a print shop that had published fliers announcing plans by city leaders to negotiate with the local American commander. Intelligence was reporting that insurgents were spreading out from the town to conduct attacks elsewhere. People leaving the city reported that gunmen snatched men from their homes and killed at least ten of them as American spies. As many as a hundred people had disappeared, taken from their homes by gunmen wearing ski masks or Arab scarves. Tribal chiefs and others cooperative with the government went to the Americans speaking of near total lawlessness. The town was a problem.

The Americans returned briefly to Samarra on September 9, under a peace deal brokered by tribal leaders, and U.S. forces agreed to provide millions of dollars in reconstruction funds in exchange for an end to attacks on American and Iraqi troops. Part of the deal was to reseat the city council that was there when the Americans left. The army had agreed to leave the city to their own devices in July along with a new interim mayor. U.S. and Iraqi commanders portrayed the deal as a success.

The preceding two months had been critical in that there was almost no law in Samarra. Kidnapping was widespread. The Shi'ite merchants became particularly upset because other Shi'a were refusing to come to the Mosque of the Golden Dome to celebrate their religious pilgrimages, which had cut business by a half.

The problem was how to keep the city council in office and working. Coalition forces started on September 13 to provide guards for the meetings. The next day, the local commander brought his civil affairs team with medical supplies and arranged to guard the City Council the day after. That guard came under attack by a man with an RPG on September 15.

On September 19, the uneasy truce ended. A four-door sedan came up to a checkpoint outside the city. As members of the checkpoint approached, the car exploded. An Iraqi soldier was killed, and three U.S. soldiers and three Iraqi National Guardsmen were wounded by the suicide car-bombing.

A 1st Infantry Division patrol was attacked September 22, with small-arms fire and mortars from a mosque in Samarra. A gun battle ensued with air power supporting. U.S. troops called in air strikes that night. Three Iraqis were killed according to Samarra's police chief. The air strikes damaged or burnt twenty-one cars, he added. U.S. forces sealed off the city, including the crucial bridge over the Tigris. As this was going on, Allawi told members of the U.S. Congress, "In Samarra, the Iraqi government has tackled the insurgents who once controlled the city."

On September 27, General Talib Abed Ghayib Najm, who was named to head the National Guard in the neighboring Diyala province just two days prior, was arrested by U.S. forces on the suspicion that he had ties to insurgent fighters. Meanwhile, the 1st Infantry Division was repositioning forces for an assault on Samarra. A battalion from the Styker brigade redeployed as a reserve if needed.

On September 28, U.S. troops briefly entered the city to deal with tribal leaders in a final effort to save the situation. What they found was dozens of masked gunmen carrying automatic rifles and rocket-propelled grenades driving through the main streets of Samarra in about twenty vehicles. Some carried the black flags of Iraq's Tawhid and Jihad, run by Abu Musab al-Zarqawi. Two of the cars carrying the gunmen were police pickup trucks that appeared to have been confiscated by the insurgents. The gunmen stopped some cars and asked passengers to hand over music tapes, giving back tapes with recitations from the Muslim holy book, the Koran, in exchange. Perhaps realizing that such a display was likely to provoke a U.S. military response, after a two-hour drive-through, the convoy dispersed around noon and the gunmen disappeared from the streets.

If it were not clear before, action would have to be taken quickly or Samarra would follow Fallujah and the example would quickly spread to the other Sunni cities. Operations to retake the city would start. It would be called Operation Baton Rouge.

A brigade-size force of U.S. 1st Infantry Division and nearly 2,000 Iraqi National Guard troops attacked in the early morning, and were in the center of the city before the end of the day after heavy fighting. Supported by tanks and aircraft, troops were going through the city sector by sector, clearing buildings and mosques. Forces cut electricity to some sections. U.S. military officials estimated that more than 2,000 Iraqi insurgents and 250 foreign fighters were in the city, although most escaped, jumping into cars and filtering out with the families fleeing the combat. The fight was a lopsided one with considerable damage to the city.

The most sensitive aspect of the operation was the taking of the Golden Dome Mosque which the insurgents used as an arms depot. Around noon of the second day, the Iraqi National Guard came forward to lead the assault into the Shi'a mosque. Twenty-five insurgents had stayed to fight. The U.S. forces breached the gate but the Iraqis led the way after that. The operation went off without much damage to the historic mosque.

The people of Samarra who had not left, their electricity and water supplies cut off, took shelter in their homes. The reception was mixed in that a large portion of the population was Shi'a and had been terrorized by the Sunni militias. Still, many came complaining loudly to the press, claiming that they saw U.S. soldiers killing babies in their mothers' arms. The offensive did not come without loss. The shooting was heavy and although the operation was well planned, one U.S. soldier (an activated National Guard member) fell victim to a sniper.*

The U.S.-led force imposed a curfew and began house-to-house searches, kicking and sometimes shot-gunning doors open. At one point, troops broke into a bewildered wedding party that had not noticed that American forces were overrunning the neighborhood. Mostly, the houses were empty and showed signs of a hasty departure. Iraqi officials and U.S. forces claimed success after fighting continued for two days. They had seized three quarters of the city, including the main government buildings, police station and a pharmaceutical factory. After two days, they claimed to have killed one hundred and twenty insurgents and captured another eighty-eight.

Right behind the combat soldiers came the civil affairs operators handing one and a half million dollars' worth of projects in the way of cleanup after the battle. But the quick infusion of money did not quell all of the complaints.

There was the usual accusation of U.S. snipers firing on anyone who appeared in the streets. An ambulance driver said, "Dead bodies and injured people are everywhere in the city and when we tried to evacuate them, the Americans fired on us. Later on they told us that we can evacuate only injured women and children and we are not allowed to pick up injured men."[61]

A retired schoolteacher commented to a British newspaper, "There have been a lot of deaths, and they have been of ordinary people.... They are killing us to save us."[62]

---

*KIA: Sgt. Michael A. Uvanni

The Samarra General Hospital told the media that of the seventy dead, twenty-three were children and eighteen were women. Another one hundred and sixty people were treated for wounds.

Other casualties were being treated in hospitals in nearby Tikrit or by the Red Crescent, which set up thirty tents on the road to Tikrit to provide medical aid and shelter for fleeing residents. Unnoticed was civil affairs planning and assistance to make that happen. The Tikrit Teaching Hospital reported that the casualties they treated were mostly women and children. Pointing to a young boy whose stomach was bandaged, one official told the press, "His pregnant mother was killed." In a nearby bed, a young girl had lost a foot.

Iraq's National Security Minister, Kasim Daoud, claimed to have the support of more than one hundred religious, tribal, political, and professional leaders who met with him in Baghdad the previous weekend. He made clear, however, that the attack would have gone ahead even if the delegation had objected. "It is our duty to clean this city," he declared.

One Samarra leader said that he was surprised by the attack. He believed that a deal was about to be concluded with the Baghdad government. "What we are seeing now is an effort to subdue Samarra by force and to sideline certain political forces to serve the agenda of the United States and that of its allied government. I do not think force is the answer," he said.

Prior to the U.S. invasion, the city and its tribal leaders were widely regarded as nominally Baa'thist. Traditionally, Samarra had been a rival to neighboring Tikrit, Hussein's hometown, because of Samarra's Shi'a population. Nevertheless, after the U.S. troops withdrew, the local council and police rapidly collapsed.

Speaking that weekend, Iraqi Defense Minister Hazem Shaalam boasted to al-Arabiya television: "It is over in Samarra."

The U.S. troops involved in the operation were under no illusion that the fighting was over. "The bad guys are just pulling back to see what we're going to do," an officer said, "Our guess is, this battle is going to get pretty rough and will probably last a long time."

Now Lt. Col. Greg Fischer's people moved in to start the rebuilding process. The 415th Civil Affairs Battalion was supposed to have redeployed to civilian life* by now, but there was a delay in getting their replacement, the 411th, in country. They had just arrived and were conducting the handover during this critical operation. Fischer worried about this last fight. He had lost one soldier† in the first two weeks back in February, and although his was not a combat unit, at least eleven times his

---

*415th is an army reserve unit from Kalamazoo, Michigan.
†KIA: Pfc. Nichole M. Frye, Baqubah, Feb. 16, 2003.

soldiers had driven into ambushes and had to shoot their way out, killing "bad guys." It was a wonder that they had lost only one killed in action.

The tactics turned up the heat on some Iraqi politicians. On September 30th, Iraqi President Ghazi al-Yawir strongly protested U.S. air strikes against Iraqi cities, comparing them to Israeli tactics in Gaza and branding them a form of "collective punishment."

In the headquarters of the Multi-National Force Iraq there were smiles. They had two examples of how to handle the insurgents, Tal Afar and Samarra. For the moment, the military had been able to focus on eliminating insurgents rather than gaining the population's support. This was something they understood, something for which they trained. Now, if they could just get those civilians out of Fallujah and the election would just get over back home.

Meanwhile, back in Washington, D.C., the Pentagon announced that in Iraq, eighty servicemen and one service woman were killed in action, 641 soldiers wounded in the month of September.

CHAPTER 17

The Final Days of a City-State

The decision was made to retake Fallujah, the Tal Afar and Samarra had been taken from insurgent control, and a deal with al-Sadr was a near certainty. There was a clear sense within MNFI that September 2004 was the high-water mark of the insurgency. With the American presidential election a month off and the new Iraqi battalions still undertrained, they had a month to scare out the civilians and plan the operation.

Back in Camp Victory, Baghdad, staff officers were carefully going over the after-action reviews of the operation at Samarra. They were trying to calculate just what was the most likely counter the insurgency would use to answer the assault on Fallujah. They also debated amongst themselves just what they had accomplished in the Samarra battle. Certainly they had taken back control of the ground, which was essential if there was to be even a semblance of a victory. But they had not destroyed the force, at least not in any classical military sense. The vast majority of the real fighters escaped with that part of the population that fled to avoid the battle. Under traditional military concepts, surprise was a central tool in battle, but the desire to get civilians out of the way of the fighting made that impossible.

Some staff officers analogize the operation as sweeping a pile of dirt from under one rug to another. Those with political and civil affairs experienced disagreed, saying that what was important was not killing the bad guys in the battle but denying the public support for the insurgents through operations after the city was taken. They said that it is not taking the swamp that was important, but draining it after that was done. This was unsettling to a number of officers for it meant that as of yet, they had accomplished only the conditions to start the battle, and had not won it.

The analysis being prepared for General Casey was outlining a likely and most dangerous course of action by the insurgency. Assuming al-Sadr would be defanged, which at the time was looking more likely, the chances of being tag-teamed by both Sunni and Shi'a insurgents like last April were low. But, in light of what happened both in Tal Afar and at Samarra, it was also unlikely that most of the insurgents would stand and fight. If anything, the most dangerous in Fallujah would slip out with the civilians in what was now an established practice of allowing non-combatants notice and a chance to flee prior to the battle.

What was very likely was that after the Americans were decisively engaged in Fallujah, a counteroffensive would erupt in other Sunni-dominated areas. A short-term surrender of affected urban areas might be necessary with a repositioning of forces as the battle in Fallujah progressed. There was another possibility, which MNFI dreaded. What if, instead of trying to incite a general uprising in the Sunni Triangle, the insurgents massed in Baghdad? There was less of a chance of that happening now in al-Sadr City, but amongst the other two and a half million residents the fighting could be disastrous. That possibility complicated matters. It made it critical that the First Cavalry Division keep a tight hold on the city up to the assault, and remove as many of the possible nesting places as possible.

That would be a challenge. Maj. Gen. Peter Chiarelli, the new commander of the Army's 1st Cavalry Division, believed that the Iraqi capital was far short of the numbers of Iraqi policemen needed to secure it. Baghdad only had 15,000 policemen, the majority of whom had only eight weeks of training. Both his Provost Marshal and G2 were telling him he needed at least 25,000 well-trained policemen, including 7000 to patrol the slums of east Baghdad and keep al-Sadr honest to his word. The shortfall of 10,000 policemen could not be filled before next spring or summer. The assessment was that because the police were so vulnerable, undermanned, and lightly armed, they would be useless should large numbers of insurgents appear. They would either flee or simply turn a blind eye as they had done in Najaf and Karbala.

For the State Department in the Green Zone, the upcoming battle in Fallujah was politically complicated as the end game became clear. The Kurdish leadership watched closely the interaction between the Americans and al-Sistani and were grasping quickly that this was the best time to bargain in what was becoming a clear inevitable end, elections with the Shi'a ruling Iraq. In exchange, the Shi'a would rein in al-Sadr and not kick up a fuss about what promised to be an ugly affair in Fallujah.

The Americans would need Iraqi troops to provide an Iraqi face for the destruction of what was, in fact, an independent city-state in Fallujah. The only reliable and experienced of those troops were Kurdish. If there was going to be a referendum on what the Kurds claimed as their price, Kirkuk, that claim had to be made now. The Kurds mounted big demonstrations October 2, demanding much more provincial autonomy. They wanted a popular referendum, and they wanted the oil-rich city of Kirkuk to be turned over to their "Kurdistan" province.

The Shi'a had their price; the Kurds needed their concerns met. Officials assured the Kurds that in the coming election, a non-binding referendum would be on the ballot as to Kurdish independence. That was as far as anyone could go. The Americans privately approved of the measure in any case. A warning shot across the Shi'a bow as a reminder that the Kurds expected to be treated with respect would be a good thing.

The extra month also meant that a month's bloodletting would continue. The nationalist insurgents were eager to find some way to derail what they knew to be the end game for Fallujah and maintain their control of the city. Al-Zarqawi, however, was determined to keep up the pressure. October in the al-Anbar would be particularly violent.

For the people around Fallujah at this stage everything looked much the same as before. Insurgents directed small-arms fire at two American soldiers at a traffic checkpoint on October 3, killing them.* U.S. warplanes and tanks also struck in Fallujah daily now, as much for psychological effect as for lethality. By now, more than half of Fallujah's residents had fled the city due to continuous bombings and the warnings.

October 7 continued al-Zarqawi's campaign with one of his car bombs detonating at Anah near the Syrian border, targeting recruits for the National Guard. It killed sixteen and wounded twenty-four.

The Americans shifted their action westward as well. Heavy fighting broke out in the provincial capital October 10. In Ramadi, insurgents launched a major attack with rocket-propelled grenades and machine guns. Insurgents also ambushed a Marine patrol close to nearby Hit, but the Marines struck back, killing three and wounding five. In Hit the next day, a major clash broke out between U.S. troops and dozens of local insurgents.

U.S. troops raided seven mosques in Ramadi on October 12, arresting a leading Sunni clergyman, Abdul Alim al-Saadi and his son. The night before, insurgents had fired mortar shells at city hall, starting the fighting and leaving three policemen and a civilian dead. Al-Saadi was a leader of the Provincial League of Anbar Clergy and regularly visited Fallujah. The military was now following closely what the clergy was doing and saying.

As the air strikes continued so did the claims of civilian victims, which were widely broadcasted. The strikes killed five and wounded two, according to the Fallujah hospital on October 12. The U.S. military pointed out that there were powerful secondary explosions at a building that had been struck, suggesting it had been used as a place to store explosives.

---

*KIA: Sgt. Christopher Potts, Staff Sgt. James Pettaway

The U.S. heavily bombarded Fallujah on October 15, the first day of the fasting month of Ramadan. The public affairs officers replied pointedly to criticism, stating that since the insurgent attacks had not let up on the start of the holy month, neither would they.

On October 17, Marines were stepping up their attacks, using small arms, tanks, artillery, mortars, and seven precision air strikes against insurgents. At one point the insurgents were seen taking refuge in a mosque. The Marines brought up a PSYOPS Humvee, using the loudspeakers and saying, "Come out and face us, you cowards." The Fallujah hospital officials reported four civilians wounded by U.S. bombing of this residential district, one of them a child.

On that day a statement appeared on a website used by a militant Islamic group in Iraq, declaring allegiance to al-Qaeda and Osama bin Laden. Said the statement, "We announce that Tawhid and Jihad, its prince and its soldiers, have pledged allegiance to the leader of the mujahadeen, Osama bin Laden.... The al-Qaeda leadership understood our strategy in Iraq."

To the Americans it meant little as they had been watching a trend towards cooperation for some time, but to the Fallujans it caused a stir within the leadership. There was no hiding now that the de facto city-state was in the same predicament as had been the Taliban in Afghanistan. Osama bin Laden had turned Afghanistan from establishing an Islamic state to an attack upon America. Now in Fallujah, they realized that they were no longer seen as a simple resistance to the occupation but as a part of a wider struggle.

The Marines were taking extraordinary measures to protect themselves from car bombs, which was making it difficult to score the big kills justified by the few people who were willing to commit suicide. The suicide bombers had to reach out further to find easier targets. Early on the twenty-third, a suicide bomber crashed into an Iraqi police post outside a U.S. Marine base at the small town of Baghadi in the al-Anbar, killing sixteen Iraqi policemen and wounding forty others.

Most of the action, however, bounded back and forth between al-Ramadi and Fallujah. On the twenty-fifth, three Iraqis were killed and four others injured during violent clashes between U.S. forces and armed men in eastern districts of Ramadi. The clashes erupted after a U.S. military headquarters, west of the city, was shelled.

There were black days for the Marines preparing for the assault. On October 30, eight U.S. Marines* were killed and ten others injured when

---

*KIA: Lance Cpl. Jeremy Bow, Lance Cpl. Michael Scarborough, Lance Cpl. Travis Fox, Cpl. Chistopher Lapka, Lance Cpl. John Byrd, Sgt. Kelley Courtney, Pfc. Andrew Riedel, Pfc. John Lukac

a car bomb exploded near Fallujah. That same day, the Fallujans subjected Marine positions outside the city to the strongest artillery barrage seen in weeks. The U.S. military responded by bombing Fallujah, attempting to hit a mortar emplacement. Ramadi saw further fighting on the thirtieth. The fighting left two policemen dead and four Iraqis injured. Three Marines were wounded.

On October 31, in Ramadi, a U.S. Marine* was killed and four others wounded. Three of the four were injured when a roadside bomb detonated beside their convoy. Throughout the day there was a cat and mouse game as insurgents fired rockets and mortars and fled.

For the soldiers repositioning troops to the buildup for Fallujah, just traveling the road could be exceptionally dangerous. On November 2, 2004, two platoons from Bravo Company, 1st Battalion, 160th Infantry Regiment, a California Army National Guard unit, rolled on a two-day escort mission in which troop-carrying trucks were ferrying Iraqi soldiers and equipment to Fallujah for the upcoming campaign. As they moved towards Fallujah, their convoy of nearly sixty American and Iraqi vehicles was attacked with an improvised explosive device and small-arms fire. No one was injured and only one Iraqi vehicle was disabled.

The next day, a rocket-propelled grenade slammed into one of the lead vehicles carrying Iraqi National Guardsmen. The disabled truck halted, the convoy was becoming what insurgents hoped would be easy prey. From nearby buildings and other concealed areas, insurgents opened up on the column of immobilized vehicles with two heavy machine guns, RPG's, and a hail of small-arms fire. Exposed on the four-lane highway with firing from every direction, they had to push through.

One of the trucks tried to drive around the ING vehicle that had been hit, but the Iraqi soldiers were already dismounting their trucks. The Iraqi soldiers were shooting in all directions and taking cover on the side of the road in a ditch. The trucks trying to move forward couldn't move around them. In the first truck trying to push through the kill zone was medic Spc. Gerrit Kobes. Unable to drive to the wounded, he grabbed his aid-bag and along with his platoon sergeant, ran to their position nearly a third of a mile ahead through the enemy fire. As they ran up, they found several Marines trying to organize a defense with the Iraqis. They also found four wounded Iraqis. One was badly hurt, with arterial bleeding on his right arm from shrapnel wounds. Some additional soldiers from Bravo Company's 4th platoon came up and laid down suppressive fire to repel the attackers as Kobes quickly applied a tourniquet to the wound and stopped the bleeding.

Looking around he saw that one Iraqi soldier had a head injury and

*KIA: 1st Lt. Matthew Lynch

a hole through his hand. Another's leg was bleeding and the fourth had shrapnel wounds on his face. Ignoring the combat around him, he treated the wounds. The soldier with the tourniquet appeared to be in a lot of pain so Kobes called for another American soldier, an infantryman with Bravo Company that spoke Arabic. He had the Arab-American soldier explain to the wounded Iraqi what he was doing and to told him everything was going to be all right. He also had Ibrahim tell him that Kobes was going to give him morphine to ease the pain.

By this time the leaders of the convoy had gained enough control to start the convoy on the move. Kobes once again exposed himself to fire as he loaded the wounded onto the Iraqi vehicles. The air snapped as it disappeared from bullets drilling through it, but the shooting towards their position was petering out. The ambushers were leaving.

While this was all going on Kobes found another Iraqi soldier, the one who took the brunt of the first RPG round during the attack that disabled the truck. A radioman was trying to call in a MEDEVAC helicopter for him. Kobes told them to call it off. It was too late. Kobes then ran to their vehicle and continued to Fallujah. It had happened all so fast and now it was over nearly as quickly.[*]

Meanwhile, U.S. warplanes were striking Fallujah in earnest on November 3. That day two Marines fell as the troops were massing.[†] The bombarding in preparation for the attack was not a one-sided affair. Rockets in particular were coming out of Fallujah. On November 5, one claimed the life of a soldier preparing for the assault.[‡] But there was a sense of relief. Soon, they would put an end to this waiting just outside of the hornets' nest called Fallujah.

For those outside of Fallujah there was a question to answer. Where would the counterstrike land? Each command watched the movements of the insurgents, carefully seeking a clue as to whether the insurgents would target them as the American Marines, backed by army tanks, were decisively engaged. To the south, U.S. troops were repositioning and asked that the British bring up the famed Black Watch to fill in as the American troops fought in Fallujah. This was no easy assignment, for the Americans were leaving the British Sunni enclaves that intelligence clearly showed insurgents were occupying as they were leaving Fallujah. The British agreed, but in Parliament there was considerable debate as opposition members of Parliament charged that the prime minister's move was endangering British troops to aid President Bush in his re-election effort.

---

*For Spc. Gerrit Kobes' actions he was awarded the Silver Star medal.
†KIA: Cpl. Jeremiah Baro, Lance Cpl. Jared Hubbard
‡KIA: Sgt. Carlos M. Camacho-Rivera

The 1st Cavalry Division braced itself as it was giving up forces to help in Fallujah. In and around Baghdad, a deadly battle continued, now with even higher stakes. On October 4, insurgents blew up a roadside bomb at Abu Ghraib on the western rim of Baghdad, killing one Iraqi and wounding three. Also in Baghdad, insurgents shot to death two persons working for the Ministry of Science and Technology. These attacks were by nationalist insurgents, but it was al-Zarqawi's far smaller group that was doing most of the killing.

Two massive car bombs blew up in Baghdad, killing twenty-one and wounding ninety-six. One bomb targeted recruits of the Iraqi army and police, who were lined up near the Green Zone. The other exploded near the hotels that foreigners usually stayed in.

In Baghdad on October 8, insurgents fired Katyusha rockets into the Sheraton Hotel, frequented by foreign contractors. No one was injured. But the news that jolted the intelligence people was the report of seizures of 1,500 artillery shells by U.S. troops when they stopped a truck in Baghdad. Artillery shells were commonly used in roadside bombs and car bombs. Fifteen hundred IEDs would make for the basis of a good-sized offensive in Baghdad come the start of the Fallujah campaign.

Two car bombs in Baghdad virtually at the same instant exploded, killing eleven and wounding dozens on October 10, one in the vicinity of a police academy in east Baghdad. Ten dead bodies, including three cadets at the police academy and a female officer, were brought to Kindi Hospital, along with fifteen injured. The other car bomb went off at a market as a U.S. convoy went by. This bomb killed one U.S. soldier,[*] and one Iraqi civilian, and one person was injured. Monotheism and Holy War, al-Zarqawi's group, claimed credit for the two car-bombings. Also in Baghdad, insurgents assassinated an Iraqi intelligence officer on his way to work in the morning. The 1st Cavalry was hitting back, determined to clear out Haifa Street. A sharp gun battle erupted as neither side was willing to yield the territory. In the end, American firepower won out.

The next day in southern Baghdad, insurgents fired rockets, killing two American troops[†] and wounding five other U.S. soldiers.

On October 12, al-Zarqawi broke his usual pattern with a new wrinkle. Two bombs went off at 1:00 P.M. local time in Baghdad's Green Zone, killing ten people, four of which were American. Twenty more were injured; two were soldiers shopping for souvenirs. One bomb went off in an area known as the Vendors' Alley while another went off by the Green Zone Cafe. Monotheism and Holy War claimed credit for the attack.

---

[*]KIA: Pvt. Carson Ramsey
[†]KIA: Pvt. Anthony Monroe, Sgt. Pamela Osbourne

October 13, was just another day in Baghdad, as insurgents deto-nated several roadside bombs, killing one U.S. soldier.* As was the next, with two more deaths of American troops.†

But the tensions were starting to fray nerves in the capital on Octo-ber 15th, when a spectacular car bomb detonated in Baghdad. A speed-ing car charged the police headquarters in Dura at 9:45 A.M. About 500 pounds of explosives left at least ten Iraqi civilians killed and a dozen wounded. All the dead were civilians, including a family of four travel-ing in a car in the immediate vicinity of the blast site. Also that day, a leading member of the Iraqi Islamic Party was killed when U.S. forces opened fire on his car along the highway west of Baghdad. Anyone in a car coming up too quickly could be instantly killed.

On October 16, insurgents opened fire south of Baghdad on nine Iraqi policemen in a convoy that was returning from training classes in Jordan. The next day, insurgents detonated a car bomb near a Baghdad cafe frequented by Iraqi police, killing seven persons and wounding twenty. The police were having their evening meal to break the fast dur-ing Ramadan. Then there was a car bomb next to a police convoy in Jadiriyah. The explosion left six people dead, including three policemen, and injured twenty-six.

Intelligence was watching all of this closely and could not see a pat-tern in the capital itself, but there was clearly movement just to the south. It was worrisome, for from the Sunni towns close by, insurgents could quickly move either into Baghdad or against the British to cause politi-cal trouble. On October 19, in Iskandariyah south of Baghdad, Iraqi security forces and U.S. Marines made a sweep of the area, arresting 130 suspected insurgents.

Then it was back to the grinding violence as before. In western Bagh-dad late on the 20, insurgents detonated a roadside bomb, wounding three U.S. soldiers. Also in al-Durah district of southern Baghdad, insur-gents detonated a car bomb outside an Iraqi police station, wounding ten persons, five of which were policemen. Insurgents also detonated a car bomb on the road to the airport, attempting to hit U.S. Humvees, but the driver detonated too early. The soldiers went away only unnerved.

On the road out to the airport from Baghdad on the twenty-third, insurgents set off a roadside bomb as a Bradley Fighting Vehicle passed, wounding six U.S. soldiers. In downtown Baghdad, two mortar rounds landed. They killed two Iraqi civilians and injured another.

On October 27, a British force began moving out of the southern Iraqi city of Basra in a move north to take over operations from U.S.

---

*KIA: SPC Jeremy Regnier
†KIA: David Waters, Spc. Josiah Vandertulip

forces. The 850-strong battle group, led by the 1st Battalion of the Black Watch, took up stations and waited to see what would happen. Throughout the military bases in Baghdad, commanders looked at their intelligence officers and asked: is it coming our way? Baghdad violence continued with other losses but at a measurably lower rate than in September. The answer was universal; if there was a repositioning of forces for an offensive in Baghdad, the insurgents had hidden it too well for the Coalition to see.

Throughout the Sunni triangle as well, the story was the same: continued violence but at a slightly reduced level as before. There were no large groups gathering, no big stockpiles of weapons and munitions found.

Attention, however, was focusing back on Samarra. Samarra was a poster child of what Fallujah would look like. Therefore, military officials were keen to maintain it as a success. The 1st Infantry Division was also watching the people who fled to Fallujah now coming back to Samarra, only in larger numbers as Fallujah was emptying out.

On October 20, clashes in Samarra left eleven U.S. soldiers wounded, with eight civilians killed and twelve wounded. Also in Samarra, insurgents detonated two car bombs, killing one child and wounding a translator. In the village of Ishaqi near Samarra on the twenty-third, another suicide bomber set off his payload near a checkpoint maintained by Iraqi National Guards, killing four and wounding six. Insurgents in Samarra itself set off a roadside bomb, killing two more Iraqi policemen. In Samarra on the twenty-fifth, a U.S. military vehicle was damaged after being hit by an explosive device in al-Sikak neighborhood. If it happened this way in Fallujah, most people would count the retaking of the city as a failure.

The big news of the month for Iraqis came on October 24, when the bodies of more than forty Iraqi army recruits were found following an ambush near the Iranian border in the northeast of the country. It was clearly an execution. Many were found dead lying face down by the roadside with a single bullet wound to the head. There was an uproar over the news as the recruits were assigned to a training camp under the control of the Americans. The prime minister accused the U.S. Army of incompetence. They in turn stated that the recruits had left unarmed, without an escort because they were in a hurry to go on leave.

All of the executed Iraqi soldiers were Shi'a from the south. There was a deep sense of resentment in the Shi'ite-dominated press at the coldness of the killings. Most blamed al-Zarqawi, but the anger was being directed at Baa'thist and Sunni nationalist insurgents as well. On a regular basis in the Shi'a south, the term "resistance fighter" was being dropped from the language and "terrorist" taking its place.

Intelligence was now seeing a pattern distinguishing the combined foreign and native Salafi fighters from the nationalist insurgents. Both were far more sophisticated than a year before, but the nationalists were more discriminating in their targets. They used IEDs in ambushes and indirect fire, and then melted away. Sometimes, they would resort to car bombs, but nearly always by parking them first. They then detonated them remotely.

The religious radicals, however, usually used suicide attacks and did not care how many civilians they killed. The casualties caused were about the same numbers from both, but the nationalists were far and away a larger group.

For Brigadier General Ham, Mosul was increasingly violent. Salafi groups were filtering into the Arab neighborhoods from Fallujah.

On the fourth, one of al-Zarqawi's group's suicide bombs killed three persons in Mosul. On the eleventh, a Salafi bomber detonated his car bomb in front of a U.S. military convoy, killing at least one U.S. soldier[*] and two Iraqis, and injuring twenty-seven persons. Other attackers fired at the convoy from a mosque after the explosion and then disappeared. On October 13, an army civil affairs team was targeted by a car bomb killing two.[†]

By the middle of October the violence was intensifying. October 15 brought a car bomb that killed a soldier.[‡] In Mosul, on October 17, Salafis detonated a car bomb on a bridge. They killed five Iraqis and wounded fifteen others. The next day, a car-bomber ran into a civilian convoy, leaving one dead and four wounded. In Dhuluiyah on October 19, in the north, Iraqi National Guardsmen and U.S. forces were trying to police up any trouble spots. The clashes left two Iraqis dead, ten wounded, and eighteen detained. Meanwhile, in Mosul, Zarqawi's group detonated three car bombs but only killed two Iraqi civilians and wounded three. One car-bomber was trying to get the governor of Ninevah, who was thought to be in the convoy. In fact, he was not present. Another car-bomber had aimed at a U.S. military convoy, but only managed to inflict minor injuries on one U.S. soldier.

If the Salafi groups were any indication of where the expected counterstrike might occur, General Ham believed he knew where it would happen.

But what worried the military most was the political side. Last April in Fallujah, it was not the generals that pulled the plug; it was the politicians. Even as the MNFI was making intensive preparations to take Fal-

---

KIA: Staff Sgt. Michael Burbank
†*KIA: Lt. Col. Mark Phelan, Maj. Charles Soltes*
‡*KIA: Spc. Alan Burgess*

lujah, there were almost desperate efforts by others to avoid the military onslaught.

There was a sense by a number of anti–American groups that the elections could be delayed if there were areas the interim government could not control. A delay would likely result in Shi'a cities' following Fallujah's example. With Fallujah a safe-haven other Sunni cities could be added to the number of places outside of central government control even if the Americans kept coming in to reoccupy them. As soon as the combat forces would leave, it would be back to business as usual.

This would mean that any election conducted would have to be on the terms of the Sunni, and their first term was for the Americans to leave.

On October 5, interim Prime Minister Ayad Allawi again was sounding a warning to Fallujah and the neighboring city of Ramadi to shun violence or face the consequences.

While Moqtada al-Sadr was busy dealing to save his position in al-Sadr City, negotiations were also ongoing over Fallujah. As of October 6, the Fallujans were offering to have the Iraqi National Guard maintain security in Fallujah. A so-called Fallujah protection force comprising residents of the city and nearby areas would join the guardsmen. The U.S.-led forces would continue to remain outside Fallujah, complying with a key demand of the fighters. The Fallujans promptly called al-Jazeera saying that a deal was nearly completed.

The offer was not even considered either at Camp Victory or the Green Zone. It was clear that this additional force would be used to house the insurgents and foreign fighters they saw as loyal to continued resistance.

President Ghazi al-Yawar of Iraq, a Sunni, was feverishly trying to negotiate a cease-fire though his influence with local clan elders in Fallujah in the first week of October. He was offering a similar deal being offered to Moqtada al-Sadr. He was the politician with the most to lose with another assault. But the negotiations were going nowhere due to the foreign fighters and their radicalized Iraqi recruits. The city fathers of Fallujah could not convince their followers to give up the insurgency, which they viewed as legitimate. Neither could they separate the foreigners from the draw of al-Zarqawi.

On October 13, Allawi laid out what he saw as the non-negotiable starting point to the 100-member interim parliament. "We have asked Fallujah residents to turn over Zarqawi and his group. If they don't do it, we are ready for major operations in Fallujah." Mr. Allawi in his speech was blunt: "We will not be lenient."

The military now was doing everything it could to reinforce this sense of impending battle, and it was starting to have a clear effect. Just as with Samarra, people were leaving, only in greater numbers.

On October 14, U.S. troops started encircling Fallujah and reinforcing forces in ar-Ramadi. As more troops started to marshal, there was a sense within the city that this was the last chance to leave. Military officials had no doubt that many of the males of military age who were leaving were insurgents. But they were in such large numbers that to hold tens of thousands of males on the grounds that they were from Fallujah was neither politically nor legally plausible. Besides, there was no place to put them.

There was no ID system in Iraq, although there was some talk about how to establish one in May of 2004. With no driver's licenses or ID cards other than a food ration card, there was no way to distinguish one person from another.

In the meantime, as the Americans were repositioning troops and the air strikes multiplied, a delegation of city elders and leaders pulled out of talks with the Iraqi interim government, protesting against the threats by Ayad Allawi. He was clear that the city would be invaded if it did not hand over al-Zarqawi and his supporters. In light of the continued car-bombings that were killing increasing numbers of civilians, this demand was only improving his standing for the upcoming elections.

On the Fallujan side there was defiance. One Fallujan delegate said, "Allawi and his government will bear the responsibility of the spilling of Muslim blood in Fallujah." He said delegates were close to reaching a breakthrough in talks that would allow Iraqi forces to come back into the city before Allawi imposed "impossible conditions."

In Baghdad, the government's national security adviser, Qasim Dawud, said he hoped the delegates could mediate a truce and rid the city of foreign fighters to avert a military showdown. "I hope they kick them out, otherwise we are preparing to crush them."

The government was also trying to affect the leadership of the Fallujan negotiations, hoping to seed them with people willing to turn on al-Zarqawi. At the urging of Prime Minister Ayad Allawi, on October 19, the U.S. released from custody Sheikh Khalid al-Jumaili, who had engaged in peace talks with the insurgents in Fallujah. The U.S. had arrested this negotiator and interrogated him. Al-Jumaili was leading his own militant group separate from a majority of those in the de facto city-state.

It turned out to be a mistake for as soon as he was released, al-Jumaili lost credibility and the city's insurgent leadership told him he no longer represented them. That same day, the clerics in Fallujah called for a campaign of civil disobedience across Iraqi cities to forestall an American attack.

President Ghazi al-Yawir again pressed Allawi about the possibility of reviving peace talks between the U.S. military and the leaders in

Fallujah. While negotiations were ongoing to avoid the crushing of Fallujan independence, Abu Musab al-Zarqawi had other plans on how to expand his influence both inside and outside of Iraq. He changed the name of his organization from Monotheism and Holy War to "Mesopotamian al-Qaeda."

To nearly everyone in Fallujah, the realization had come that the crisis was not going to abate and that the Americans were in fact coming. The clerics and other leaders of Fallujah held a convention to devise a common front to avoid the assault and save their independence. The Association of Muslim Scholars, the Consultative Council of Fallujah, the mayor, the delegation of negotiators with the government and "the League of al-Anbar Clerics" had all assembled in the town hall to discuss renewing negotiations with the Iraqi government. The meeting only highlighted the conflict within the Sunni groups. Some sought to dare the invasion, looking for a final battle. Others, watching the exodus, knew that without the civilians to shield the defenders, the Americans would be able to crush the city without the political outrage that saved the city before. After much arguing, some threats and intimidation, the result was a declaration of defiance.

On the twenty-first, they announced their position to the government. They urged the Iraqi government to halt the American air strikes. They had their own non-negotiable list of six conditions for renewing negotiations:

1. Bombing of the city must cease.
2. Families forced out must be allowed to return.
3. They must be paid compensation.
4. U.S. troops must withdraw from the city and from its main entryways.
5. Iraqi National Guardsmen must be the ones who provide security.
6. At least one-third of the National Guardsmen must be local Fallujans.

"We have entered the final phase to solve the Fallujah problem," Allawi told a news conference in Baghdad. "If we cannot solve it peacefully, I have no choice but to take military action. I will do so with a heavy heart." The Iraqi prime minister offered three conditions that would spare Fallujah: the exit of foreign fighters and insurgents, handing over of heavy and medium-sized weapons and allowing the government to begin the process of reconstruction. From Fallujah there was defiant silence in return.

The Sunni establishment, now desperate to fend off the attack on Fallujah, was finding no support from the Shi'ites. President Ghazi al-Yawir (a Sunni) met a delegation from (Shi'ite) Karbala on October 27. He said a way must be found for Iraqis to prevent a U.S. attack on Fallujah and other Iraqi cities. There was polite sympathy but it was clear there would not be any condemnation prior to the crushing of the city-state. When asked privately what was the reason for the lack of support, one word was repeatedly uttered: Zarqawi.

United Nations special envoy to Iraq, Ashraf Jahangir Qazi, held talks that same day with Shaikh Muhammad Bashar al-Faydi, a leader of the Association of Muslim Scholars. The UN wanted to discuss the AMS's attitude toward the January elections. They, in turn, wanted to talk about Fallujah. Qazi said that the UN was willing to take a more active negotiating role in Iraq if it might avert a Sunni Arab boycott of the elections. AMS was urging a boycott, in contrast to the Iraqi Islamic Party, which wanted Sunnis to come out in force. Neither came away with anything other than pleasantries.

The sense of abandonment by the Sunnis was now in the open. Shaikh Mahdi al-Sumaid'i of the Association of Muslim Scholars preached before hundreds of worshipers at the Ibn Taimiyah Mosque in Baghdad. He said that a meeting would be called to address the "marginalization of the Sunnis" and the crushing of their personality. He said that during the Najaf crisis, they had stood as a single man against the American operation.

The signals from the Shi'a were only all the more discouraging for the Sunni. Grand Ayatollah al-Sistani met with the Chaldean Patriarch, a Christian Reader. The grand ayatollah urged Christian Iraqis to vote and condemned attacks on Christian churches by what he called "kafirs." The militant, radical Muslim fundamentalists often declared other Muslims to be unbelievers. The practice of declaring some Muslims to actually be "kafirs" or infidels was controversial and unusual for al-Sistani.

Muhammad Bashar al-Faidi, a spokesman of the Association of Muslim Scholars, warned on November 2 that if there was an assault on Fallujah his clerical group would use "mosques, the media and professional associations" to proclaim a civil disobedience campaign and a boycott of the January elections.

Just as the Marines were entering into their final stages before the invasion, UN Secretary General Kofi Annan sent in a letter to the United States, Britain and Iraq officials criticizing the impending invasion of Fallujah. Within MNFI, there was outrage at the last-ditch effort to stop the battle. When pressed by the media, Annan declined to comment on the letter but suggested that the offensive would make it harder for some Iraqis to accept any result from the election.

U.S. State Department spokesman Richard Boucher acknowledged differences with Annan, saying, "In this regard, frankly, we differ. The

Iraqi government has made very clear that they do have a strategy for resolving the problems of these towns like Fallujah."

With the end of the election in the United States, the politicians on board, and careful preparations, General Casey was ready to start the battle which he hoped would set the stage for the upcoming elections. His arguments that just sitting back passively would increase casualties, while taking it to the enemy would save both American and Iraqi lives, seemed to be justified. For the entire month of October there were fifty-six killed in action and 641 wounded, a significant drop from September. The fighting in November would likely double that but with the safe-haven eliminated the cost in American lives would decrease. Once the elections were over, he felt sure that most of the cost in blood for a democratic Iraq would be from Iraqis.

The early days of November were proving the prediction of casualties too true. Zarqawi had ordered a series of car bombs just prior to the invasion of Fallujah. Seven soldiers and Marines died.*

---

*KIA: Spc. Cody Wentz, Pvt. Scott McArdle (Brit. Army), Pvt. Paul Lowe (Brit. Army), Lance Cpl. Jared Hobb and, Sgt. Stuart Gray, Cpl. Jeremiah Baro, Pvt. Justin Yoemans

CHAPTER 18

The Fall of Fallujah

As the final preparations for the assault were made, the C9 (Directorate of Civil Military Operations) was preparing its estimates of the civilians likely to be in the way. Imagery suggested that the warnings had been nearly completely successful in draining the city. The place looked deserted from the air. At most, thousands was the guess that might be in the way, maybe not even that. Nearly every able-bodied man in the sights of the Marines and soldiers would be combatants, was the estimate. "Five thousand is my bet," said a colonel on the general staff. That many could be cared for with food and water by the civil affairs teams without interfering with combat operations, removing the need to bring in outsiders. Things were ready for a real battle. Now, would the insurgents only stand and fight?

U.S. commanders estimated that 2,000 to 2,500 fighters were inside the city and its surrounding areas. The MNFI, C2 figured that another 10,000 men could fight elsewhere, although they were not sure where. Some 20,000 U.S. and Iraqi troops had been massing around Fallujah since mid–October and the offensive was about to erupt.

U.S. artillery shelled Fallujah on the second, after overnight air and tank attacks. The targets now were fighting positions. An intense half-hour bombardment of eastern and northwestern areas by AC-130 planes and tanks shook the city late the next night.

The Iraqi battalions preparing to invade were of a different sort than the ones that mutinied en masse last April. But the results were mixed. The Iraqi troops, established as Special Operations, were eager to start the fight. But one Iraqi battalion had shrunk from over 500 men down to 170 over the past two weeks, with 255 members quitting. One was the commander. Meanwhile another GI fell in Fallujah.*

On November 6, the Marines and army were starting in earnest the preparation for the battle through targeted artillery strikes. This was different from the wholesale use of the 155mm guns used in conventional

---

*KIA: Sgt. Carlos Camacho-Rivera

war, often firing just one gun at a time at a single target. But the sound of continuous incoming artillery was a clear signal. The Americans were coming.

Allawi, who spoke excellent English, visited some of the 12,000 troops staged to actually invade the city. "The people of Fallujah have been taken hostage just like the people of Samarra and you need to free them from their [the insurgents'] grip," he told the soldiers.

"Your job is to arrest the killers, but if you kill them then let it be," he said, warning the soldiers not to harm civilians.

On November 7, Allawi declared martial law for two months. He also ordered a curfew in Fallujah and the closure of Baghdad's international airport. That day, U.S. forces bombed Fallujah and advanced on the city. Two Marines were injured by a car bomb near a Fallujah checkpoint, and a U.S. soldier was wounded when a roadside bomb exploded south of Fallujah. The casualties were thus far light.*

Loudspeakers on top of PSYOPS Humvees declared in Arabic as they drove around the outskirts of the city. "Attention, attention! All men aged between 15 and 50 are forbidden from entering or exiting. Only women and children are allowed to leave on condition that they will not return until order is restored." Leaflets were also being dropped telling males how to surrender to U.S. troops without being shot, should combatants wish to do so.

All expected that starting the next day the death notices for U.S. servicemen would start streaming to homes in America. But that day came with its own cost with a loss of two.† Three additional British soldiers were killed three days before.

In the city of Ramadi, just west of Fallujah, insurgents massed on the main street after U.S. snipers withdrew from their positions and banners were hung in the windows proclaiming solidarity with insurgents in the neighboring city. Throughout the Fallujah fighting, Ramadi was a problem. "Almost every time we went out, we got hit. It was unreal," said one navy corpsman stationed there.

An explosion of violence in Ramadi on the seventh and eighth left thirty dead and some sixty wounded, including fourteen wounded Marines. One Marine QRF responding to an attack on Echo Company had it particularly rough. The patrol rolled into a daisy chain of several 155mm shells as IEDs. A series of explosions rocked the first armored Humvee.‡ The IEDs blasted the vehicle with shrapnel, tearing chunks out

---

*Sgt. Michael Smith was mortally wounded and died twenty days later.
†KIA: Lance Cpl. Sean M. Langley and Spc. Brian Baker
‡In the Humvee were Sgt. Sam Pennock and Cpl. David Kammerer, of the U.S. Marines, and HM2 Nathan McDonell, of the U.S. Navy. Cpl Mark O'Bien stayed in the Humvee to man the machine gun to cover the others and was severely injured.

of the armor plating and blowing holes through the rear fenders. With their Humvee crippled by the IEDs, three crewmembers quickly dismounted and began laying down suppressive fire with their M-16s while the fourth stayed in the vehicle to shoot back with the machine gun.

These insurgents were well trained and well disciplined, not anything like the amateurs that fought in al-Sadr City. The insurgents had used the attack of Echo Company as bait for this ambush. The insurgents stayed and fought it out at close range with the Marines. Then came the RPGs.

One rocket-propelled grenade hit the first Humvee and the explosion severed the leg of the Marine manning the machine gun. The corpsman got up and ran through the fire to pull the wounded Marine from the line of fire. The patrol fought for a good two to three hours before the insurgents were forced to withdraw, leaving their dead and wounded.

Late on November 8 a two-pronged assault on Fallujah began. The hospital and two bridges over the Euphrates River were the first targets in the assault. U.S. forces seized the hospital first to provide medical care but also in the expectation that the presence of embedded reporters at the hospital would prevent inflated reporting of civilian casualties.

The troops detained about fifty men of military age inside the hospital, but about half were later released. The troops used special tools, powered by .22 caliber blanks, to break open door locks with a rifle-like crack. Many patients were handcuffed until troops determined whether they were insurgents hiding in the hospital. A barrage of rocket, mortar, and gunfire rained down as Iraqi troops tried to raise the new Iraqi flag above the hospital.

The first casualty reports were also coming in. A Marine* was killed when his bulldozer flipped over into the Euphrates River. He was busy preparing a fighting position when the ground gave way. Those handling the big dozers would turn out to be some of the bravest and most useful troops of the battle. The huge machines, as large as a small house, would flatten defensive positions while the defenders were still in them.

Some troops, backed by the 1st Cavalry Division's tanks and armor, advanced slowly on the northwestern Jolan neighborhood, a maze of alleyways where insurgents had dug in. At the same time, some 4,000 troops, backed by tanks and armor, went into the northeastern Askari district. Intelligence had plotted a number of IEDs, so as they entered Jolan, the Marines smashed through a railway line and advanced through fields to avoid using the main roads. They moved house-to-house through the neighborhood, seen as the heart of rebel activity in Fallujah, spraying rounds of machine-gun fire at buildings from where militants fought back with small-arms fire. Not a civilian was in sight. Chickens and a few farm animals ran around amid a constant clatter of AK fire and explosions.

*KIA: Cpl. Joshua D. Palmer

The Marines called the offensive "Phantom Fury." The more politically sensitive Iraqis didn't like the name. Iraqi Defense Minister Sheikh Hazem Shaalan said. "We've called it Operation Dawn. God willing, it's going to be a new, happy dawn for the people of Fallujah."

By the end of the eighth of November, the staffs of the various assault elements were recapping the day's events. The attack was going ahead of schedule. There was some stiff resistance in places, but it was not as heavy as they expected. The casualties among the Americans were not as high either. The Marines had lost in combat only three.[*]

"Either they're falling back or they are not there in the first place," said one lieutenant colonel. "I think they might have left, but to where? Someone will have hell to pay."

One of those places turned out to be in Babil Province. The Marines lost four more[†] to insurgents and the British one. In Baghdad as well the cost was high with three soldiers lost.[‡]

By midnight, one element of troops advanced 800 yards into the city as they picked their way past the IEDs with few casualties. But others came under heavy fire and spent hours breaking through a single line of houses. There too were intense street clashes in the denser neighborhoods. U.S. troops moved roof-to-roof to secure buildings as machine gun-equipped Humvees patrolled the streets already secured.

The mosques were where the resistance was heaviest. The 1st Battalion of the 8th Marine regiment found one large insurgent element that was willing to put up a determined defense. Before the mosque was secured the Marines killed 70 in one building alone.

U.S. troops surged into rubble-strewn districts in the heart of Fallujah on the ninth, after seizing one third of the city after hours of street fights. "As for casualties on the insurgents' side, I can tell you that they are dying. A lot of them are dying and this is a good thing," Marine spokesman Lieutenant Lyle Gilbert said.

The troops on the ground were amazed at the tactics the insurgents were using. Modern armies are centered on teamwork, combined arms, and discipline. The insurgents tried to make up for a lack of that with courage and a form of volunteerism that was foreign to the Americans.

As expected, each of the mosques was an outpost for the insurgents. But they were also command and control centers as well. In each were snipers that would serve as forward command posts. As the American troops and Marines approached, the snipers would take the attackers

---

[*]*KIA: Staff Sgt. David G. Ries, Cpl. Robert P. Warns II, Lance Cpl. Thomas J. Zapp*

[†]*KIA: Cpl. Nathaniel T. Hammond, Lance Cpl. Branden P. Ramey, Lance Cpl. Shane K. O'Donnell*

[‡]*KIA: Spc. Don A. Clary, Spc. Bryan L. Freeman, Staff Sgt. Clinton L. Wisdom, Sgt. Quoc Tran*

under fire. The small force in the mosque then raised a black flag and started to call on others in the city to come to the battle using the loud-speakers each mosque had for the call to prayer. Groups of insurgents, sometimes as many as fifty, more often in the tens or only a few, would race to the battle and counter-attack in a disjointed manner. Sometimes no one would show up at all.

Soldiers and Marines would assault these command posts having to pay even more attention to their flanks and rear than the defended mosques. The counterattacks, though disconcerting, were not effective. On a regular basis, the infantry squads would stop the attacks and a new firefight would ensue in the direction of the buildings where the coun-terattackers took refuge. The loss to the insurgents using this tactic was ghastly and more often than not, dozens of insurgents would be killed with no loss to the Americans. But then, the clearing operation would occur. It was here that the casualties mounted.

IEDs were common. While many of the insurgents when wounded would surrender, others were willing to play dead only to rise and throw a grenade. The use of a white flag to fake surrender only to open fire was common.

In the planned assaults, along with attacking troops were units of Iraqi National Guard, solely for storming the mosques. Soldiers and Marines would secure the area around a mosque and only then the ING squad would appear, busting through the door. As it became clear that all of the mosques were so dangerous, and the ING were still so green, things were going too slowly with each mosque. The tactic was modified. Once in the mosque itself, the Americans took over and cleared the build-ing. The tactic was done to avoid the bad press but the only ones there reporting were the embedded press, who seemed not to care that much.

There were mixed results as far as the Iraqi troops were concerned. Some fought well, while others cowered or were so undisciplined with their fire that they frightened the American troops. There as well were several incidents where insurgents, dressed in ING uniforms, attacked American troops. But where the Iraqis worked best was securing the rear and checking out the houses, although several commanders noted that the reason they excelled in clearing the houses once the fighting passed was that they were in fact burglarizing them.

Meanwhile, to the south of Fallujah, elements of the 1st Cavalry Division, the Black Watch, and Iraqi forces set up blocking positions to intercept insurgents that escaped the fighting.

The political fallout was starting in reaction to the fighting in Fallu-jah. On November 8, the al-Sadr movement issued a statement forbid-ding the participation of Iraqi troops in the attack on Fallujah. The statement said, "We direct an appeal at the men in the Iraqi forces, whether national guards or others, the majority of whom are Muslim, calling upon them to refrain from committing this enormous sin under the banner of forces that do not respect our religion or any principles of basic humanity, and we ask them to view this war as illegal." It called a "ploy" the assertion that the attack was merely on foreign fighters at Fallujah.

The Association of Muslim Scholars, an influential Sunni clerical group, condemned the assault on Fallujah. The group had threatened to boycott elections. "The attack on Fallujah is an illegal and illegitimate action against civilian and innocent people. We denounce this operation which will have a grave consequences on the situation in Iraq," said spokesman Mohammed Bashar al-Faidhi.

The insurgents were doing their best to recreate the conditions that were so effective in April with phoned interviews claiming that twenty doctors were killed when the Americans bombarded a clinic erected to take the place of the hospital. The Arab press widely publicized the accounts, but were unable to provide the images, so there was not the sense of outrage as before.

Just how different the Fallujah battle was playing politically was now becoming apparent. In April, the threat of a pullout by the Sunnis sent the CPA leadership into a panic. Lt. General Sanchez and L. Paul Bremer would meet for hours trying to balance military factors with political considerations. Repeatedly, a sour General Sanchez would leave the meeting dejected over the restrictions placed upon his Marines.

The Association of Muslim Scholars forbade Iraqis to participate in the attack on Fallujah with the Americans. In a communiqué, the AMS said that for Iraqis to take part with "raiding forces" in the assault on a city the population of which was Muslim (such as Fallujah) would be considered the most mortal of mortal sins. The Sunni AMS told Iraqis, "You sinned when you participated with occupation forces in the assault on Najaf, and beware lest you repeat this same sin in Fallujah. Remember that the Occupation is ephemeral."

The Iraqi Islamic Party, led by Muhsin Abdul Hamid, was threatening to pull out of the Allawi caretaker government, just as it had with L. Paul Bremer the April before. The IIP had also been the main force urging Sunni Arabs to participate in the elections scheduled for January, and had been opposed in this stance by the Association of Muslim Scholars.

The Iraqi Islamic Party made good on its threat to pull out of the Allawi government over the assault on Fallujah. The IIP, less popular than the AMS, had tended to cooperate with the Americans.

The Iraqi Islamic Party had expelled from its ranks Hajim al-Hasani, the Minister of Industry, because he declined to resign from Allawi's cabinet as demanded by the party leadership. Throughout the leadership there was a sense of "Let them leave," and "So?" with each Sunni threat.

The AMS publicly blamed Allawi for what it characterized as the bloodletting in Fallujah, trying to turn up the political heat. "The interim Government of [Prime Minister] Ayad Allawi bears full legal and historical responsibility for the war of annihilation Fallujah is exposed to today at the hands of the occupation forces and militias of some parties in the interim Government." The Association of Muslim Scholars had been calling for a boycott of the election for some months.

A military spokesman estimated the number of insurgent dead as a result of the bombing and of artillery fire at ninety. Fallujah hospitals said that twelve civilians had been killed and seventeen wounded.

Ten U.S. troops died* in the fighting at Fallujah on the ninth, along with two Iraqi National Guardsmen. MNFI felt that so far they were getting off easy, even if another four servicemen were killed elsewhere in Iraq.† The fighting continued unabated on the tenth with all of the killed in action Marines or corpsmen.‡ In MNFI there was now an eye out for where the counterstrike would occur, but with action elsewhere scattered and only the loss of two others** there was still no clue.

Later on November 11, the U.S. arrested Sheikh Mahdi al-Sumaidi, a leader of the Salafi (Sunni fundamentalist) movement, who had denounced Grand Ayatollah Ali al-Sistani for declining to intervene in the Fallujah crisis. He also called for armed resistance against the Americans. The Americans raided the Ibn Taymiyah Mosque to get him (Ibn Taymiyah was a medieval-minded imam who preached Muslim intolerance of Christians).

On the fourth day, Marines found and detained Al-Saadi, an al-Arabiya reporter, inside a mosque. He was later released after questioning, but was not given access back into Fallujah. There was Arabic TV coverage of the fighting in Fallujah, however. Al-Iraqiya, the new Iraqi government-sponsored network, gave regular reporting and visual images to Iraqi TV stations. In the "cold war" days the U.S. military spend much of its training and tactical development on getting inside the decision cycle of an opposing commander, making the right decision before the enemy could react. After April, the Americans had painfully learned the importance of getting inside of the media cycle, effectively getting its political view of events out before its enemy could react.

---

*KIA: Marine Sgt. David Caruso, Cpl. William C. James, Lance Cpl. Nicholas Larson, Lance Cpl. Juan E. Segura, Lance Cpl. Abraham Simpson, Staff Sgt. Russell L. Slay, Sgt. Lonny D. Wells, Lance Cpl. Nathan R. Wood, Staff Sgt. Todd R. Cornell, Command Sgt. Maj. Steven W. Faulkenburg

†Master Sgt. Steven Auchman, Spc. Travis Babbitt, Maj. Horst Moore, and Sgt. John Trotter

‡KIA: Lance Cpl. Wesley J. Canning, Lance Cpl. Erick J. Hodges, Cpl. Romulo J. Jimenez II, 1st Lt. Dan T. Malcom Jr., Lance Cpl. Aaron C. Pickering, Staff Sgt. Gene Ramirez, Petty Officer 3rd Class Julian Woods, Cpl. Joseph Heredia

**KIA: Pfc. Dennis J. Miller Jr., Staff Sgt. Michael C. Ottolini

Al-Sistani and most other Shi'ite leaders refused Sunni pleas to denounce the invasion. Even Moqtada al-Sadr, who issued a communiqué, was not enthusiastic in opposing the Americans as he had been with the first battle of Fallujah.

With the majority of the city of Fallujah now effectively in American hands, Grand Ayatollah Ali al-Sistani called for a peaceful resolution of the conflict in Fallujah. His representative in Karbala, Ahmad al-Safi al-Najafi, said that the position of the grand ayatollah was that a peaceful resolution of the conflict was required. Speaking before thousands of worshipers at the Mosque of Imam Husain in Karbala, he said that the grand ayatollah had the same attitude to the fighting in Fallujah as he had to that in Najaf. There should be a peaceful solution on the basis of the sovereignty of the regime, law, and the evacuation of foreign forces and of gunmen with unlicensed arms. Al-Sistani also condemned all loss of innocent life. But he only called for peace in Fallujah when the result of the battle was a foregone conclusion. The evenhandedness of the criticism of the fighters was not what the Sunnis wanted.

On the 11th, two U.S. Super Cobra helicopters were downed in separate missions near the battle. A previously unknown group, the Green Brigade, member of the 1920 Revolution Brigades, claimed responsibility. The most dangerous part of the operation now was not over the city, but flying to and from the battle from the base. One of the most disappointing aspects of the operation since the start had been the failure of the military to clear Iraq of its anti-aircraft missiles. The military had offered to buy, no questions asked, any turned in by Iraqis. But the insurgents regularly paid twice the price the Americans offered.

The fighting in Fallujah had cost eighteen U.S. servicemen killed and 178 wounded. Five Iraqi soldiers were killed and 34 were wounded. Staff officers were warning that the cost would be much higher. So long as the defenders could withdraw, they would pull back. Hunting them down in determined defensive positions would be more costly.

On the eleventh, troops found a slaughterhouse for people and an Iraqi man chained to a wall in northeastern Fallujah. Bruised and starving, he told Marines he was a taxi driver abducted ten days prior and that his captors had beat him with cables. In the building there was a small, windowless room with straw mats covered with blood on the floor. Also found were a computer and a wheelchair, likely used to move bound hostages. There were documents of hostages, along with CDs showing beheadings and the black clothes like those worn in videotapes airing the executions. The Americans lost six more Marines and elsewhere two more soldiers.*

---

*KIA: 2nd Lt. James Blecksmith, Cpl. Theodore Bowling, Lance Cpl. Kyle Burns, Cpl. Peter Giannopoulos, SSG Theodore Holder II, Lance Cpl. Justin Reppuhn, SSG Sean Huey, Spc. Thomas Doerflinger

On the twelfth, U.S. soldiers started their advance into southern Fallujah. They now controlled eighty percent of the city, but the southern part was the most heavily fortified. But now that they were concentrated and the civilians were out of the way, the Marines were able to make better use of their artillery.

Now that they were getting into the hard core of the city the casualties were increasing. Six marines and two soldiers were lost that day.* The losses elsewhere showed a slight increase in activity with two other KIAs.† The next day the losses were slightly down with nine combined army and Marines dead.‡ The real question was where was the counterblow to land. The next day the action had been light with MNFI losing only one other soldier** to a mortar attack in Baghdad.

By November 14, there had been intense combat against the Fallujah insurgents. U.S. warplanes, tanks, and mortars left a shattered landscape of gutted buildings and bodies. Telegraph poles were down, human remains littered the vacant streets, concrete houses were flattened, mosques lay in ruins, power and phone lines hung slack in the rubble. Cars lay crushed in the middle of streets by the American tanks. The stench of human remains hung heavy in the air. The few remaining civilians said that most had left a long time ago.

The military leadership tallied the cost so far to thirty-eight Americans and six Iraqis killed in the assault and more than 200 U.S. soldiers injured for 1,200 insurgents killed. Another 400 had been captured.

The staff was particularly pleased with the lack of losses that day. The Marines had lost only four.†† "I suspect we will start seeing a lot more surrenders as we close in on the last," said one intelligence staff officer. "But, the fighting is not over."

As U.S. and Iraqi troops mopped up the last vestiges of the insurgency in the city, residents who stayed on through last week's offensive were emerging and telling harrowing tales.

Posters still hung on the walls bearing decrees from insurgent commanders to be heeded on pain of death. One decree, dated November 1, gave vendors three days to remove nine market stalls from outside the city's library or face execution. The troops were finding improvised jails in houses throughout the city.

*KIA: Cpl. Nathan R. Anderson, Lance Cpl. Nicholas H. Anderson, Sgt. Morgan W. Strader, Lance Cpl. David M. Branning, 1st Lt. Edward D. Iwan, Sgt. James C. Matteson, Lance Cpl. Brian A. Medina, Sgt. Jonathan B. Shields

†KIA: Spc. Raymond L. White, Cpl. Jarrod Maher

‡KIA: Lance Cpl. Benjamin S. Bryan, Cpl. Kevin J. Dempsey, Lance Cpl. Justin M. Ellsworth, Lance Cpl. Victor R. Lu, Lance Cpl. Justin D. McLeese, Sgt. Byron W. Norwood, Capt. Sean P. Sims, Spc. Jose A. Velez, Sgt. Catalin Dima

**KIA: Sgt. Catalin Dima

††Cpl. Dale A. Burger Jr., Lance Cpl. George J. Payton, Cpl. Andres H. Perez, Cpl. Nicholas L. Ziolkowski

Another hard-line cleric, Abdullah Junab, warned all women that they must cover up from head to toe outdoors, or face execution. Two female bodies discovered suggested that such decrees were enforced.

U.S. forces continued attacking diehard positions in south Fallujah, including an underground bunker complex of steel-reinforced tunnels. The Iraqi Red Crescent was planning to come in but abandoned plans after being refused entry by U.S. forces, who denied that there was any humanitarian emergency. Civil affairs teams had things well under control. The seven-truck convoy instead headed to nearby villages, where tens of thousands of refugees from Fallujah were housed.

Not all of the people they came upon were hostile. There were people happy to see the retaking of Fallujah, and the Marine Public Affairs officers were eager to get them in front of embedded news reporters. An elderly man, in only his underwear and suffering from shrapnel wounds, cursed the insurgents as he greeted the advancing Marines. "I wish the Americans had come here the very first day and not waited eight months," he said, trembling.

One member of the Sufi sect, followers of a mystical form of worship deemed non–Islamic by the hardliners, told how he and other members of his order had lived in terror inside their homes for fear of the Salafis. Another elderly man said he was detained by the militants and held for four days before being freed. He said, "We suffered from the bombings. Innocent people died or were wounded by the bombings. But, we were happy you did what you did because the Mujahadeen had suffocated Fallujah. Anyone considered suspicious would be slaughtered. We would see unknown corpses around the city all the time."

Marines were now able to offer tours to mosques that had been used as weapons stores and fighting positions by the defenders.

Fighting continued in Fallujah on November 15, as some insurgents fought to the death. That day, Ayad Allawi announced that he was sure there had been no civilian casualties in Fallujah. Both his people within the Iraqi ministries and the Americans were saying that they had overestimated the numbers of non-combatants in Fallujah prior to the battle. There was a consensus that the numbers not participating in the fighting were in the hundreds, not thousands.

The most dangerous job was clearing Fallujah's houses. The fighting sometimes became intense and personal. On November 15, one of the first Marines to enter one of the houses, Sergeant Rafael Peralta, was shot in the face by an AK47 from a room near the entry door. The wounded Marine did not have to take part in the clearing of the building in the first place, being assigned to another job, but volunteered to go in with the other Marines. Moments later, a fragmentation grenade rolled into the room where the wounded Peralta and other Marines were seeking cover. Two other Marines scrambled to escape the blast, banging against a locked door. Peralta grabbed the grenade and cradled it into his body. One of the other Marines was badly wounded by shrapnel from the blast, but both of Peralta's comrades survived. The casualties reflected just how difficult the fighting was becoming. Twelve Marines were lost that day.*

The stories of heroism were becoming commonplace. One involved the grandson of famed test pilot Chuck Yeager, who was a corporal in the Marines. As the Marines cleared an apartment building, they got to the top floor and the first man kicked in the door. As he did so, an enemy grenade and a burst of gunfire came out. The explosion and enemy fire took off the point man's leg. He was then immediately shot in the arm as he lay in the doorway.

Corporal Yeager tossed a grenade in the room, which would take five seconds to explode, then ran into the doorway and into the enemy fire in order to pull his comrade back to cover. As he was dragging the wounded Marine, his own grenade came back through the doorway.

Without pausing, he reached down and threw the grenade back through the door while he heaved his buddy to safety. The grenade went off inside the room and Cpl. Yeager threw another in. He immediately entered the room following the second explosion. He gunned down three enemy, all within three feet of where he stood, and then let fly a third grenade as he backed out of the room to complete the evacuation of the wounded Marine.

The losses on November 16 slowed down with two more Marine deaths in Fallujah[†] and another two elsewhere.[‡] Artillery and mortars pounded Fallujah on November 17, and troops hunted insurgents. The question on most of the military's minds was whether they had gotten lucky and al-Zarqawi had stayed. From the beginning, intelligence assumed that he was gone along with the leaders of his organization.

Meanwhile, in Ramadi, nine Iraqis were killed and fifteen wounded when U.S. forces confronted large groups of rocket and mortar-firing gunmen who fanned out through the streets. But the casualties of the day were uncharacteristically light throughout Iraq with Fallujah providing the only death.[**] The next day only another two were lost.[††] From the distance, the picture looked rosy, and there was a sense that the whole Fallujah operation was settling into a remarkable and, in relative terms, bloodless success. The MNFI C2 people were still pointing out that there

---

*KIA: Lance Cpl. Jeramy A. Ailes, Lance Cpl. Travis R. Desiato, Lance Cpl. Shane E. Kielion, Lance Cpl. William L. Miller, Lance Cpl. Bradley L. Parker, Sgt. Rafael Peralta, Capt. Patrick Marc M. Rapicault, Cpl. Marc T. Ryan, Lance Cpl. Antoine D. Smith, Lance Cpl. James E. Swain, Cpl. Lance M. Thompson, Cpl. Nicholas L. Ziolkowski.
†Sgt. Christopher T. Heflin, Lance Cpl. Louis W. Qualls
‡1st Lt. Luke C. Wullenwaber, Pfc. Jose Ricardo Flores-Mejia
**KIA: Lance Cpl. Michael W. Hanks
††KIA: Lance Cpl. Luis A. Figueroa, Sgt. Joseph M. Nolan

was another shoe to drop, it just hadn't yet. On the nineteenth, five Marines were lost* in what was still heavy fighting in room-to-room searches. The twentieth looked better throughout Iraq with two lost in Fallujah† and one elsewhere.‡ Then, on the twenty-first, mouths dropped open when not a single serviceman died in Iraq. The next day they lost two,** and the day after they lost only one.††

By now the operation in Fallujah was avoiding all of the pitfalls of the April before, and the leadership was starting to congratulate itself. Then a videotape of a Marine shooting what appeared to be an unarmed wounded man circulated from an embedded reporter.

A group of Marines had earlier fought their way into a mosque and wounded several Iraqis. After providing first aid, they left the wounded to be picked up by follow-on forces. A second team of Marines came into the mosque. Upon seeing the wounded Iraqi, one Marine started shouting that the wounded man was pretending to be dead and shot him. This second team of Marines had not known that a previous team had left these wounded insurgents in the mosque for subsequent medical pickup, assumed that they were active combatants, and that one of them might be a suicide bomber only pretending to be dead.

The Arab press expressed horror and outrage. Unlike U.S. news outlets, al-Jazeera and other news stations actually showed the prisoner being shot, which made the footage more powerful. For the MNFI commander, the incident created an immediate diversion from the fighting. General Casey assured the prime minister that an urgent inquiry was underway and that he would share its findings with the Iraqi government in full and with complete transparency.

Execution of wounded, unarmed combatants violated Article Three of the Geneva Convention, Relative to the Treatment of Prisoners of War, which stated in part that "persons taking no active part in the hostilities, including members of armed forces who have laid down their arms and those placed hors de combat by sickness, wounds, detention, or any other cause, shall in all circumstances be treated humanely."

Ambassador to Iraq John Negroponte apologized to Prime Minister Ayad Allawi and vowed that "the individual in question will be dealt with." Lieutenant General John F. Sattler, commander of the 1st Marine Expeditionary Force in Iraq, added in an interview, "We follow the law of armed conflict and hold ourselves to a high standard of accountability."

---

*KIA: Cpl. Bradley T. Arms, Lance Cpl. Demarkus D. Brown, Lance Cpl. Michael A. Downey, Lance Cpl. Dimitrios Gavriel, Lance Cpl. Phillip G. West
†KIA: Spc. David L. Roustum, Cpl. Joseph T. Welke
‡KIA: Cpl. Joseph J. Heredia
**KIA: Cpl. Michael Cohen
††KIA: Sgt. Benjamin Edinger

The instant controversy highlighted a contradiction in the lives of those in combat. The rules as applied to the reality of war in Iraq were not clear at all, especially in an environment where suicide bombers did everything they could to appear as non-combatants and wounded combatants would feign death to continue combat. Some called the practice of shooting at fallen combatants "dead-checking."

When clearing rooms, each body would be shot to keep up the momentum as the fighting progressed. To stall combat by checking each person for weapons in the middle of a clearing operation would endanger everyone in the unit. Speed and shock were critical to clearing a building because if given time, the defenders would reposition to the oncoming threat, or worse, take advantage of the pause to toss a grenade into the room. There also was the ever-present threat of the wounded producing an easily concealed grenade and attacking from the rear.

At the same time troops were now being drilled not to use suppressive fire when they came under fire. Suppressive fire was the military tactic of shooting into suspected enemy positions in order to force the enemy to keep their heads down, making it impossible to shoot as the Americans maneuvered to a place where a killing shot could be acquired. Stung by the repeated complaints and the damage caused by civilian casualties, the military issued orders to always identify a target, discouraging suppressive fire. Soldiers and Marines were regularly coming under fire and not answering back for fear of hitting civilians. The disciplined and necessary response often created in the minds of soldiers and Marines a contradiction, which under the stress of combat induced adrenaline, fear, and lack of sleep. The order seemed incomprehensible and unattainable. This dilemma of war acted itself out repeatedly not only in the direct combat of Fallujah but on checkpoints and guard posts throughout Iraq. On a regular basis, guards would face an oncoming car with less than a second to decide whether or not to fire. Mistakes regularly occurred with innocent families shot to death and with soldiers blown apart by car bombs.*

Throughout the Sunni Triangle and Baghdad there had been an increase in violence but not to the degree the commanders feared. The attacks that came were easily handled in all but one place, Mosul.

Armed clashes broke out in several northern Iraqi cities on the tenth, leaving some twenty-two persons dead in Mosul, Baiji, and Tuz. Fighting was heavy around the headquarters of the Patriotic Union of Kurdistan party in Mosul. An hour-long battle left six assailants dead before the insurgents withdrew.

---

*On May 4, 2005, the Marine Corps issued a report on the shooting in the mosque in Fallujah with the findings that the Marine who fired the shots had a reason to believe that the victim was faking his death and was concealing something, thus exonerating the Marine. No legal action was taken against the Marine.

But for all the fighting the casualties were remarkably few. Only one American serviceman died in Mosul on November 11. There had been careful planning in anticipation of a counterstroke by General Ham's staff.

Outnumbered, the American troops along with the Iraqi National Guard withdrew from the center of Mosul but maintained control of bridges that split the city in two. The police had disappeared. Within both the Iraqi security service and the U.S. military there was considerable anger over the performance of the police. Not only had the police not provided any early warning of the attacks, but the Arabs readily fled or changed sides. The Allawi government fired the police chief of Ninevah province.

The insurgents who took control of the city's streets burned all the police stations and released from jails all the criminals. In the center of Mosul, the offices of government service agencies and economic targets were set ablaze. A number of shops were attacked and looted. Armed men roamed the streets and manned checkpoints between city quarters. Mosque preachers called on Mosul residents to flood into the streets to protect their quarters, government offices, and shops.

By November 13, the insurgents were wandering freely around Iraq's second largest city. They were busy salting the center of the city with IEDs in an effort to fortify the city in what would be a sure battle once the Americans returned in force.

In response, additional forces were dispatched, but the fighting was not as nearly heavy as expected. At the appearance of the American armor, the insurgents gave way with only scattered ambushes, withdrawing into the residential areas. Rather than fight his way into the Arab neighborhood, the commander was satisfied with just retaking the center of the city and the business districts. There would be plenty of time to clean out the insurgents at a time and manner of their choosing. Much had changed in the mentality of the Americans since their first entrance into Iraq. Thus, the feared counterstroke that would light up the whole of the Sunni Triangle never happened at all.

Meanwhile, the fighting in Fallujah centered on mopping up operations, avoiding political problems, and trying to figure out what to do now with an empty and destroyed city. The UN Office of the High Commissioner for Human Rights on the sixteenth stated that they were "deeply concerned" about the situation of civilians caught up in the ongoing fighting in Fallujah.

The UN was pushing to get into Fallujah to have access to the civilians. Apart from the security issue, which the military considered real, they were not about to risk a repeat of any of the publicity of the prior April. The few civilians they were finding were well within the ability of the military to feed and care for, which met its legal obligations.

The Marines were making what news was coming out of Fallujah. Lt. Gen. John Sattler, commander of the First Marine Expeditionary Force in Fallujah, said the offensive had "broken the back of the insurgency." Meanwhile, on November 19, at a Pentagon press briefing, Lt. Gen. Lance Smith, deputy commander of the U.S. Central Command, said that U.S. forces were finding evidence in house-to-house searches showing that Fallujah was a haven for "former-regime elements."

The U.S. military found what had been a headquarters for Abu Musab al-Zarqawi. U.S. troops found documents in the house, including letters from al-Zarqawi with instructions to his lieutenants, along with medical supplies and boxes of ammunition. A black-and-white mural painted on the wall was like that which appeared in videos showing the beheading of foreign hostages.

With the fighting over, the Red Crescent was allowed into Fallujah. Its spokesman said that less than 200 civilian families appeared to still be there.

But staff officers were warning that any significant withdrawal of troops from the Iraqi city of Fallujah would strengthen the insurgency. The assumption was always that the assault forces would turn the city over to the Iraqi National Guard. From the beginning, staff officers had argued that the political imperative of a quick turnover to Iraqi control of the city was just not attainable. The insurgents would just move back.

The battle over the place was still dangerous. On November 25 three more Marines were lost.* November 26 cleanup operations cost another two Marines.† In an empty city, there were still plenty of places to hide for a few remaining holdouts. By the close of November, the month in Iraq had cost the Americans 137 dead and 1350 wounded, the bloodiest of the Iraqi war.

Every one of the city's 77 mosques had been used as a weapons storage facility or a fortress. A Marine unit found 91 caches and 432 IEDs. As a comparison, in October throughout all the rest of Iraq, the coalition found 130 arms caches and 348 IEDs. But in the aftermath there was a realization that most of the real "bad guys" had escaped. Gen. George Casey, commander of the U.S. military in Iraq, said that his troops had come upon only fifteen foreign fighters in Fallujah among 1000 fighters killed who were Iraqi. All of their leadership escaped.

His staff was more optimistic as to the total number of insurgents tallied, placing the number of captured fighters at 1052 (with 1600 killed). It was about half of what they hoped when they planned the battle. They wanted to destroy some 4000 to 5000 combatants. The Americans vowed to "liberate" the residents of Fallujah from these "criminal elements,"

*KIA: Pfc. Ryan J. Cantafio, Lance Cpl. Jeffery S. Holmes, Cpl. Gentian Marku
†Lance Cpl. Bradley M. Faircloth, Lance Cpl. David B. Houck

described as "mugs and thugs" by the Marine commander. Still, the numbers were impressive. "If there are 20,000 hard core fighters, we just clipped that number by five percent right here in a few days. I call that progress," said one staff officer.

As the Fallujah campaign appeared to be winding down with no serious counterstrike, Moqtada was negotiating with al-Sistani over how many seats his movement would get if it joined the Shi'a political movement. The fundamentals of the campaign had been achieved. The Kurds and the Shi'a would hold their election. Power and responsibility would be split between those who would participate. Nothing could stop that now.

There was a political cost. Forty-seven Iraqi political parties, including many with a religious base, announced that they would boycott the planned January elections. The Sunni would not at this juncture enter into negotiations over the smoldering ruins of Fallujah. The Americans were skeptical, however. "They would have boycotted anyway, demanding that we leave before the election and that the Sunni get a veto over the Shi'a majority. Al-Sistani would have never agreed to the latter and the former would have meant no elections at all," said one military political advisor.

Unlike before, the military had deftly handled the publicity and avoided the scenes of suffering civilians. Just as valuable was the treasure trove of evidence of atrocities left by the foreign fighters. Privately, one public affairs officer said, "Thank God for Zarqawi. We couldn't have done it without him."

On June 8, 2006, approximately 17 months after the fall of Fallujah, Zarqawi was killed when U.S. planes dropped two 500-pound bombs on a safe house where he had been spotted, near the town of Ba'qubah, some 30 minutes northeast of Baghdad.

Some Fallujans were furious at the "mujahadeen" who fought the Americans using their city as a base. One who remained said that if a holy warrior proffered his hand, he'd "rip it to pieces with his teeth." The Iraqi Defense Ministry put the total death toll of both combatant and non-combatant at 2085 Iraqis killed in the course of the U.S. assault on Fallujah.

The Fallujans weren't the only ones angry. Late in November, in a recording published on an Islamist website, al-Zarqawi attacked the ulemas, the Sunni clerics, for not coming to his defense. "You have let us down in the darkest circumstances and handed us over to the enemy.... You have quit supporting the Mujahadeen.... Hundreds of thousands of the nation's sons are being slaughtered at the hands of the infidels because of your silence."

It was December 23 before Prime Minister Allawi gave the go-ahead for citizens to return. Heads of households were being paid a $200 humanitarian assistance payment to help them buy necessities and reestablish themselves. Each had to prove his residence and was given an identification card. The first day, 921 citizens returned to the city and 12 government workers showed up. Civil affairs teams signed contracts with local contractors to clear debris and help with the water situation. They set up six humanitarian sites for aid.

But many of the residents took one look at the city and left, some in disgust and others heartbroken. Between the insurgents who took advantage of the chaos in the last days before the battle, and the destruction caused by the fighting, most found their homes unlivable. Many of the houses were nothing more than rubble. Some of the houses had been destroyed after the fighting. Iraqi forces were unforgiving if they found evidence of insurgents in the home. A number were burned to the ground in retaliation.

By mid–January, only 9,400 citizens went through the five checkpoints, and 640 government workers showed up to help. Eight battalions of Iraqi Security Forces were inside Fallujah (six from the Ministry of Defense and two police battalions from the Ministry of the Interior).

The invasion force was reduced to three U.S. Marine battalions and a regimental combat team headquarters, working side-by-side with Iraqi forces.

Six weeks later, by the close of February 2005, only 10,000 of the citizens had returned to Fallujah to stay. Over 100,000 had returned at one point or another, but most went back to relatives or the displacement camps that had sprung up in nearby towns. Families who went back had no electricity or water, and many houses needed repairs. "The Iraqi government is working hard with U.S. troops to soon give safety and adequate conditions for the residents to be back in their homes," said Colonel Peter Smith of the Marine 1st Division.

There were still mines and unexploded ordnance (UXOs) in some houses. Children were most at risk as they explored through the clutter. A few shops were open, and some fruit and vegetables sellers were at street corners. Electricity and water was still not running. Families relied upon aid agencies, who filled water tanks distributed throughout the city. Some children ran after the armed Marines who offered soccer balls and candy to them, showing some signs of reconciliation. But most of the adults stood in the doors of their homes, just watching in silence.

Notes

1. Ian Fisher, *New York Times*, "U.S. Troops Fire on Iraqi Protesters, Leaving 15 Dead," April 29, 2003.

2. CBS News, "U.S. Pullout In Fallujah," July 12, 2003.

3. CBS News, "U.S. Pullout In Fallujah," July 12, 2003.

4. Al-Jazeera, "US faces 'ball of fire' in Fallujah, says an Iraqi cleric," September 18, 2003.

5. *Jordan Times*, Thursday, September 18, 2003.

6. Conversation with author and CJTF-7 C9 staff, September 2003.

7. Al-Jazeera, "Iraqi Tribal Revenge Fuels Fallujah's Anti-US Rage," November 7, 2003.

8. Al-Jazeera, "Iraqi Tribal Revenge Fuels Fallujah's Anti-US Rage," November 7, 2003.

9. Sewell Chan, *Washington Post*, "Descent Into Carnage In A Hostile City," April 1, 2004.

10. Rory McCarthy, *The Guardian*, "Uneasy truce in the city of ghosts," April 24, 2004.

11. *The Guardian*, "Getting aid past U.S. snipers is impossible," April 17, 2004.

12. Eric Schmitt, *New York Times*, "U.S. General At Falluja Warns A Full Attack Could Come Soon," April 22, 2004.

13. Pamela Constable, *Washington Post*, "Marines Try to Quell 'a Hotbed of Resistance,'" April 9, 2004.

14. CPA, unclassified political report, 20 April 2003.

15. Rory McCarthy, *The Guardian*, "Uneasy truce in the city of ghosts," April 24, 2004.

16. CPA, unclassified news summary from a number of printed sources, 17 April 2003.

17. Rory McCarthy, *The Guardian*, "Uneasy truce in the city of ghosts," April 24, 2004.

18. Rory McCarthy, *The Guardian*, "Uneasy truce in the city of ghosts," April 24, 2004.

19. Rory McCarthy, *The Guardian*, "Uneasy truce in the city of ghosts," April 24, 2004.

20. Rory McCarthy, *The Guardian*, "Uneasy truce in the city of ghosts," April 24, 2004.

21. *The Guardian*, "Getting aid past U.S. snipers is impossible," April 17, 2004.

22. Dahr Jamail, *The New Standard*, "Iraq Dispatches: Accounts of Atrocities Emerge from the Rubble of Fallujah," May 11, 2004.

23. CNN, "Iraqi forces patrolling Fallujah," May 1, 2004.

24. Darrin Mortenson, *North County (CA) Times*, "Fallujah's Farms Offer Respite From City Fighting," April 23, 2004.

25. Darrin Mortenson, *North County (CA) Times*, "Fallujah's Farms Offer Respite From City Fighting," April 23, 2004.

26. Darrin Mortenson, *North County (CA) Times*, "Fallujah's Farms Offer Respite From City Fighting," April 23, 2004.

27. Interview with the author, April 29, 2003.

28. Said in presence of the author.

29. Darrin Mortenson, *North County Times*, April 25, 2004.

30. Associated Press, "Fallujah residents told that fighting may resume," April 22, 2004.

31. Tony Perry and Patrick J. McDonnell, *Los Angeles Times*, "Marines Warn Of Battle In Fallouja," April 23, 2004.

32. Darrin Mortenson, *North County Times*, "Pendelton Marine Receives Silver Star," May 5, 2005.

33. Dahr Jamail, *New Standard*, "Iraq Dispatches: Fallujans Declare Victory," May 11, 2004.

34. Reuters, "International staff of Help is leaving Iraq," September 21, 2004.

35. Fox News, "Clashes Break Out in Heart of Baghdad," September 29, 2004.

36. Bonnie Adams, *Times Leader*, "Emotional recall of soldier's Iraq death," November 11, 2004.

37. James V. Walker, *Jackson* (MS) *Clarion-Ledger*, "When Death Knocks At The Door," March 26, 2003.

38. James V. Walker, *Jackson* (MS) *Clarion-Ledger*, "When Death Knocks At The Door," March 26, 2003.

39. Keith Eldridge, KOMO News, an interview with wounded soldier Trevor Phillips, September 17, 2004.

40. CNN.com, "Kirkuk bombing latest attack on Iraqi forces," September 18, 2004.

41. AP, Suicide bombing, fierce fighting rocks Baghdad, September 22, 2004.

42. CNN.com, "Kirkuk bombing latest attack on Iraqi forces," September 18, 2004.

43. Associated Press, September 10 2004.

44. 2nd Lt. Rick Caldwell, 1st platoon leader for the 39th Brigade's C Company, 1st Battalion, 153rd Infantry Regiment, Matthew Cox, *Army Times*, September 20, 2004 .

45. Headquarters United States Central Command Press Release, September 18, 2004.

46. VOA, September 15, 2004.

47. Associated Press, "U.S. renews effort to secure insurgency hotbed," September 28, 2004.

48. RFE/RL, "U.S. Warplanes Strike Baghdad, Al-Fallujah," September 28, 2004.

49. Rajiv Chandrasekaran, *Washington Post*, September 21, 2004.

50. Rajiv Chandrasekaran, *Washington Post*, September 21, 2004.

51. Rajiv Chandrasekaran, *Washington Post*, September 21, 2004.

52. Rajiv Chandrasekaran, *Washington Post*, September 21, 2004.

53. Rajiv Chandrasekaran, *Washington Post*, September 21, 2004.

54. Marwan Naamani, *Time*, "The Enemy With Many Faces," September 27, 2004.

55. Michael Isikoff and Mark Hosenball, *Newsweek*, September 29, 2004.

56. VOA, "Iraqi Ministers and Academic Community Face Up to Security Threats," September 21, 2004.

57. VOA, "Iraqi Ministers and Academic Community Face Up to Security Threats," September 21, 2004.

58. VOA, "Iraqi Ministers and Academic Community Face Up to Security Threats," September 21, 2004.

59. Samantha Quigley, *AFSI*, "War in Iraq Moving in the Right Direction, Says CENTCOM Leader," September 26, 2004.

60. VOA, September 15, 2004.

61. *The Independent*.

62. The Independent.

Index